PowerPoint 2016 Complete
Student Edition

30 Bird Media
510 Clinton Square
Rochester NY 14604
www.30Bird.com

PowerPoint 2016 Complete

Student Edition

CEO, 30 Bird Media: Adam A. Wilcox

Series designed by: Clifford J. Coryea, Donald P. Tremblay, and Adam A Wilcox

Managing Editor: Donald P. Tremblay

Instructional Design Lead: Clifford J. Coryea

Instructional Designer: Robert S. Kulik

Keytester: Kurt J. Specht

COPYRIGHT © 2016 30 Bird Media LLC. All rights reserved

No part of this work may be reproduced or used in any other form without the prior written consent of the publisher.

Visit www.30bird.com for more information.

Trademarks

Some of the product names and company names used in this book have been used for identification purposes only and may be trademarks or registered trademarks of their respective manufacturers and sellers.

Disclaimer

We reserve the right to revise this publication without notice.

PPNT2016-A1-R10-SCB

Table of Contents

Introduction 1
   Course setup 2

Chapter 1: Fundamentals 3
   Module A: Exploring the PowerPoint environment 4

Chapter 2: Creating a presentation 17
   Module A: Creating a presentation 18
   Module B: Creating and modifying slide content 24

Chapter 3: Formatting 47
   Module A: Working with slide masters and layouts 48
   Module B: Formatting slides and text 73

Chapter 4: Working with shapes and images 95
   Module A: Creating and formatting shapes 96
   Module B: Working with images 116

Chapter 5: Working with charts and tables 129
   Module A: Working with charts 130
   Module B: Working with tables 146

Chapter 6: Customization 159
   Module A: Slide transitions 160
   Module B: Additional text options 165
   Module C: Printing 174

Chapter 7: Advanced formatting 187
   Module A: Inserting and formatting SmartArt 188
   Module B: Additional formatting options 213

Chapter 8: Animation, time effects, and media 229
   Module A: Animating slide content 230
   Module B: Inserting and formatting media 251

Chapter 9: Reviewing content, tracking changes, and saving in other formats 271
   Module A: Reviewing content and tracking changes 272
   Module B: Saving a presentation in other formats 296

Chapter 10: Custom slide shows 315
   Module A: Working with notes pages 316
   Module B: Configuring, rehearsing, and presenting slide shows 330

Chapter 11: Sharing, collaborating, and security 343
   Module A: Protecting your presentations 344
   Module B: Sharing your presentations 352

Alphabetical Index 373

Introduction

Welcome to *PowerPoint 2016 Level 1*. This course provides the basic concepts and skills that you need to start being productive with Microsoft PowerPoint 2016: How to create, navigate, format, and customize PowerPoint presentations. This course and the Level 2 course map to the objectives of the Microsoft Office exams for PowerPoint 2016. Objective coverage is marked throughout the course, and you can download an objective map for the series from http://www.30bird.com.

You will benefit most from this course if you want to accomplish basic workplace tasks in PowerPoint 2016, or if you want to have a solid foundation for continuing on to master PowerPoint. If you intend to take a Microsoft Office exam for PowerPoint, this course is a good place to start your preparation, but you will also need to complete the Level 2 course to be fully prepared for either exam.

The course assumes you know how to use a computer, and that you're familiar with Microsoft Windows. It does not assume that you've used a different version of PowerPoint or any other presentation program before.

After you complete this course, you will know:

- How to open and interact with PowerPoint and how to save and close presentations
- How to modify the structure of a presentation, and arrange and format its various elements
- How to work with shapes and images
- How to import and create charts and tables
- How to create custom slide presentations, and create WordArt from text
- About printing options

This is the first course in a series. After you complete it, consider going on to the next one:

- *PowerPoint 2016: Level 2*

Course setup

To complete this course, each student and instructor needs to have a computer running PowerPoint 2013. Setup instructions and activities are written assuming Windows 10; however, with slight modification the course works using Windows XP Service Pack 3, Windows Vista Service Pack 1, or Windows 8 or 8.1.

Hardware requirements for Windows 10 course setup include:

- 1 GHz or faster processor (32- or 64-bit) or SoC
- 1 GB (32-bit) or 2 GB (64-bit) RAM
- 25 GB total hard drive space (50 GB or more recommended)
- DirectX 9 (or later) video card or integrated graphics, with a minimum of 128 MB of graphics memory
- Monitor with 1280x800 or higher resolution
- Wi-Fi or Ethernet adapter

Software requirements include:

- Windows 10 (or alternative as above)
- Microsoft PowerPoint 2016 or any Microsoft Office 2016 edition that includes PowerPoint
- The PowerPoint 2016 Level 1 data files and PowerPoint slides, available at http://www.30bird.com

Network requirements include:

- An Internet connection in order to complete the sharing exercise and the exercise on downloading and using a template (which can be skipped or demonstrated by the instructor)

Because the exercises in this course include viewing and changing some PowerPoint defaults, beginning with a fresh installation of the software is recommended. But this is certainly not necessary. Just be aware that if you are not using a fresh installation, some exercises might work slightly differently and some screens might look slightly different.

1. Install Windows 10, including all recommended updates and service packs. Use a different computer and user name for each student.
2. Install Microsoft PowerPoint 2016, using all defaults during installation.
3. Copy the PowerPoint 2016 Level 1 data files to the Documents folder.

Chapter 1: Fundamentals

You will learn how to:

- Use the PowerPoint interface to interact with the program and its presentations

Module A: Exploring the PowerPoint environment

When you start PowerPoint, at the top of the screen you'll see a set of tools called *the ribbon*. You click the commands and buttons on the ribbon to get work done.

You will learn:

- How to start PowerPoint
- To identify basic features of a presentation
- How to exit PowerPoint

Starting PowerPoint and opening a presentation

In Windows 10, you can start PowerPoint by clicking either its tile in the Start menu or its icon on the Task bar. When you start PowerPoint, you're first greeted with the Open Presentation window. From here, you can open either an existing presentation or a blank one.

1. Click **Start** to open the Start menu.
2. There are a couple of ways to start PowerPoint from here:
   - Find and click the PowerPoint 2016 tile.
   - Click **All Apps > PowerPoint 2016**.
     You can also set up icons on the desktop—or anywhere else you like—for starting PowerPoint.

   The Open Presentation window is displayed.

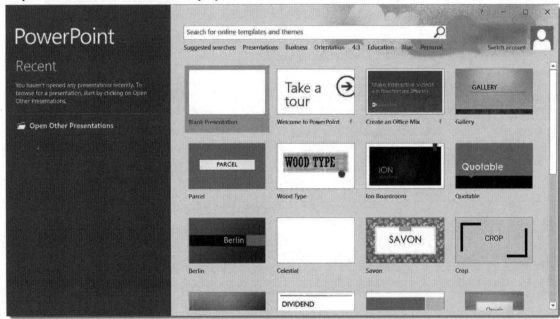

3. Click **Open Other Presentations**.
   In the left pane of the window.

The Open options are displayed.

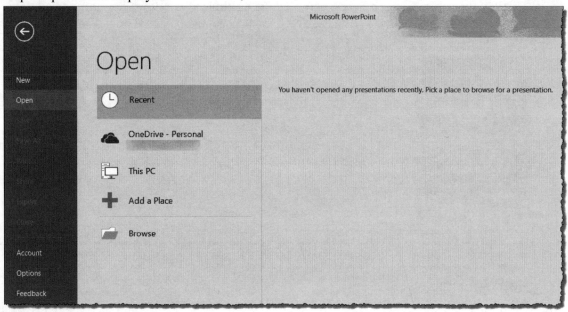

4. Click **Browse**.

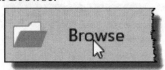

The Open window is displayed.

5. Navigate to the folder containing the presentation you want to open, click the presentation, then click **Open**.
   Or double-click the file name to open the file automatically.

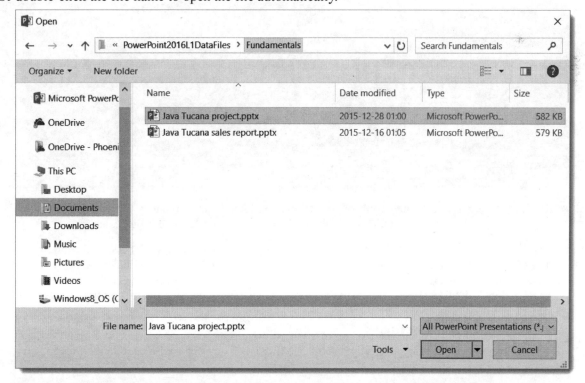

The file opens in the PowerPoint window.

Note: The first time you open a presentation file, the PowerPoint window opens maximized to fill your screen. You can toggle between this maximized-window view and a smaller window by clicking the Maximize/Restore Down icon, respectively, in the upper-right corner of the window.

The PowerPoint interface

If you've never used PowerPoint, the interface might be intimidating. But if you break it into pieces, it's fairly straightforward.

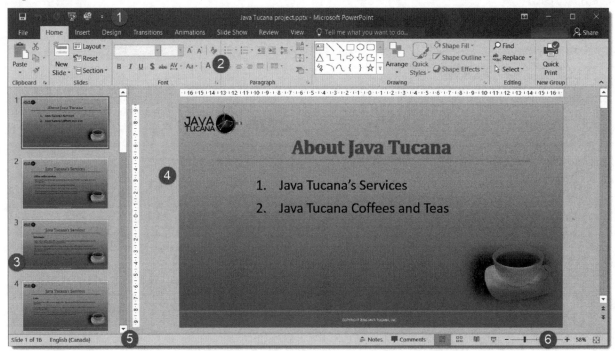

1. The *Quick Access toolbar* contains only the most common PowerPoint commands, but you can customize it any way you like. To the right of the toolbar, in the horizontal center, the file name is displayed.

2. The *ribbon* contains groups of buttons, lists, menus, and commands that give you access to the most relevant actions you might want to take. They are *context-sensitive*, meaning that they change depending on where you are and what you're doing. The ribbon is organized into *tabs* (File, Home, and so on), and then within tabs by *groups* (Clipboard, Slides, Font, and so on). Get more information about any tool by pointing to it to display a *tooltip* with information about the tool.

3. The *slides pane* displays thumbnail versions of all the slides in a presentation sequentially, from top to bottom. However, its contents can vary, depending on the current view. This pane is also commonly referred to as the *thumbnail pane*.

④ The *current slide pane*, or *main pane*, displays the slide selected in the Slides pane. This is where you edit the slide selected in the slides pane.

⑤ The *status bar* displays information such as the number of the currently selected slide, the number of slides in the presentation, the current language and view, and other features.

⑥ The *zoom bar* provides a quick way for you to zoom in on or out from the current slide.

You work on a particular slide by first selecting it in the Slides pane, then manipulating it as you wish in the main part of the window.

Exploring views

In PowerPoint, there are a number of different views. A *view* is a particular organization of elements in the PowerPoint environment. Each view is suited to particular kinds of tasks. Also, there's more than one way to open each view. On the View tab, in the Presentation Views group, are the view buttons. Simply click the corresponding button to change to that view. A few of these views are also represented on the status bar.

  MOS PowerPoint Exam Objective(s): 1.5.2

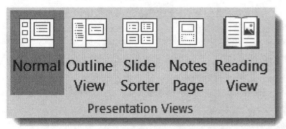

- *Normal view*: The view you'll likely spend most of your time in while working on PowerPoint presentations. You can also click [icon] on the status bar.

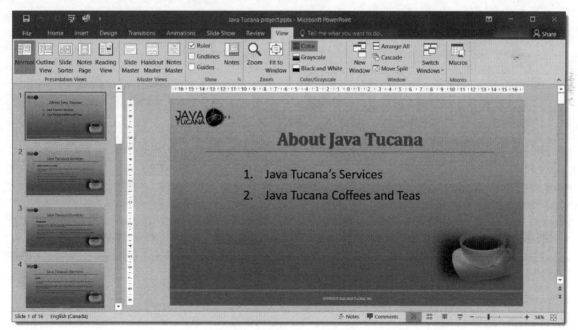

- *Outline view*: Useful for creating an outline of your presentation or exploring storyboard ideas.

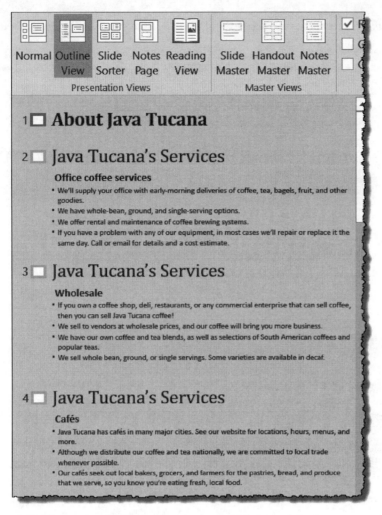

- *Slide Sorter view*: Particularly suited to organizing the slides in your presentation. You can move slides simply by clicking and dragging them to new positions, much as if they were a deck of cards.

  You can also click on the status bar.

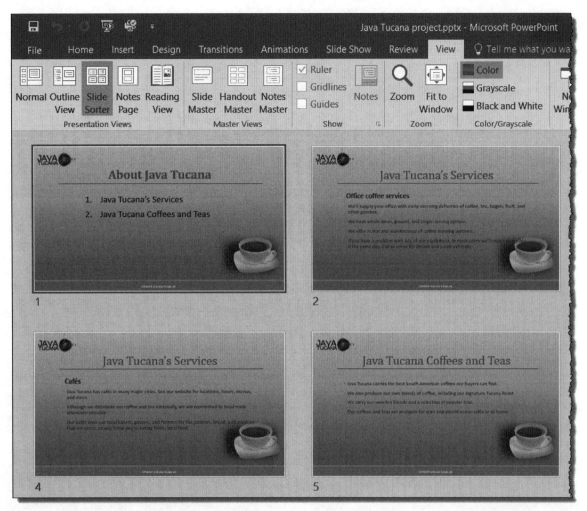

- *Notes Page view*: Opens a page associated with each slide, that allows you to enter and display notes for that slide. Notes pages can be printed for your own use and/or for your audience, and they can be displayed on screen or hidden from view. Accessing Notes view from the ribbon produces a larger notes page under the slide. Clicking ≜ Notes on the status bar displays a smaller Notes area.

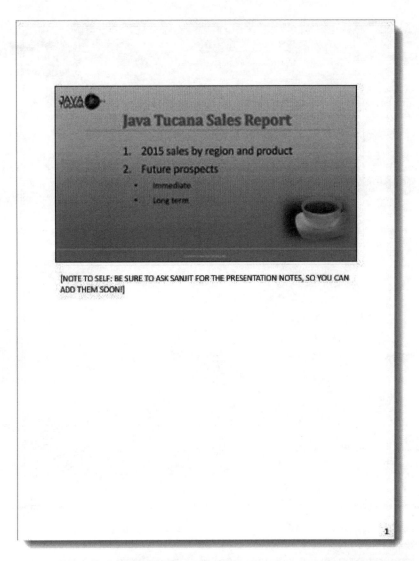

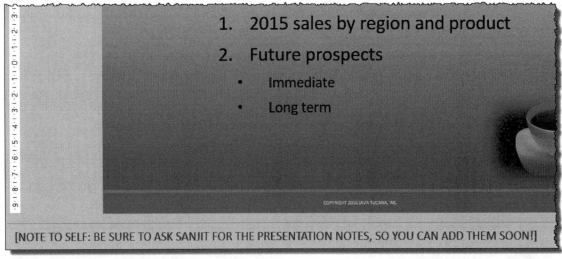

- *Slide Show view*: What you use to play your presentation for an audience. Each slide displays in full screen, and any controls, transitions, effects, and so on that you've added to it will show up here. Obviously, this isn't the view to use when you want to make changes to your presentation. To get to Slide Show view, click 🖥 on the status bar.

- *Reading view*: You'll probably spend the least amount of time in this view. It's similar to Slide Show view, except that you'd use it to play the presentation for yourself, rather than for an audience. You can also get to Reading view by clicking ![icon] on the status bar. In Reading view, controls for navigation and switching to other views are displayed in the status bar.

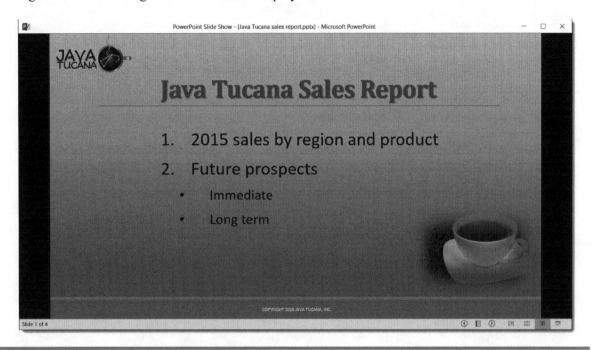

Getting help

To get help in PowerPoint 2016, use the Tell Me box.

1. Click **Tell me what you want to do**.
   To the right of the View tab's name.

   The insertion point is in the Tell Me box.
2. Begin typing the topic you'd like information for.
3. In the list of context options, click the one that most closely matches your topic.
4. If the options listed aren't what you're looking for, you can always click **Get Help**.

The PowerPoint 2016 Help window opens with additional information that hopefully matches your topic.

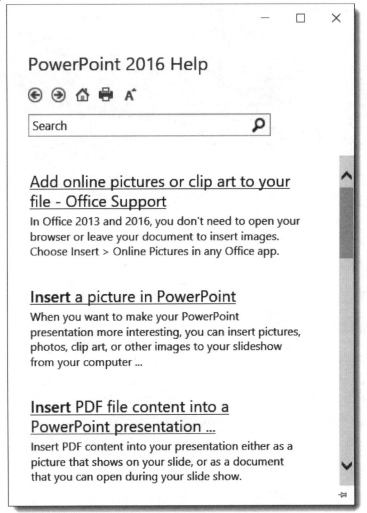

5. Scroll to view the displayed, linked topics, then click to select the desired topic.
   You can also type additional search text in the Search box, then press **Enter** for even more information.

6. When you're finished with your search, close the help window.

Exercise: Checking out PowerPoint

Before you start, be sure that your computer is on and Windows is running. You'll start PowerPoint and take a look around its interface.

Do This	How & Why
1. Follow your instructor's directions to start PowerPoint.	If necessary. The method you use depends on your version of Windows and how it is set up. In Windows 10, you can simply click the PowerPoint icon on the taskbar at the bottom of the screen, or click **Start** and then click the PowerPoint 2016 tile.
2. Navigate to the folder containing the data files for this course, and open `Java Tucana project.pptx`.	If you've just started PowerPoint, click **Open Other Presentations**, and click **Browse**. In the Open window, navigate to the `Fundamentals` data folder, and double-click **Java Tucana project.pptx**.
3. Observe the PowerPoint window.	Most of the window consists of the Slides pane and the current slide.
4. Observe the Slides pane.	All the visible slides of the presentation are displayed.
5. Observe the current slide in the main pane.	The first slide in the presentation is selected and its contents are displayed.
6. Click on another slide.	In the Slides pane. You can also use the Up Arrow and Down Arrow keys to move sequentially through the slides.
7. Observe the status bar.	The number of the selected slide is displayed as you select each one, as well as the total number of slides in the presentation.
8. Use your mouse pointer to grab the zoom bar slider and drag it left and right.	Press and hold as you drag. As you drag the slider left, the slide is reduced in size; as you drag right, it's enlarged. Its current size is represented as a percentage at the right edge of the zoom bar.
9. Observe the ribbon.	This is the large area of buttons, lists, menus, and palettes at the top of the window. It's organized into tabs (File, Home, Insert, and so on), and within in a tab, into groups.
10. Observe the Home tab.	When you open a presentation, the Home tab is selected by default. It contains the most common commands, organized into groups (Clipboard, Slides, Font, Paragraph, and so on). The commands in the Font and Paragraph groups are currently grayed out.
11. Select slide 1 in the presentation.	Click it in the Slides pane. You might need to use the pane's scroll bar to scroll quickly to the top of the presentation.

Do This	How & Why
12. Click on any text in either bulleted item in the list.	In the main pane.
13. Observe the ribbon.	

The commands in the Font and Paragraph groups are now available because you've selected slide text.

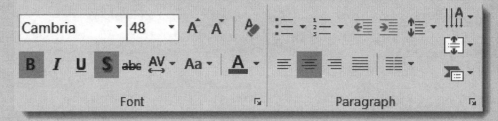

14. Point to the **Bold** button.	To display a tooltip, explaining what the tool does. 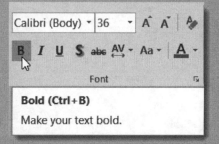
15. Observe the Quick Access toolbar.	This is the small toolbar at the top left.  It has just a few of the most useful commands. You can customize it however you like.
16. Display the presentation in different views.	Use the Presentation Views group buttons on the View tab, as well as the icons on the status bar. To exit Slide Show view at any time, you can press the **Esc** key. 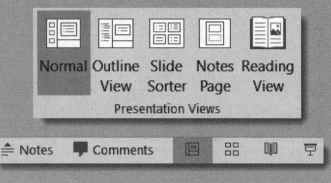

Do This	How & Why
17. Exit PowerPoint without saving the presentation.	Click the **Close** button.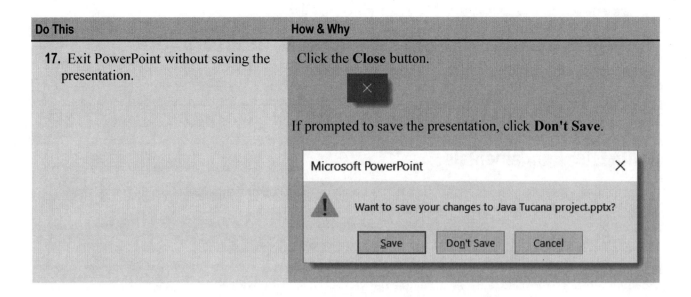If prompted to save the presentation, click **Don't Save**.

Assessment: Exploring the PowerPoint environment

1. Which of the following are ways to interact with PowerPoint? Choose all that apply.

    - Click buttons on the ribbon.
    - Use the Control Panel.
    - Use the Start menu.
    - Click buttons on the ribbon.
    - Click buttons on the Quick Access toolbar.

2. True or false? You edit a slide in the Slides pane.

    - False
    - True

3. You've opened a PowerPoint presentation and selected a slide in the Slides pane. In the Home tab's Paragraph group, the commands are grayed out and therefore unavailable. Why?

    - You need to wait until PowerPoint warms up.
    - Slides can be edited only in the Slides pane.
    - Ribbon commands become available only after all slide elements are created.
    - Ribbon commands become available when you click on a slide element to which they are applicable.

Summary: Exploring the PowerPoint environment

You should now know how to:

- Start PowerPoint, use the PowerPoint interface to interact with the program and its presentations, navigate among the elements of the PowerPoint window, and close the program

Synthesis: Fundamentals

In this chapter synthesis exercise, you'll start PowerPoint, open a slide presentation, and navigate in the window. Then you'll close the presentation without saving it.

1. Start PowerPoint, and open the `Java Tucana project` presentation.
    From the `Fundamentals` data folder.
2. Scroll through the entire slide presentation and view each slide individually.
3. Zoom in on and out from a selected slide.
4. Do what's necessary to enable the Font group's commands, so that they're no longer grayed out.
5. Open `Java Tucana sales report`.
6. Scroll through and view each slide in the presentation.
7. Select the individual elements of each slide, and observe the effects of doing so on the ribbon.
8. Explore the presentation in different views.
9. Close PowerPoint without saving any changes you might have made to either presentation.

Chapter 2: Creating a presentation

You will learn how to:

- Create a presentation
- Create and modify slide content

Module A: Creating a presentation

In PowerPoint, there is more than one way to create a new presentation, depending on whether you want to do so completely from scratch, or by using an existing structure. Either way, PowerPoint provides you with powerful and helpful tools for creating a presentation.

You will learn how to:

- Create a blank presentation
- Create a presentation from a template

Types of new presentations

PowerPoint provides you with powerful options for creating a presentation. You can create a blank presentation with a completely empty "canvas" for your full creative expression, or you can start with a PowerPoint template. In addition, if you have a particular style of template in mind for your presentation, you can search for one that meets your needs.

Backstage view

As in all Microsoft Office applications, PowerPoint's *Backstage view* is a central location from which you can create, open, and manage your presentations, among other things. You access Backstage view by clicking the File tab on the ribbon.

- When you first click the File tab, the *Info* pane is displayed, containing information about the current presentation.
- The *New* pane contains options for creating a new presentation, including many templates. When you wish to create a blank presentation and PowerPoint's already open, in the New pane, click **Blank Presentation**.

Creating a blank presentation

There are two ways to create a blank presentation in PowerPoint: when opening PowerPoint, and via Backstage view.

MOS PowerPoint Exam Objective(s): 1.1.1

1. Close PowerPoint.
   If necessary. You'll see how to create a blank presentation when opening PowerPoint.
2. Open PowerPoint.
   Click the PowerPoint 2016 tile; or in the Start menu, find and click **PowerPoint 2016**. PowerPoint's opening window provides you with options for creating a presentation.
3. Click **Blank Presentation**.

The PowerPoint window opens with a new, blank presentation.

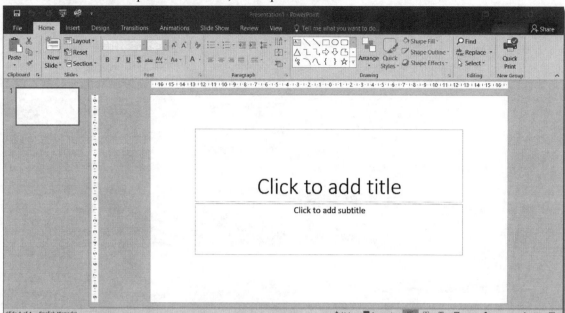

4. Observe the blank presentation.
   It contains only one slide.

5. Display Backstage view.
   On the ribbon, click the **File** tab.

6. Click **New**.
   In the left pane.

The New pane opens.

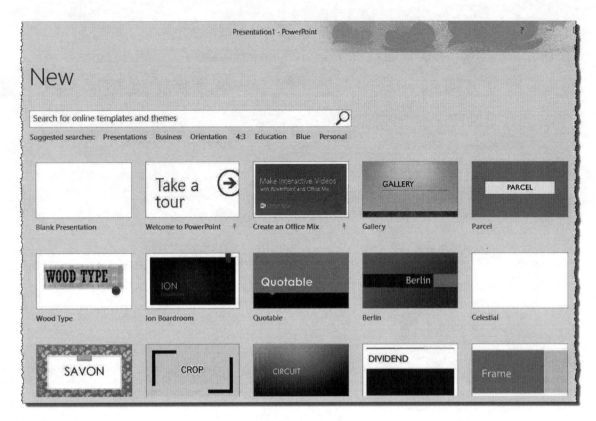

7. Click **Blank Presentation**.

    A second window opens with a new, blank presentation.

8. Observe the window titles.

    The presentations are given temporary names ("Presentation1" and "Presentation2"). Once you save the presentations, their new names replace the temporary ones.

9. Close the Presentation2 window.

    Click its  button.

    Only the Presentation1 window remains open.

Creating a presentation from a template

PowerPoint provides you with a number of template designs you can use to create your own presentations.

 MOS PowerPoint Exam Objective(s): 1.1.2

1. In Backstage view, click **New**.

    The New pane opens.

2. Scroll to view all the available template options.

    You can also use the Search box to narrow your template options, or search online for even more templates.

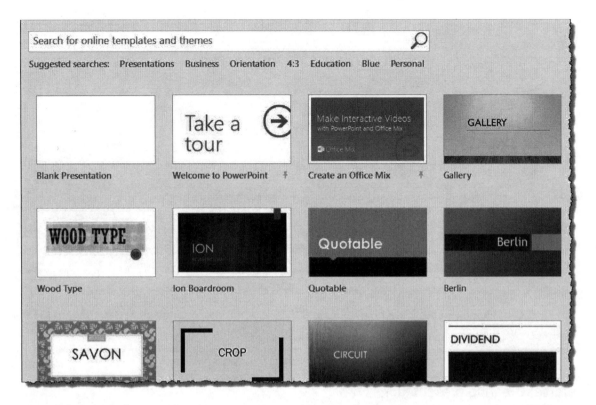

3. Click on a template design to select it.

   A window opens, displaying a magnified preview of how a slide will look with the selected design. Two sets of scroll arrows allow you to flip through more designs using the preview: Use the arrows on either side of the preview window to preview other designs. Use the More Images arrows to display other types of slides using the current design.

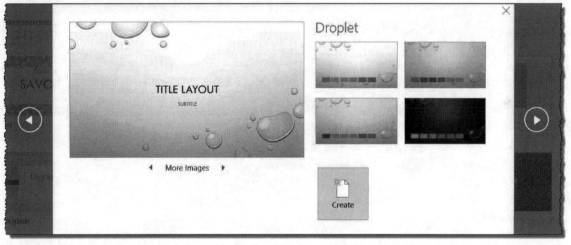

4. Use any of the scroll arrows to preview other designs and/or other types of slides.
5. Once you've selected a design you like, click **Create**.

   The presentation opens in a new PowerPoint window, temporarily titled "Presentation3." PowerPoint numbers presentations consecutively, starting at "1" each time you start the program. It continues to "remember" the sequence even after you save (and thus rename) any of them.

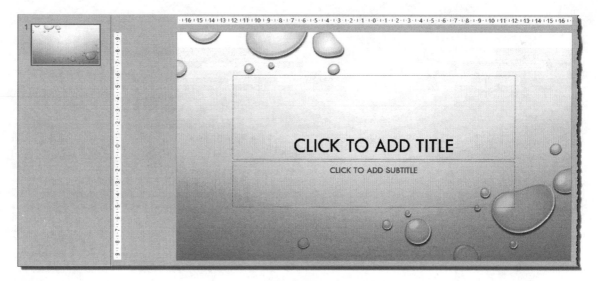

6. Observe the new presentation.

   The design appears on the selected slide, and the presentation contains only one slide. In the main pane, rulers are displayed along the top and left side of the current slide.

Exercise: Creating presentations

Before you begin, PowerPoint is running on your computer. You'll create two new presentations: one blank, one template-based.

Do This	How & Why
1. Click **File**, then click **New**.	To display the options for creating a new presentation in Backstage view's New pane.
2. Click **Blank Presentation**.	A new, blank presentation appears on the screen.
3. Open Backstage view again, and view the available template options.	Click **File** > **New**. Scroll to view the available templates. You can use the Search box to search for a specific design type. If you have an Internet connection, you can also search online for additional templates.
4. Select a design.	Click on a template. The design opens in a preview window.
5. Use the scroll arrows on either side of the window.	To preview additional designs.
6. Use the More Images scroll arrows.	To preview other types of slides in the current design.
7. Once you've selected a design, click the **Create** button.	In the preview window. The template-based presentation opens in a new window.
8. Close the new, template-based presentation without saving it.	Click [×] in the upper-right corner of its window.
9. Save the blank presentation as `My Cafe Presentation`. a) Click **File**, then click **Save As**.	

Do This	How & Why
b) Click **Browse**, then navigate to the `Creating a presentation` data folder.	Your instructor can help you find it.
c) In the File name box, type `My Cafe Presentation`.	
d) Click **Save**.	
e) Keep My Cafe Presentation open, but close any other open presentation windows without saving.	

Assessment: Creating a presentation

1. True or false? To open, create, or save a PowerPoint presentation, you use Backdoor view.
   - True
   - False

2. What is the command sequence for creating a blank presentation in PowerPoint?
   - Backdoor, New, Blank Presentation
   - File, New, Blank Presentation
   - Open, New, Blank Presentation

3. True or false? When previewing presentation template designs, you can use the More Images arrows to display each sample slide in a different template.
   - True
   - False

Module B: Creating and modifying slide content

PowerPoint makes it easy for you to add text or other design elements to slides. In addition, you can add as many slides as you like to your presentation.

You will learn how to:

- Insert text on a slide
- Add, delete, and hide slides in a presentation
- Insert a hyperlink
- Insert shapes and images

Slides and their elements

A slide is essentially a blank canvas on which you can place text, shapes, or images in order to convey information relevant to your presentation. A presentation can contain any number of slides, but rather than merely deciding on a number, it's best to have a good idea of the salient points, topics, subtopics, and so on that will make the presentation as clear and meaningful as possible. You can always add (or remove) slides later, as needed.

By default, slides contain *placeholders*: special areas designated for holding *objects* such as text, shapes, images, and graphs. Most slides come with one placeholder for the slide's title, and another for a subtitle or body text. However, you can add more placeholders to any slide, as needed. Likewise, you can delete any placeholder.

When deciding on the contents of each slide, it's good to keep in mind a few general guidelines.

- Try to convey or illustrate a single idea, whenever possible. Cluttering a slide with too many different ideas—or simply too much information—can obscure what you're trying to show.
- For any text that isn't a heading, use bullet lists whenever possible, to keep each item concise and memorable. Try to avoid placing a whole paragraph (or more) of text on a slide. If you feel that all the information in the paragraph should be there, simply rewrite the information in the form of a bullet list.
- Graphical elements (shapes, images, and so on) can add esthetic value to a presentation when used prudently, as when illustrating a point. However, try to avoid too many illustrations or, worse yet, pointless ones. For example, a slide intended to show company sales figures might not benefit from a picture of a duck.

Inserting text on a slide

You enter text on a slide by clicking a text placeholder, then typing. Once you click in a text placeholder, it becomes a *text box*, a container for text. When typing text, you can use all the usual word processing tools, such as the Backspace and Delete keys, arrow keys, and so on. You can also select the text and format it as you wish.

 MOS PowerPoint Exam Objective(s): 2.1.1

You can change the size of a text box by dragging its handles, which appear at its corners and sides.

1. Click to select the slide on which you wish to enter text.
   In the Slides pane.

The slide's placeholders are displayed in the main pane: one for a title, the other for a subtitle or body text.

2. Click in the title placeholder.

   The placeholder becomes a text box with handles, an insertion point appears centered in it (replacing the "click to add title" message), and the mouse pointer changes to an *I-beam*, which signals that you can enter text.

3. Type the title text in the box.
4. Drag the text box handles to change its size.
   - Dragging any corner handle allows you to reduce or enlarge the box's length and width at the same time. As you hover over a corner handle, the mouse pointer becomes a diagonal double-headed arrow. As you drag the handle, the mouse pointer becomes crosshairs.

   - Dragging the left or right side handle reduces or enlarges the box's width. Dragging the top or bottom handle reduces or enlarges the box's height. As you hover over any side handle, the mouse pointer becomes a horizontal or vertical double-headed arrow. As you drag the handle, the mouse pointer becomes crosshairs.

- To maintain the text box's dimensional symmetry, press and hold the **Ctrl** key as you drag a handle. This keeps the box centered in its original position on the slide.
    - **Ctrl**+drag a corner handle to change the size of left-right and/or top-bottom sides.
    - **Ctrl**+drag a left/right handle to change the width of the box equally from both sides.
    - **Ctrl**+drag a top/bottom handle to change the height of the box equally from the top and bottom.

5. Press the **Esc** key, or click anywhere in the slide outside the selected text box.

    The text box, its handles, and the title placeholder itself are no longer visible. Only the new title text is visible.

Adding, deleting, and hiding slides in a presentation

Every new PowerPoint presentation comes with only one slide. But there are many ways to add slides to a presentation. Deleting slides is quite simple. However, you can also simply hide one or more slides, so that they're not deleted, but they don't display in the presentation.

 MOS PowerPoint Exam Objective(s): 1.2.2, 1.2.3, 1.2.4

1. Add a new slide to the presentation by using one of the following techniques.
    - On the Home tab, in the Slides group, click the upper part of the **New Slide** button.

    - Right-click in the Slides pane, and from the context menu, select **New Slide**.

- Press **Ctrl+M**.

  A second, new slide is added in the slides pane. Like the first slide, it contains placeholders only for a title and for a subtitle or other content.

2. This time, click the lower part of the New Slide button.

   On the Home tab, in the Slides group.

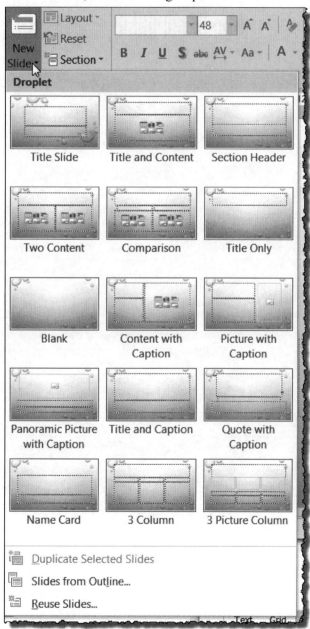

The Office Theme gallery opens, displaying various options for prearranged slide content. Additional menu choices are displayed below the gallery.

- *Duplicate Selected Slides*: Automatically duplicates the format and contents of any selected slide.
- *Slides from Outline*: Opens the Insert Outline window, from which you can navigate to a Word or other text document in outline form. On inserting that document, its outline is automatically rendered as PowerPoint slides.
- *Reuse Slides*: Opens the Reuse Slides pane, which assists you in reusing/salvaging slides from another PowerPoint presentation or other source.

3. Click on a gallery option.

    To add the new slide to the presentation.

4. Right-click the slide you wish to delete.

    It's easiest to do this on slide thumbnails in Normal view or Slide Sorter view. Press and hold **Ctrl** to select multiple slides. Then right-click anywhere in the selection.

    A context menu opens.

5. Click **Delete Slide**.

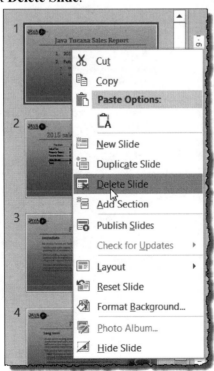

6. Right-click the slide you wish to hide from display in the presentation.
   Or multiple selected slides.
7. Click **Hide Slide**.

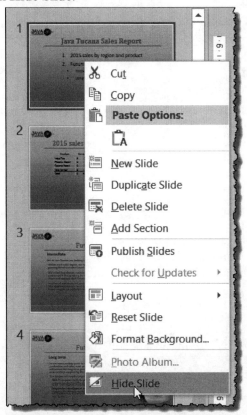

Navigating a presentation

Once your presentation contains more than one slide, there are several handy ways to navigate it.

1. Navigate a multi-slide presentation using one of these methods.
   - In the Slides pane, click the desired slide. Use the Slides pane scroll bar to quickly move through longer presentations.
   - In the lower right of the main pane, click a double-headed arrow to move sequentially through the slides in the direction of the arrow.

   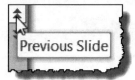

   - In the main pane, use the scroll bar to drag to the desired slide in the presentation. As you drag the scroll box, a tooltip indicates the number and title of the current slide.

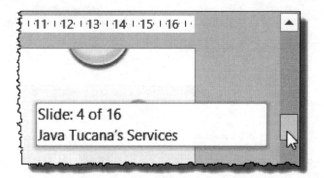

- On the keyboard, use the **PgUp** and **PgDn** keys to navigate through the presentation one slide at a time.

Inserting a hyperlink on a slide

 MOS PowerPoint Exam Objective(s): 2.1.6

A *hyperlink* is specially formatted text or a graphic object that's linked to other data in another location. In PowerPoint, you can insert a hyperlink on a slide to link to, for example, another slide (in the same presentation or in another one), another Microsoft Office document, or even a website.

 Note: It's important to remember that hyperlinks become clickable only in Slide Show view.

1. Select the source object—the text or other object—you wish to link to a destination.

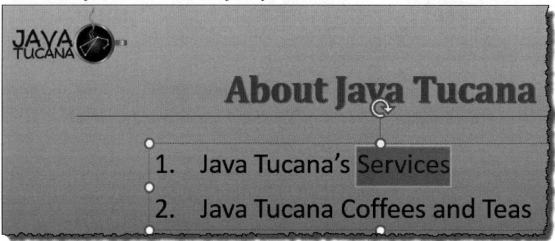

2. Format the text as a hyperlink.
    - On the ribbon's Insert tab, in the Links group, click **Hyperlink**.

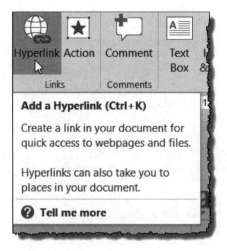

- Press **Ctrl+K**.

   The Insert Hyperlink window opens.

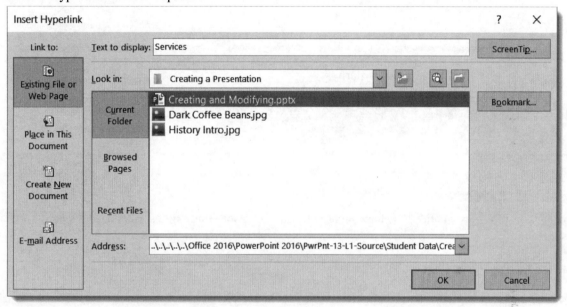

3. Select the destination to which you wish to link the source.

   Use the buttons under "Link to" and "Look in" as necessary. For example, to link to another slide in the current presentation, under "Link to," click **Place in This Document**. The Insert Hyperlink window then lists the slides in the presentation. Select the name of the destination slide in the window, and click **OK**.

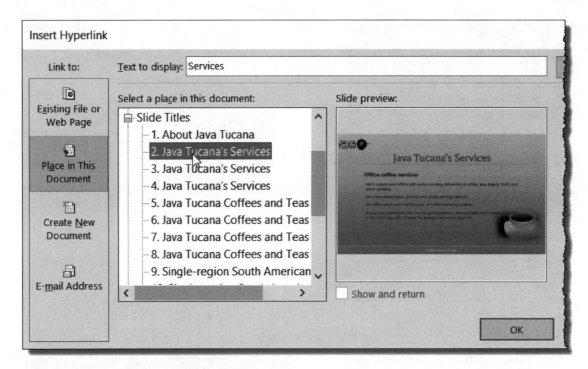

The selected source is now a hyperlink.

Inserting shapes

PowerPoint provides a gallery of shapes that you can insert onto your slides. Shapes are accessible from the Insert tab.

 MOS PowerPoint Exam Objective(s): 2.2.4

1. Select the slide onto which you'd like to insert a shape.
2. Insert a shape from the Home tab or the Insert tab.
   - On the ribbon's Home tab, in the Drawing group, click the Shapes gallery's **More** button.

   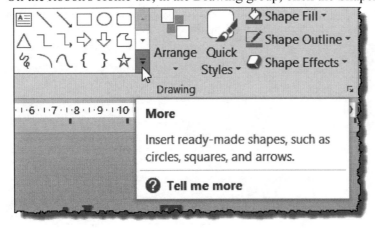

   - On the Insert tab, in the Illustrations group, click **Shapes**.

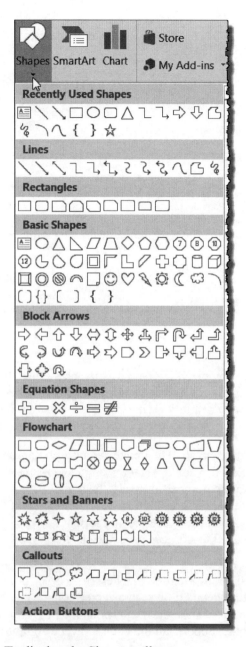

To display the Shapes gallery.

3. Click to select the shape you want to insert.
4. Click on the slide where you'd like to place the shape.

The shape appears on the slide, and the box enclosing it indicates that it is selected. At the sides and corners of the box are selection handles, which you can use to change its dimensions.

5. Hover over the shape with your mouse pointer.

   The mouse pointer becomes a four-headed arrow, indicating that the shape can be moved in any direction.

6. With the four-headed arrow displayed, click and drag the shape to place it in the desired location on the slide, then release the mouse button.
7. Press **Esc** or click in a blank area of the slide.

   To deselect the shape.

Types of images

You want your slide presentations to have visual appeal and convey meaning. One way to accomplish this goal is to include images on your slides, where it's appropriate and useful to do so. Fortunately, PowerPoint allows you to insert many kinds of images, or pictures, in a variety of file formats. PowerPoint categorizes image files into two types: bitmap images and vector graphics.

- A *bitmap image* is a file that contains an image made up of *pixels*. The image can be a photograph, a scanned drawing or form, and so on. The number of pixels per unit area (for example, per square centimeter) determine the image's resolution: the greater the number of pixels, the higher the resolution. PowerPoint supports more than a dozen different picture file formats, including .bmp, .jpg, .gif, and .png. However, whenever possible, it's a good idea to use the .jpg format, as its considerable file compression allows you to conserve valuable storage space and can keep your presentations "lean and mean."

- A *vector graphic* is a drawing that contains highly detailed information that describes every point in it in mathematical terms. Thus, the resulting image is highly detailed. In fact, a vector graphic can be enlarged to any degree and maintain all of its resolution. So it shouldn't be surprising that vector graphics are heavily used in the design world. PowerPoint supports all the common vector-graphic file formats, including .cdr, .drw, .eps, and .emf.

In PowerPoint, you can insert an image from a file on your computer or other storage device. However, from the ribbon, you can also download online images.

Inserting an image from a file

The procedure for inserting an image onto a slide is the same for both bitmap images and vector graphics.

1. Select the destination slide for the image.
2. Click **Pictures**.

   On the Insert tab, in the Images group.

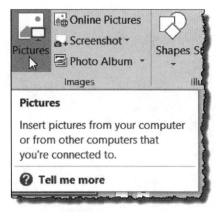

The Insert Picture window opens.

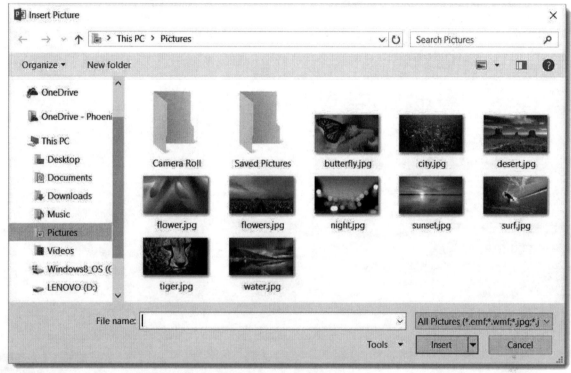

3. Navigate to the location of the image file you wish to insert.
4. Select the image file, and click **Insert**.

    The image file is inserted onto the current slide.
5. Drag the image to position it in the exact location desired.

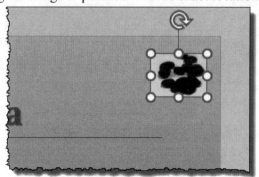

Inserting online images

You can download images from online sources and insert them onto your slides.

1. Select the slide onto which you wish to insert your downloaded image.
2. Click **Online Pictures**.
   On the ribbon's Insert tab, in the Images group.

   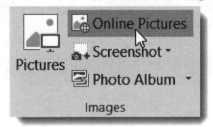

   The Insert Pictures window opens. Its available options will differ, depending on your current online connection and services.

   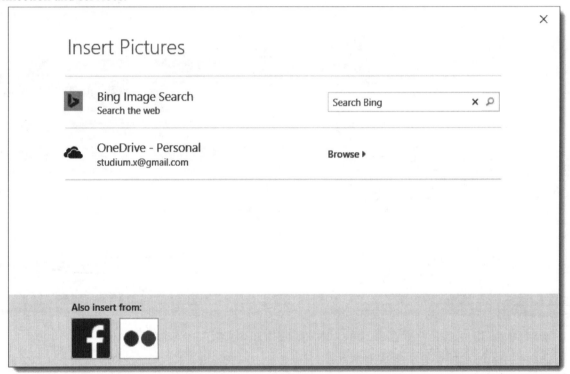

3. Choose a connection to obtain an image.
   - Select an available source, such as OneDrive, and click **Browse**. Then navigate to the desired location and download the image.

- Click in the search box (for example, using Bing Image Search), type a keyword or search string, and press **Enter**. Select an image, and click **Insert**.

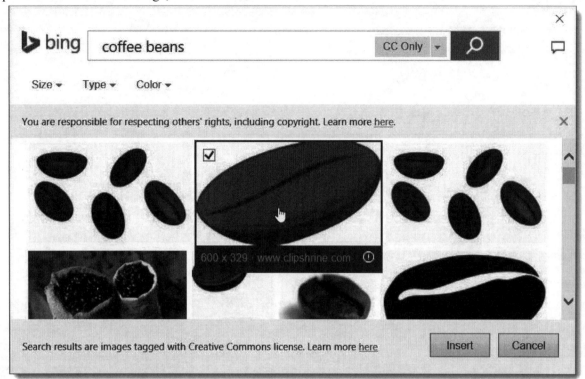

The image appears on the selected slide.

4. Drag the image to position it exactly where you want it to appear.

Exercise: Creating and modifying slide content
You'll add slides to a presentation, and you'll add text and graphics.

Do This	How & Why
1. Open `Creating and Modifying.pptx` and save it as `My Creating and Modifying.pptx`.	It's in the `Creating a presentation` data folder.
2. Scroll through the presentation.	Use either the Slides pane or the main pane. The presentation contains different types of slides ordered and grouped to cover topics and subtopics.
3. View slide 5.	Currently the first slide in the Java Tucana Coffees and Teas section of the presentation. It would be helpful to have a slide that provides a brief overview of this section.
4. View slide 4.	The last slide of the Java Tucana's Services section. You'll insert a slide after this one to begin the next section.

Do This	How & Why
5. Click **New Slide**. On the Home tab, in the Slides group.  A new, blank slide 5 is inserted and selected.  6. Click in the upper text box. Where it reads "Click to add title." The placeholder text is replaced with an insertion point, and the cursor becomes an I-beam. 	
7. Type `Java Tucana Coffees and Teas`.	The heading's font, size, and color is preformatted to match the other slides.
8. Now click in the lower text box.	Which reads "Click to add text." The insertion point appears, aligned at the left edge of the box.

Do This	How & Why
9. Click the arrow to the right of the Bullets button.	On the Home tab, in the Paragraph group. A gallery of bullet styles opens.
10. Select the Filled Round Bullets style.	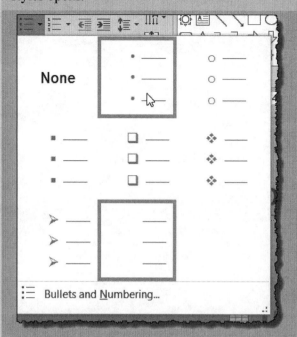 A bullet of the selected style appears at the insertion point.
11. Type `Java Tucana carries the best South American coffees our buyers can find.` Then press **Enter**.	The statement appears as a bullet item. Pressing Enter inserted a second bullet on a new line.
12. Create a second bullet item that reads `We also produce our own blends of coffee, including our signature Tucana Roast.` Then press **Enter**.	
13. Create another bullet that reads `We carry our own tea blends and a selection of popular teas.` Then press **Enter**.	
14. Create a final bullet item that reads `Our coffees and teas are available for your enjoyment in our cafés or at home.`	If you want to include the accented "é" in "cafés," on the Insert tab, in the Symbols group, click **Symbol**. There's no need to press Enter, as this is the final item in the list.

Do This	How & Why
15. Deselect the text box, and observe the bullet slide title and list you've created. Click in another part of the slide.	

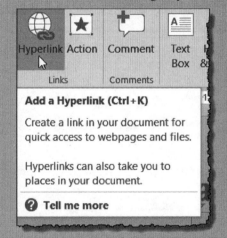

16. On slide 1, format "Services" as a hyperlink to slide 2.	
a) Select slide 1.	
b) Select **Services**, then click **Hyperlink**.	On the Insert tab, in the Links group.
c) Click **Place in This Document**.	In the Insert Hyperlink window, under "Link to."

Do This	How & Why

    d) Click **2. Java Tucana's Services**.

From the list of slide titles under "Select a place in this document."

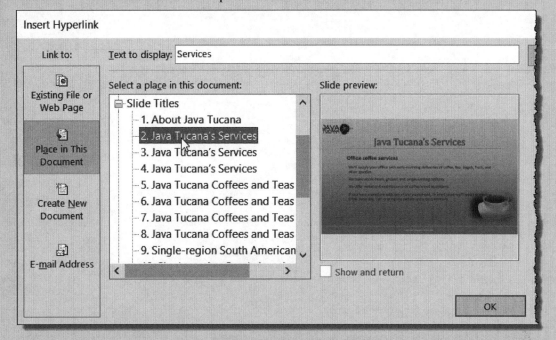

e) Click **OK**.	The Services hyperlink appears on the slide.

17. Also on slide 1, format Coffees and Teas as a hyperlink to slide 5.

Use the same procedure as in the previous step. This time, under "Select a place in this document," select **5. Java Tucana Coffees and Teas**. The two new hyperlinks now appear on the slide.

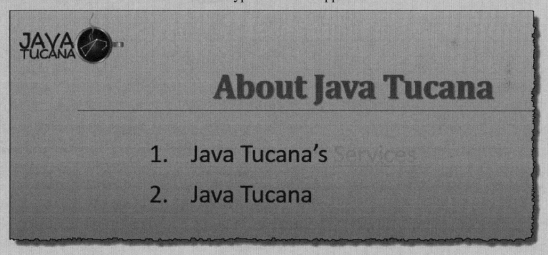

18. Display slide 9.	The first slide titled "Single-region South American coffees." You'll add a shape to this slide as a visual accent.
19. Click **Shapes**.	On the Insert tab, in the Illustrations group.

PowerPoint 2016 Level 1   41

Do This	How & Why
20. Click the **Sun** shape.	Under Basic Shapes. 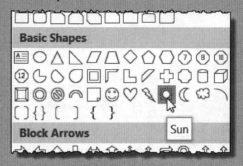
21. Click anywhere under the bullet list.	To insert the shape.
22. Drag the shape where you think it should be placed on the slide.	As you hover over the shape, as long as the mouse pointer is a four-headed arrow, you can drag the shape anywhere on the slide. Also, guide lines, or rules, appear in different places on the slide, which tell you when an object is centered, aligned with another object, and so on.
23. Resize the shape as you see fit.	Use the shape's handles.
24. Elsewhere on the same slide, insert the picture file **Dark Coffee Beans.jpg**.	
a) On the Insert tab, in the Images group, click **Pictures**.	
b) Navigate to the `Creating a presentation data` folder.	
c) Select **Dark Coffee Beans.jpg**, and click **Insert**.	The image appears on the slide.

Do This	How & Why

25. Drag the image to an appropriate location on the slide, and resize it as you see fit.

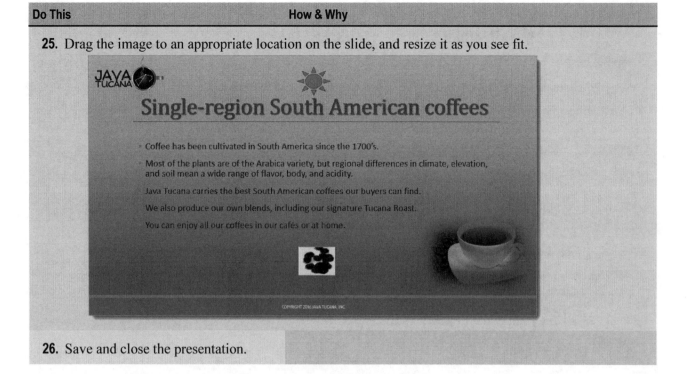

26. Save and close the presentation.

Assessment: Creating and modifying slide content

1. When you use the New Slide command, the new slide does which of the following?

    - It replaces the selected slide.
    - It's inserted immediately following the current slide.
    - It's inserted immediately preceding the current slide.
    - It's inserted as the last slide in the presentation.

2. True or false? You can insert text simply by clicking anywhere on a slide and typing.

    - True
    - False

3. True or false? A hyperlinked slide object can link to a destination on the World Wide Web, to another file, or to another location in the same presentation.

    - True
    - False

4. Which of the following statements is true for any images inserted on a slide?

    - Before you insert the image, you must specify its final destination and size.
    - Before you insert the image, you must specify its final destination, but you can resize the image at any point after you've inserted it.
    - Before you insert the image, you must first select a destination slide, but you can move the image and/or resize it afterwards.
    - Before you insert the image, you must first select a destination slide and specify the image's exact size, but you can move it freely afterwards.

Summary: Creating a presentation

You should now know how to:

- Create a blank presentation, and create a presentation from a template
- Create and modify slide content by navigating the presentation, adding slides, formatting slide objects as hyperlinks, and inserting shapes and images

Synthesis: Creating a presentation

In this chapter synthesis, you'll create a new presentation, add text to a slide, add slides to the presentation, create a hyperlink that links to another slide, and insert a shape and an image.

1. Create a new presentation—either a blank one, or one from a template.
2. On slide 1, enter the text as shown.

   History of Coffee
   - Introduction
   - Origins
   - Geography

3. Add a second slide to the presentation, and enter the text as shown.

   History of Coffee: Introduction
   - 10th century (or earlier) origins
   - Believed to have originated in Ethiopia
   - Earliest documented drinking of coffee in 15th century, in Yemen
   - Spread throughout Africa and the Middle East by the 16th century
   - Shortly after, coffee use spread throughout Europe

4. Add a third slide, and enter the text as shown.

   History of Coffee: Origins
   - Etymology
   - First use

5. Add a fourth slide, and enter the text as shown.

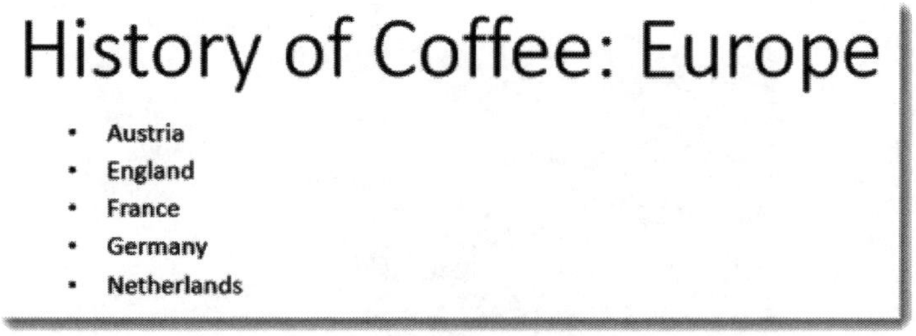

> **History of Coffee: Europe**
> - Austria
> - England
> - France
> - Germany
> - Netherlands

6. Add a fifth slide, and enter the text as shown.

> **History of Coffee: Americas**
> - Caribbean
> - Central America
> - South America
> - North America

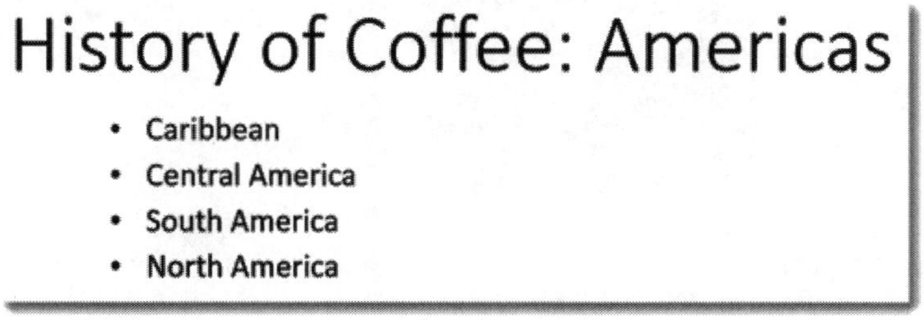

7. Add a sixth slide, and enter the text as shown.

> **History of Coffee: Asia**
> - India
> - Japan
> - South Korea
> - Indonesia

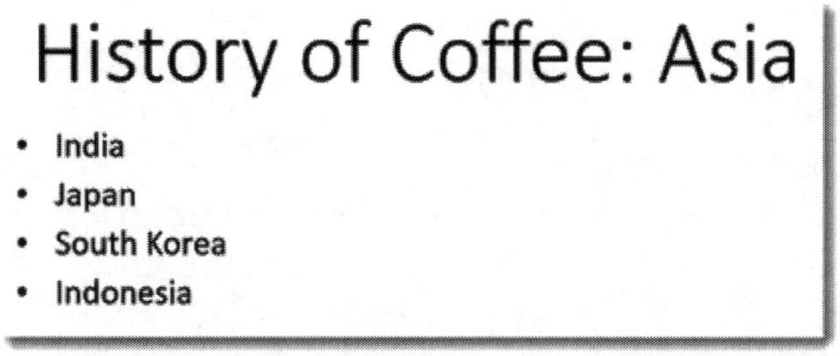

8. Insert a new slide 4 in the presentation, and enter the text as shown.

> **History of Coffee: Geography**
> - Europe
> - Americas
> - Asia

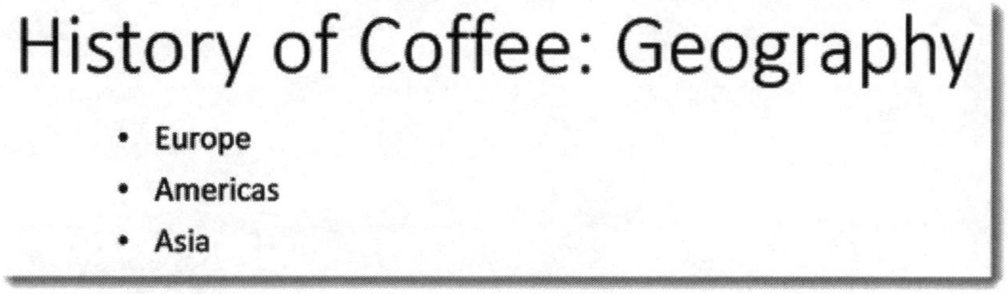

9. On slide 1, format each bullet item as a hyperlink.

   a) Link "Introduction" to slide 2.

   b) Link "Origins" to slide 3.

   c) Link "Geography" to slide 4.

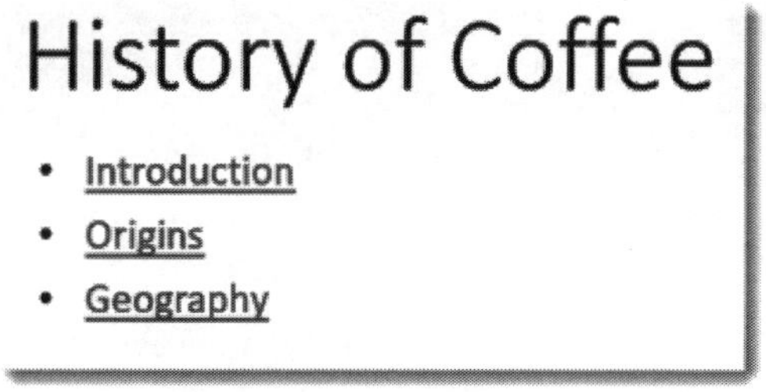

> **History of Coffee**
> - Introduction
> - Origins
> - Geography

10. On slide 2, insert the **History Intro.jpg** picture (from the `Creating a Presentation` data folder).

11. Size and position the image as you would like it to appear on the slide.

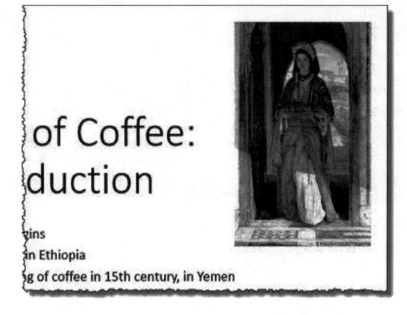

12. Insert, size, and position an image from an online source on the slide of your choice.
13. On the slide(s) of your choice, insert some graphic shapes to add visual interest.
14. Size and position the shapes as you see fit.
15. Save the presentation as `My Coffee History.pptx`.

Chapter 3: Formatting

You will learn how to:

- Control the overall look of a presentation with slide masters and layouts
- Format individual slides and their text

Module A: Working with slide masters and layouts

In PowerPoint, you can format individual slides to make them all conform to a theme or look. However, a much simpler and quicker way to make your slides conform to a theme or style is by using slide masters and layouts.

You will learn how to:

- Modify the slide master
- Use the slide master to change a layout

About slide masters

When you want to format or tweak all the slides of your presentation at once, the easiest way to do so is via the slide master, which every presentation created in PowerPoint contains by default. The *slide master* is a single slide that governs the way all its subordinate slides look. Any colors, graphics, and text elements you add to the slide master are automatically applied to all the slides in the presentation that are governed by it. The slide master can also contain one or more layouts. A *layout* governs the arrangement of slide elements, such as text and graphics.

Note: Prior to PowerPoint 2013, presentations contained a Title Master, which governed the format of all title slides. In PowerPoint 2013 and 2016, a Title Slide layout element can be included in the slide master itself. Any title slides will follow the format of the title layout.

The Slide Master tab

When you display Slide Master view, the Slide Master tab is also displayed on the ribbon. The Slide Master tab contains all the important tools for working with and modifying a slide master and its layouts.

- The *Edit Master* group contains tools for editing the slide master, including adding layouts.
- The *Master Layout* group allows you to edit a layout by adding or removing slide elements.
- The *Edit Theme* group contains only the Themes tool, which allows you to apply a theme to a master or layout.
- The *Background* group allows you to further enhance the appearance of the slides by applying a background style, as well as by modifying slide colors and fonts or adding special effects.
- The *Size* group contains only the Slide Size tool, which allows you to change the slides' aspect ratio to Standard or Widescreen (the default), or change its size to a custom value.
- The *Close* group contains only the Close Master View button.

Modifying the slide master

In Normal view, a presentation's slide master isn't visible. So, before you can work with it, you need to display it.

MOS PowerPoint Exam Objective(s): 1.3.2

1. Click **Slide Master**.

On the ribbon's View tab, in the Master Views group.

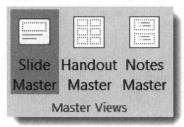

Slide Master view is displayed. The Title Slide layout is selected by default. It contains placeholders for a master title and subtitle, as well as three additional placeholders along the bottom of the slide: the Date area, the Footer area, and the Number area.

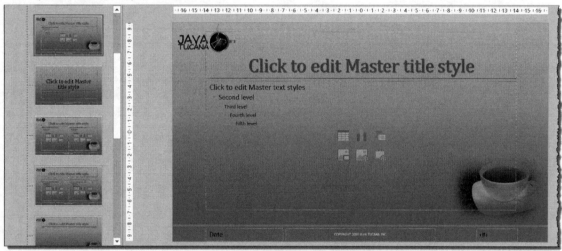

The Slide Master tab is displayed in the ribbon. In Slide Master view, by default, the Slides pane contains a single slide master, called the Office Theme Slide Master. Subordinate to it are individual slide "layouts."

2. Select the slide master.

Scroll up in the Slides pane, or press the up arrow. To modify the slide master, you must select the master itself, not one of its layouts.

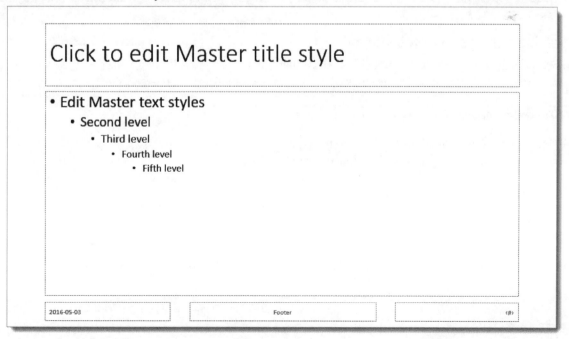

3. Make any desired formatting changes.

   Click in the appropriate placeholder/area to make your changes.

4. Insert any recurring elements.

   For example, you can insert a text box on your slide master by clicking Text Box on the Insert tab, then typing the text and formatting it. You can likewise insert images, sound clips, and video files. Just keep in mind that everything added to the slide master will recur on every slide in the presentation.

5. Change the size and/or position of elements.

   Click an element to select it, then drag to place it wherever you wish on the master slide. Use the element's handles to resize it.

6. Delete any elements you don't want to appear on every slide.

   Click an element to select it, then press **Delete**.

    Note: To delete a text box, first click to select it; next, click on its border; and then press **Delete**.

7. Return to Normal view.

   - On the Slide Master tab, click **Close Master View**.

   - In the status bar, click the **Normal** icon.

   If you wish to override a slide master element on a particular slide, select the slide (in Normal view), select the element or create a new one, and alter it as necessary. Any changes you make affect only the current slide.

Applying a theme to a presentation

You can enhance your presentation using themes that are applied globally to all slides. To do so, your presentation must be in Slide Master view. Use the same method to modify the theme.

 MOS PowerPoint Exam Objective(s): 1.3.1

1. Display your presentation in Slide Master view.

   On the Slide Master tab, click **Slide Master**.

2. Click **Themes**.

   On the Slide Master tab. There's no need to select the slide master in the Slides pane. A theme is applied globally to a master slide and its layouts, thus all are automatically affected.

   A gallery of themes and options opens. *Browse for Themes* allows you to search online for additional themes. *Save Current Theme* allows you to save a selected theme to the location of your choice.

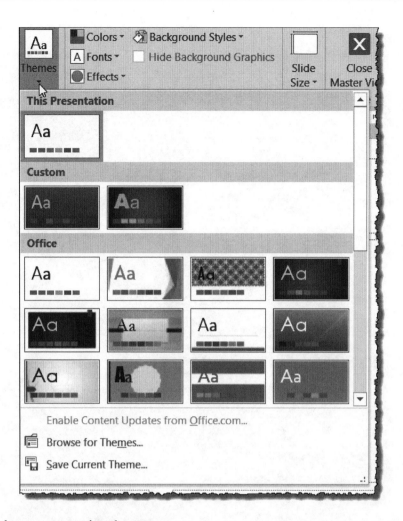

3. Select a presentation theme.

   The selected theme is applied to the slide master and its layouts.

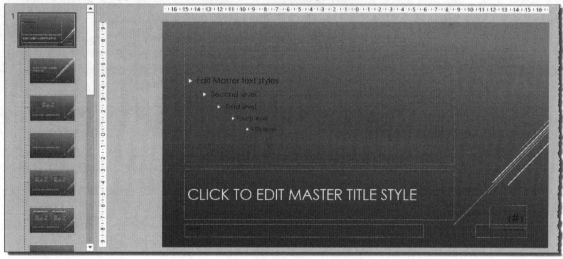

Exercise: Working with slide masters

Do This	How & Why
1. Open **JT Slide Master.pptx** and save it as **My JT Slide Master.pptx**.	From the `Formatting` data folder.
2. Scroll through the presentation's slides, and observe some of its features.	It consists of 16 slides, all of which use the same layout, colors, and graphics, including a recurring copyright footer element. Slide 1 also contains three hyperlinks.
3. Switch to Slide Master view.	
a) Click **View**.	To display the View tab.
b) Click **Slide Master**.	In the Master Views group. The presentation opens in Slide Master view, and the Slide Master tab is displayed.

4. Hover over the slide master.

In the Slides pane. A tooltip informs you that the master has a theme named Retrospect applied to it, which is used by slides 1–16.

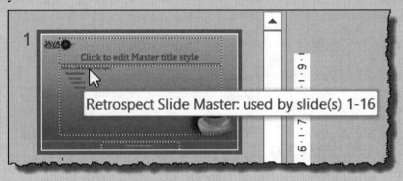

Do This	How & Why
5. Hover over the slide layout directly below the slide master, and observe the tooltip.	In the Slides pane. The tooltip informs you that this layout governs the title slide. Note that the Title Slide layout isn't currently being used by any of the presentation's slides.

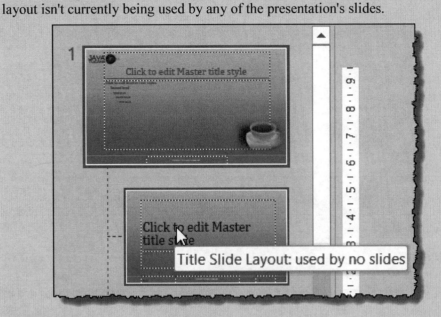

6. If necessary, select the **Title Slide** layout.	This slide doesn't contain any graphics. Because it's used to govern the layout of only the title slide, the only features of the slide master that it retains are the theme and the copyright footer.

7. Select the **Slide Master** and observe its elements.	In the Slides pane. It contains text boxes used for editing the master title and master text styles, as well as the logo and coffee-cup graphics.

Do This	How & Why
8. Click the Java Tucana logo.	To select it. Once it's selected, you can move or resize it however you wish.
9. Move and/or resize the logo on the slide master.	
10. Likewise, select the coffee-cup graphic, then move and/or resize it.	
11. Apply a new theme to the presentation.	
a) Click **Themes**.	In the Edit Themes group. The Themes gallery and options are displayed.
b) Hover over the themes in the gallery.	Scroll to view them all. As you hover over each of the themes, the slide master changes to reflect it.
c) Select a theme.	Click it in the gallery.
12. Observe the new theme in Slide Master view.	The slide master and all layouts are updated to reflect the new theme.
13. Use the **Colors**, **Fonts**, and **Effects** buttons to further enhance your theme.	In the Background group.

Do This	How & Why
14. Return to Normal view.	On the Slide Master tab, click **Close Master View**, or click the **Normal** icon in the status bar.

15. Observe the presentation, scrolling through its slides.

All the slides have been updated to reflect the new theme and modified graphics.

16. Save and close the presentation.

Headers and footers

 MOS PowerPoint Exam Objective(s): 2.3.1

Headers and footers provide a convenient way to place important recurring information in presentations. In PowerPoint, a *header* is recurring information displayed at the top of a handout or notes page. A *footer* is recurring information displayed at the bottom of a slide, handout, or notes page.

PowerPoint slide masters include three placeholders for displaying special information:

- The *Footer area*, for displaying special text that recurs on slides
- The *Date area*, for displaying the date and time
- The *Number area*, for displaying the slide number

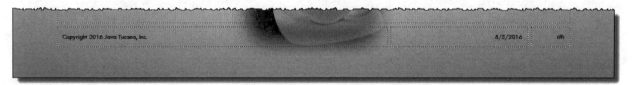

Handout and Notes masters also contain these placeholders, plus one more: the *Header area* displays at the top of handouts and notes pages.

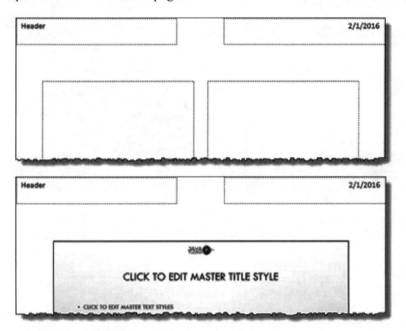

 Note: The Footer, Date, and Number areas appear at the bottom of slides and masters by default. However, you can position them elsewhere—for example, at the top—by switching to Slide view or Slide Master view, then dragging them to their new location.

Inserting footer information on a slide

Use the Header and Footer window to insert footer, date, and number information on one or more slides.

 MOS PowerPoint Exam Objective(s): 1.2.7

1. Select the slide on which you wish to include footer, date, and/or number information.

   This step is necessary only if you wish to apply the information to a single slide.

2. Click **Header & Footer**.

   On the Insert tab, in the Text group.

   The Header and Footer window opens with the Slide tab displayed.

   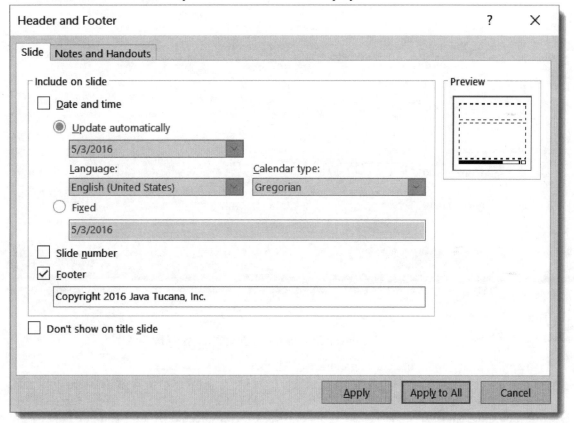

3. Click **Date and time**.

   Under "Include on slide."

   The option is now checked.

4. Click **Update automatically**, and select the date format from among the available choices.

   Under "Update automatically."

    Note: The *Fixed* format option allows you to type date and/or time information exactly as you would like it to appear. Keep in mind that doing so also prevents this information from automatically updating.

5. Select the Language and Calendar type (if available) from their respective fields.

6. Click **Slide number**.
    To display the slide number.

7. Click **Footer**.
    To display footer information.

8. Type the footer exactly as you'd like it displayed.
    In the footer box.

9. Check the **Don't show on title slide** option.
    The options you've set in the Header and Footer window won't appear on the title slide. To have this information appear on the title slide, simply click this option once again to uncheck it.

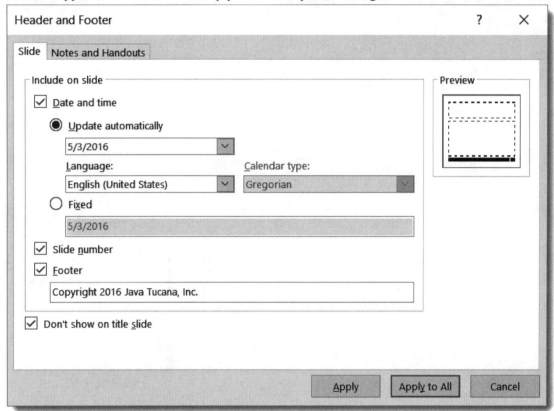

10. Apply the new settings.

    - To apply the settings to all the slides in the presentation, click **Apply to All**.

    - To apply them only to the current slide, click **Apply**.
    If you use the Apply to All option, and you later decide to suppress the display of this information on a slide, first select that slide, then use the Header and Footer window's Slide tab to deselect those options for that slide. Make sure that **Don't show on title slide** is selected (so that you don't alter its prior setting), then click **Apply**.

Headers and footers on handouts and notes pages

To add a header and/or footer to handouts and notes pages, use the Header and Footer window's Notes and Handouts tab. This tab contains essentially the same options as those on the Slide tab. However, the Notes and Handouts tab provides the additional option of adding a header at the top of each page. Once you've entered your settings, click **Apply to All**.

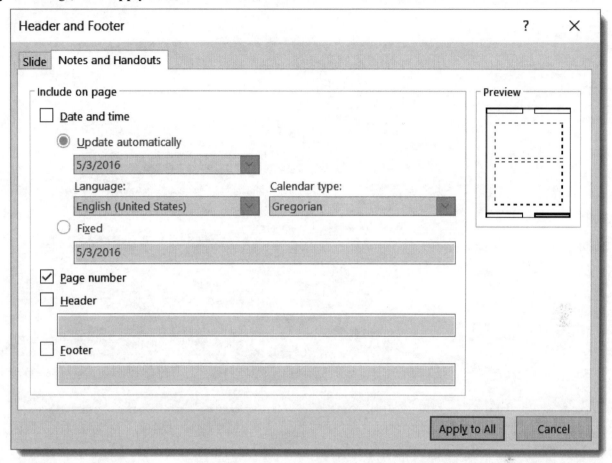

To edit text in header and footer placeholders directly, display the master containing the placeholder you wish to edit: Slide, Notes, or Handout. Then click in the placeholder and type or edit the text as you would normally.

> **Note:** Placeholders that you've set often contain special field codes that PowerPoint uses to display information. For example, <#> is the code for slide number. You can add text before and/or after these codes, but be sure to keep the codes themselves intact. Otherwise, the information they represent won't display properly.

Exercise: Adding and modifying a footer

Be sure to complete the exercise *Working with slide masters*.

Do This	How & Why
1. Open **JT Headers and Footers**, and save it as `My JT Headers and Footers`.	In the `Formatting` data folder.
2. Navigate through the presentation, and observe the footer information on each slide.	

Every slide shows the same footer in the lower left, which currently consists of only a copyright statement. There's no date or slide number.

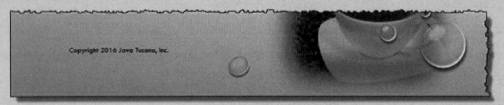

3. Display the presentation in Slide Master view.	On the View tab, in the Master Views group, click **Slide Master**.

4. Select the slide master.	Scroll up and click **Droplet Slide Master** (as displayed in the tooltip), or press the up arrow key to move up to it.
5. Observe the master slide's footer placeholders.	

On the left is the Footer area, on the right is the Number area, and between them is the Date area. Although the date and slide numbers aren't currently set to display in the presentation, they do have their own placeholders.

Do This	How & Why
6. Return to Normal view.	On the Slide Master tab, click **Close Master View**; or, in the status bar, click **Normal**.
7. Click the **Header & Footer** button.	On the Insert tab, in the Text group. The Header and Footer window opens, and the Slide tab is displayed.
8. Click **Date and time**.	Under "Include on slide," to check this option.
9. Click **Update automatically**.	Under "Date and time," to select its radio button.

Do This	How & Why
10. Open the date format dropdown list, and select a date format.	Click [v] to display the choices, then click on a format to select it. 5/3/2016 5/3/2016 Tuesday, May 3, 2016 3 May 2016 May 3, 2016 3-May-16 May 16 May-16 5/3/2016 11:22 AM 5/3/2016 11:22:23 AM 11:22 11:22:23 11:22 AM 11:22:23 AM
11. Click **Slide number**.	Under "Include on slide," to have the slide number displayed on each slide.
12. Observe that the Footer option is checked.	This made the Footer area visible in the presentation when you first opened it.
13. Shorten the current footer to read `Copyright 2016 Java Tucana`.	In the Footer box.

14. Check the **Don't show on title slide** option.

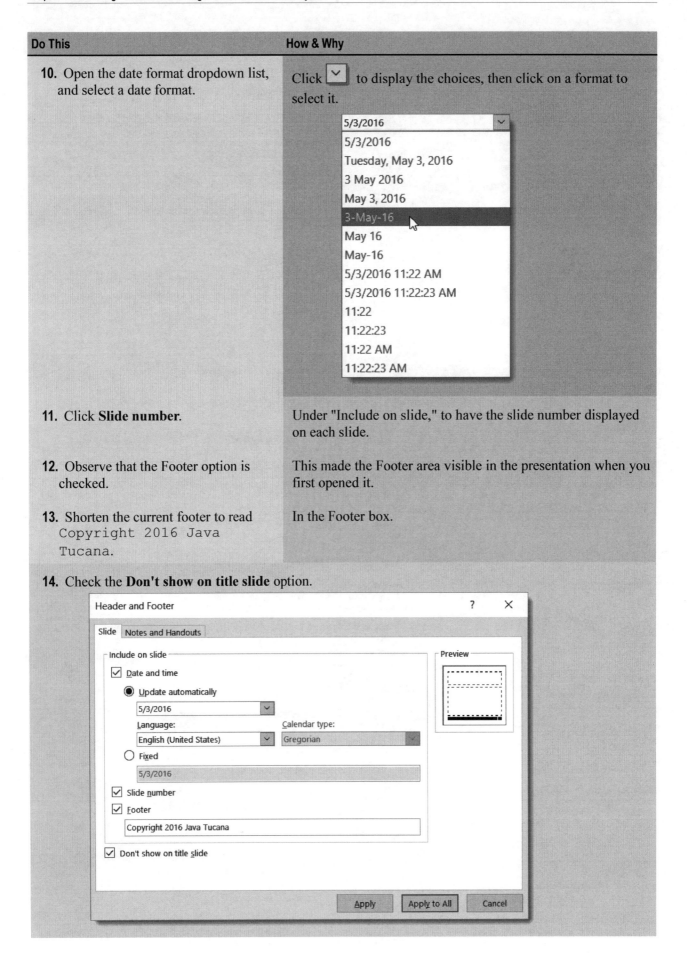

Do This	How & Why
15. Click **Apply to All**.	
16. Navigate the presentation.	
a) Observe slide 1.	No footer is displayed.
b) Observe the remaining slides.	
Slides 2 through 17 all display the same footer in the same way. The slide number changes with each slide.	
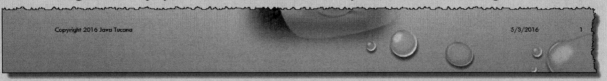	
17. Display Slide Master view.	On the View tab, click **Slide Master**.
18. Select the slide master.	Navigate to the Droplet Slide Master. You'll make the slide numbers larger and move the copyright statement closer to the lower-left corner of the slides.
19. Select the Date area of the footer.	In the Date area, click the <#> field code. 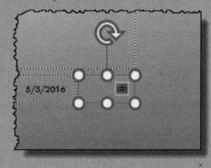 A rotation tool and sizing handles enclose the area.
20. Change the size of the date display to **12** points.	
a) Display the Home tab.	
b) Open the Font Size box, and select **12**.	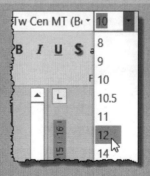
21. Drag the Footer area to the lower-left corner of the slide.	

Do This	How & Why
a) Click on the text in the Footer area, and observe the mouse pointer.	An insertion point appears in the text, and sizing handles border the area.

b) Hover over the Footer area border, and observe the mouse pointer.

It becomes a four-headed arrow, indicating that you can click the area and drag it in any direction.

c) Press and hold the mouse pointer at this position, and drag the Footer area toward the lower-left corner of the slide.

When the left and bottom Footer area borders align roughly with those of the slide, release the mouse button.

22. Return to Normal view, and observe the completed footer.

Still visible only on slides 2 through 17. The slide number is now slightly larger, and the copyright statement now appears closer to the lower-left corner.

23. Save and close the presentation.

About layouts

In Slide Master view, by default, the Slides pane contains a single slide master, called the Office Theme Slide Master. Subordinate to it are 11 individual slide "layouts": Title Slide, Title and Content, Section Header, Two Content, Comparison, Title Only, Blank, Content with Caption, Picture with Caption, Title and Vertical Text, and Vertical Title and Text. By default, only the Title Slide layout is applied to an actual slide (slide 1).

Using the slide master to change a layout

You change a layout in Slide Master view.

 MOS PowerPoint Exam Objective(s): 1.3.3

1. Display Slide Master view.
   On the View tab, click **Slide Master**.

   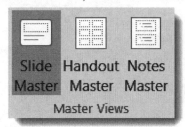

2. Select the layout you wish to change.
   In the Slides pane.

3. Add, remove, or alter any element you wish to change.
   To alter an element, first click in it to place the insertion point. Use the tools on the Slide Master tab to make your changes.

4. Return to Normal view.
   Click **Close Master View**, or click **Normal**.

   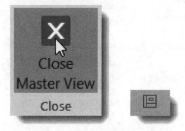

Applying a layout to a slide

You can apply any available layout to an existing slide or to a new slide.

 MOS PowerPoint Exam Objective(s): 1.2.1, 1.2.5, 1.3.4

1. Display the presentation in Normal view.
   In the status bar, click the **Normal** icon, if necessary.

2. Select a slide to receive the new layout.
   - Select the destination slide in the Slides pane.

- Add a new slide to receive the layout.
    i. In the Slides pane, select the slide that will precede the new slide.
    ii. On the Home tab, in the Slides group, click **New Slide**. The new slide appears and is automatically selected.

3. Click **Layout**.

    On the Home tab, in the Slides group.

    The Layout gallery opens.

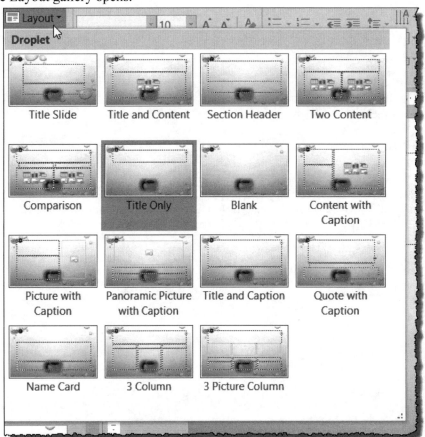

 Note: A slightly shorter method of applying a layout to a selected slide is to click the lower part of the New Slide button, which opens the Layout gallery. From there, you can choose a layout directly.

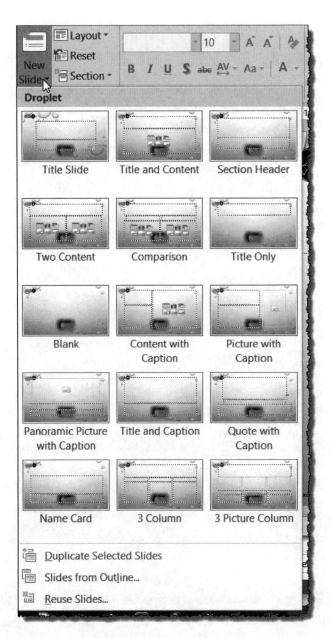

4. Click to select the layout for your slide.

The layout is applied to the selected slide.

Exercise: Working with layouts

Do This	How & Why
1. Open `JT Layout.pptx`, and save it as `My JT Layout.pptx`.	From the `Formatting` data folder.
2. Scroll through the presentation's slides, and observe its theme, features, and layout. Notice also its title and text styles.	
3. Switch to Slide Master view.	On the View tab, in the View Masters group, click **Slide Master**.
4. Click on each of the various layouts provided.	Each type of layout can be used to control different features of a presentation, and each can be applied to specific slides.
5. Hover over the Title Slide layout.	The tooltip informs you that this layout is currently not in use by any slide.
6. Click to select the Title Slide layout.	

7. Select the text prompting you to edit the master title style.

In the main pane, triple-click **Click to Edit the Main Title Style**.

A text formatting toolbar is displayed.

8. Click the arrow to the right of the Font box.	To display available fonts.

Do This	How & Why
9. Select the **Garamond** font.	
10. Change the type size to **54**.	The placeholder text reflects the formatting changes.
a) With the formatting toolbar still displayed, click the arrow to the right of the Font Size box.	
b) Select **54**.	
11. Return to Normal view.	On the Slide Master tab, click **Close Master View**, or click the **Normal** icon in the status bar. You'll add a new main title slide to the presentation.
12. Right-click slide 1, and select **New Slide**.	From the context menu. 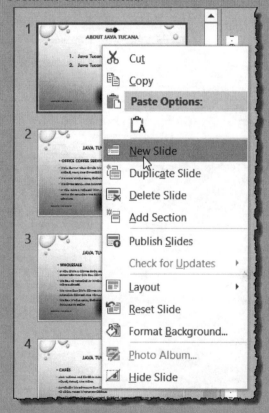 The new slide is inserted after the selected slide.
13. Click and drag the new slide 2 to place it at the top of the slides pane.	The new slide is now slide 1 of the presentation.
14. Click the **Layout** button.	On the Home tab, in the Slides group. To open the Layout gallery. Note that the layouts all fall under the Droplet theme, the current theme of the presentation.

Do This	How & Why

15. Select the **Title Slide** layout from the gallery.

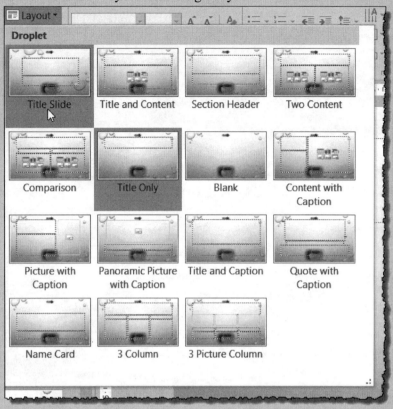

The layout is applied to the new slide, and placeholders for a title and subtitle are displayed.

16. Add the title `Java Tucana`.	Click in the title placeholder, then type the text. The new title is inserted in Garamond 54-point type. Note that although you typed the name in initial capitals, it appears in all capitals. This is because the titles in the Droplet theme were automatically formatted to appear in all capitals.

Do This	How & Why
17. Add the subtitle `Only the Best`.	The subtitle also appears in all capitals.
18. Change the color of the slide's title to **Dark Red**.	
a) Select the title.	Drag over "JAVA TUCANA" or triple-click it.
b) Click the arrow next to the Font Color button.	To open the Font Color gallery.
c) Select **Dark Red**.	Under Standard Colors. 

19. Deselect the text boxes.

Click in a blank area of the slide outside the text boxes. The new title and subtitle are displayed on the slide.

20. Save and close the file.

Assessment: Working with slide masters and layouts

1. True or false? The easiest way to modify the formatting of all slides in a presentation at once is by modifying the slide master.

    - True
    - False

2. Which of these actions would you perform to change the theme of a presentation?

    - In Normal view, choose SmartArt on the Insert tab.
    - In Normal view, choose Outline on the View tab to open the gallery.
    - In Slide Master view, choose Themes on the View tab, and select a theme from the gallery.
    - In Slide Master view, choose Themes on the Slide Master tab, and select a theme from the gallery.

3. True or false? One of the benefits of Slide Master view is that you can change all layouts from a single slide master.

    - True
    - False

Module B: Formatting slides and text

You can change the appearance of text on one or more slides in your presentation. Also, even after you've applied a theme to your presentation, you can change the appearance of a slide background and apply effects such as textures.

You will learn how to:

- Format text and apply text styles
- Apply slide backgrounds and effects

About text styles

A text *style* is its font, size, color, spacing, alignment, and orientation. As you have seen, when you apply a theme to a slide master, the text style associated with it is automatically applied to all the slides governed by that master. Similarly, if you alter the master slide's text style, all slides that it governs will display the alteration.

You can, however, modify text styles of individual slides without affecting others in the presentation. But you can only do so in Normal view.

Changing master text styles

In Slide Master view, text style changes that you apply to a slide master affect all slides governed by that master.

 MOS PowerPoint Exam Objective(s): 2.1.2

1. Display your presentation in Slide Master view.
   On the View tab, in the Master Views group, click **Slide Master**.

2. Select the slide master.
   Not one of the layouts.

3. Edit the master title style.

   a) In the master title placeholder, select the text **CLICK TO EDIT MASTER TITLE STYLE**.

   b) To make changes in font, size, color, spacing, or alignment, use the context formatting toolbar; or, on the Home tab, use the tools in the Font and/or Paragraph groups.

   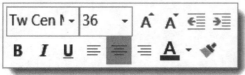

   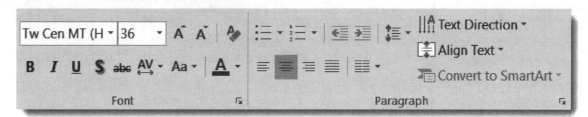

   c) For special text effects, such as text shape styles and WordArt styles, use the tools on the Drawing Tools Format tab.

4. Edit the master text styles.

   a) Change the main text style.

   Select the placeholder text **CLICK TO EDIT MASTER TEXT STYLES**, then use one (or more) of the methods in step 3 to change the text format.

   b) Change the style of any subordinate text levels.

   Select the desired text level—for example, the **SECOND LEVEL** placeholder text—and use the formatting tools to change the text style as you wish.

In Normal view, the text on all presentation slides governed by the altered slide master appears in the new format.

Changing text styles of individual slides

You can change the style of text on individual slides without affecting any other slides.

 MOS PowerPoint Exam Objective(s): 2.1.6

1. Display your presentation in Normal view.

   If necessary, click in the status bar.

2. Select the slide containing the text you want to format.

3. Apply any formatting changes.

   Doing so overrides the master text style for only that slide.

In the event that you want to revert an individually formatted slide to the master style (determined by the slide master), in the left pane, right-click that slide to display a context menu. Then click **Reset Slide**.

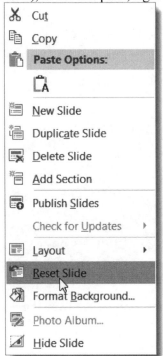

Creating bulleted and numbered lists

Creating bulleted and numbered lists in PowerPoint is quite simple.

 MOS PowerPoint Exam Objective(s): 2.1.5

1. Select the text you wish to convert to a bulleted or numbered list.
2. Click the **Bullets** or **Numbering** button.
    On the Home tab, in the Paragraph group.

3. You can further customize the bullet or number type.
    - To select another bullet type, click the arrow to the right of the Bullets button, and make a selection from the gallery. To further customize your selection, click **Bullets and Numbering**. On the Bulleted tab of the Bullets and Numbering window, you can change the size and/or color of an existing bullet type. In addition, you can click **Picture** to navigate to an image that you'd like to use as a bullet; or, click **Customize** to open the Symbol browser, from which you can select a symbol to use as a bullet.

    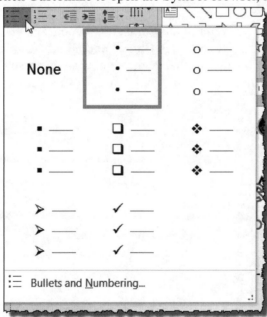

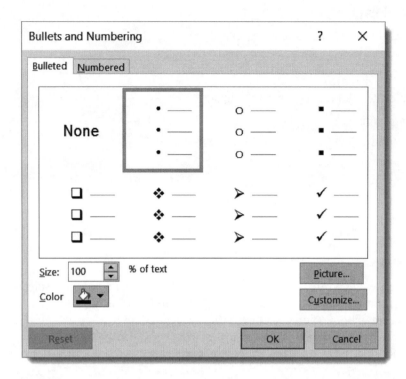

- To select another numbering type, click the arrow to the right of the Numbering button, and make a selection from the gallery. To further customize your selection, click **Bullets and Numbering**. On the Numbered tab of the Bullets and Numbering window, you can change the number style, as well as its size and color. In addition, you can specify the starting number for the first item in your list.

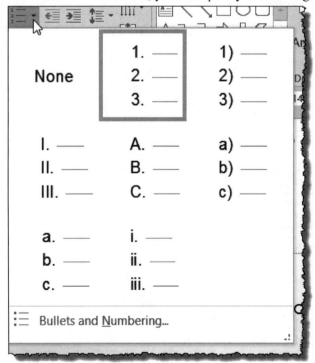

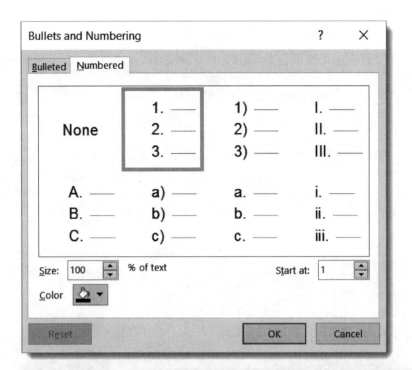

1. 2015 sales by region and product
2. Future prospects
   - Immediate
   - Long term

Exercise: Working with text styles

In this exercise, you'll change a master title style, and you'll format some text on individual slides.

Do This	How & Why
1. Open JT Text Styles.pptx and save it as My JT Text Styles.pptx.	In the Formatting data folder.
2. Navigate and observe the slides in the short presentation.	The titles of all the slides are currently very small and require enlargement. Also, a couple of the slides contain lists that could benefit from bullets and/or numbers.
3. Display Slide Master view.	On the View tab, click **Slide Master**.
4. Display the Retrospect Slide Master.	Select it in the left pane.
5. Select the text **Click to edit Master title style**.	
6. Change the size of the master title to 44 points.	Use the context formatting toolbar or the Home tab's Font group, open the Size list, and select **44**.
7. Return to Normal view.	Click on the status bar.

78   PowerPoint 2016 Level 1

Do This	How & Why

8. View all the slides.

The title of each is enlarged. However, the slide 1 title is intended as the main one of the presentation, so it should probably stand out a bit more. You need to override the master title style for this slide to make its title appear different from the others, all of which are governed by the master title style.

9. Select the slide 1 title, **Java Tucana Sales Report**.	You're still in Normal view.
10. Make the title bold.	On the context formatting toolbar, or on the Home tab, in the Font group, click the **Bold** button.

11. Deselect the title, observe the result, and compare it to the other slides in the presentation.

Click a blank area of the slide outside the title text box to observe the title. Only the slide 1 title appears bold. Now, you need to make the other items on this slide stand out a bit more.

12. Enlarge the first two (main) list items to 36 points.	Drag over **2015 sales by region and product** and **Future prospects**, open the Size list (in the context toolbar or on the Home tab), and click **36**. The two items are enlarged. Now, however, the indented list below them looks ridiculously tiny.
13. Enlarge the two indented items to 28 points.	Select **Immediate** and **Long term**, and from the Size list, select **28**.

14. Deselect and observe the items on slide 1.	2015 sales by region and product
	Future prospects
	    Immediate
	    Long term

Do This	How & Why

15. Format the first two items as a numbered list.
 	
  a) Select both items.
 	
  b) Click the **Numbering** button.
	
	On the Home tab, in the Paragraph group.

16. Format the indented items as a bulleted list.
 	
  a) Select both **Immediate** and **Long term**.
 	
  b) Click the **Bullets** button.
	
	On the Home tab, in the Paragraph group.

17. Deselect the list, and observe the results.

The items appear as numbered and bulleted lists.

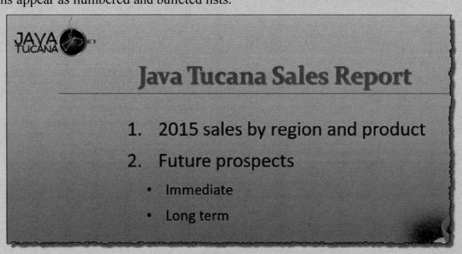

18. Observe slide 3.	The last three items aren't aligned properly in relation to the other text elements. Plus, they could use a bit of visual spice.
19. Format the last three items as a bulleted list.	The items begin **Within**, **We're**, and **In terms of**. Select all the items, then click the **Bullets** button.

Do This	How & Why
20. Deselect the list, and observe the results.	The items were indented slightly, but no bullets are displayed. You need to troubleshoot!

Immediate

We at Java Tucana are looking to futu

Within each sales region, we're maki growing list of customer countries an

We're building deeper, sustainable re partner with new growers, to expand shape and support their future grow

In terms of end users, we are in the p into additional markets in all regions brand recognition and presence. |
| 21. Select the three items again, then open the Bullets gallery. | Click the arrow next to the Bullets button. The Custom bullets option is selected, which, unfortunately for us, only indents the text slightly but does not actually display any bullets. You need to remedy this situation! 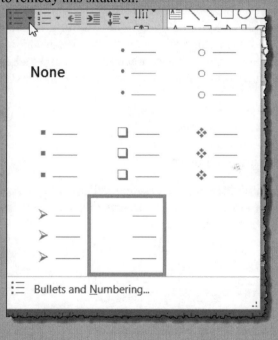 |
| 22. Select the **Filled Round Bullets** option. | 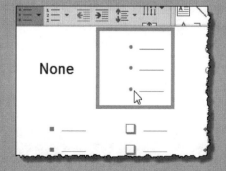 |

Do This	How & Why
23. Deselect the text, and observe the results.	**Immediate** We at Java Tucana are looking to future in a va[...] Within each sales region, we're making a conc[...] growing list of customer countries and clients. We're building deeper, sustainable relationship[...] partner with new growers, to expand our inver[...] shape and support their future growth. In terms of end users, we are in the process of[...] into additional markets in all regions, to increa[...] brand recognition and presence.
24. Save and close the presentation.	

About slide backgrounds

MOS PowerPoint Exam Objective(s): 1.2.6

You can apply a slide background, then you can modify it to make it look the way you want. Simply select the desired slide and, on the Design tab, in the Customize group, click **Format Background**. This opens the Format Background pane, which is context sensitive, and makes available many different kinds of settings, depending on whether you've selected a slide, clicked in a text box, clicked an object, and so on.

When you select a slide in the left pane of Normal view, only the Fill settings are visible in the Format Background pane. These settings control the background fill effects, and those in the lower part of the pane change, depending on whether you've selected a *Solid*, *Gradient*, *Picture or texture*, or *Pattern* fill. The settings for each fill type allow you to tweak it in many ways.

- *Gradient*: Provides fill settings such as Presets; Type, such as Linear, Radial, and Rectangular; Direction; Color, Position, and Transparency; as well as Gradient stops, which allow you to specify a precise gradient using three sliders.

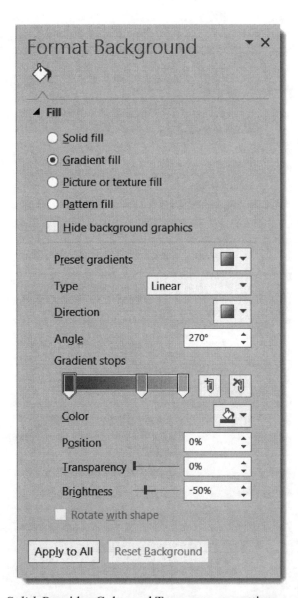

- *Solid*: Provides Color and Transparency settings.

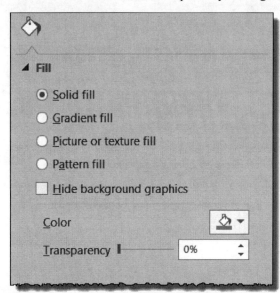

- *Picture or texture*: Allows you to use a suggested texture, or open or download a picture file to use as a background. Included are additional options, such as Texture; Transparency; and orientation offset, size, and alignment settings.

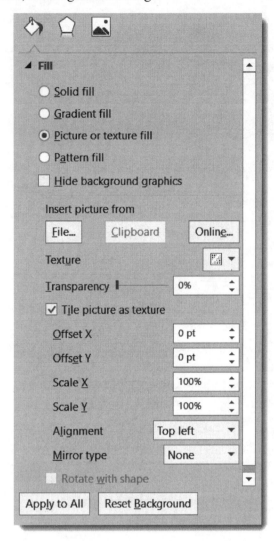

- *Pattern*: Allows you to select a fill pattern, and modify foreground and background pattern colors.

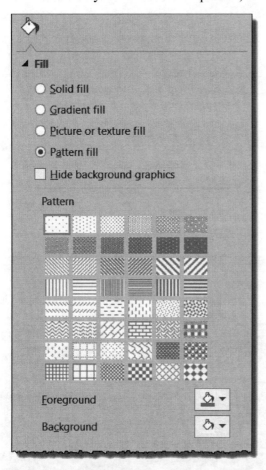

- The **Hide background graphics** option removes any background pictures from view. Keep in mind that doing so also removes the graphics from the final presentation.

Besides affecting the selected slide, any changes you make can be applied to all slides in the presentation. To do so, once you've made your changes, click **Apply to All**.

Once you change settings, the **Reset Background** button serves as a kind of "panic button" that allows you to revert the background to its original settings, should your artistic impulse have taken you to unwanted territory.

Gridlines

When you're working with the many visual elements available in PowerPoint, the rulers can help you to assess relative sizes and positions of objects, and so on. But especially when moving objects around on slides, some people find it helpful to display gridlines. *Gridlines* are evenly spaced horizontal and vertical dotted lines that provide a visual reference. You can view them in Normal, Outline, or Notes view. Gridlines don't display in the final product, however—they're merely a kind of preview.

 MOS PowerPoint Exam Objective(s): 2.3.4

To display gridlines, on the View tab, in the Show group, click **Gridlines** to check the option. To remove the gridlines, click **Gridlines** again to uncheck it.

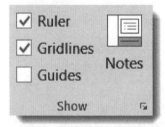

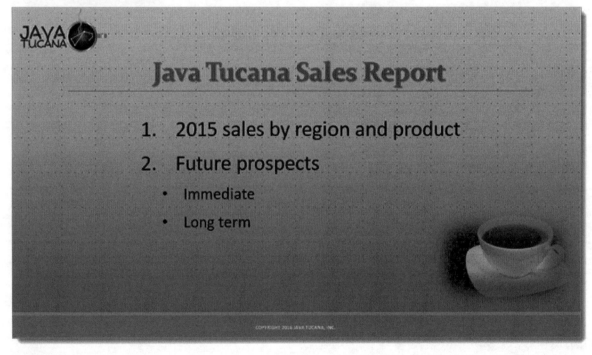

Exercise: Working with slide backgrounds

Do This	How & Why
1. Open `JT Background.pptx`, and save it as `My JT Background.pptx`.	In the `Formatting` data folder.
2. Navigate through this short presentation, and observe the appearance of slide text and graphics in relation to backgrounds.	The presentation looks pretty good, but the text and bullets could stand in better contrast to their background. This is especially noticeable in slides 3 and 4, which contain more text than the others. The lack of contrast compromises their readability.
3. Select slide 2.	
4. Open the Format Background pane.	On the Design tab, in the Customize group, click **Format Background**. 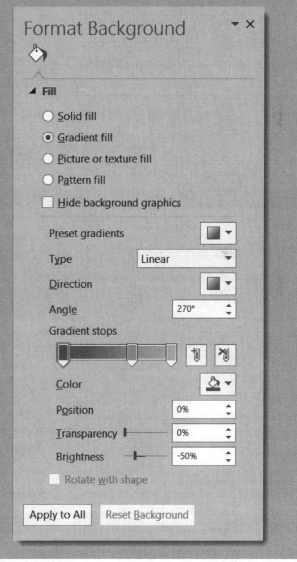

Do This	How & Why
5. Click the Preset gradients box, and select the **Top Spotlight - Accent 2** preset. 	

The chart background on slide 2 is a little brighter, making the chart figures more readable.

Do This	How & Why
6. Select slide 3.	The Format Background should still be open; if not, click **Format Background**.
7. Click the **Picture or texture fill** option.	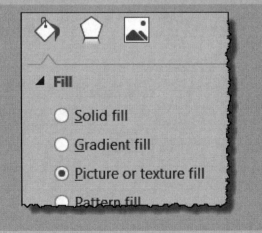
8. Select a texture.	
a) Click on the **Texture** box.	The Texture gallery opens.

Do This	How & Why

b) Click a texture.

Do This	How & Why

9. Adjust the transparency of the textured background, so that the text is easily readable.

- Drag the Transparency slider left to decrease texture transparency, or drag it right to increase transparency.

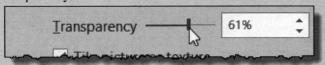

- Next to the Transparency percentage box, use the increment or decrement arrow buttons to increase or decrease texture transparency, respectively.

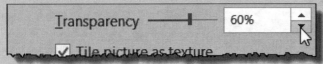

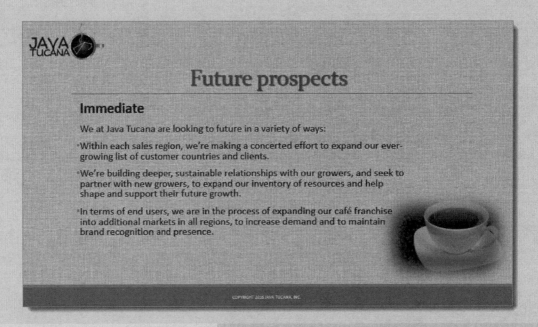

Do This	How & Why
10. Select slide 4, and click **Picture or texture fill**.	In the Format Background pane. The appearance of this slide might be too "busy." A preset texture is already applied to the slide, but you'll change this option shortly.
11. Check the **Hide background graphics** option.	The logo and coffee cup images are removed from the slide.
12. Select the **White Marble** texture from the gallery.	
a) Click the **Texture** box.	

Do This	How & Why

b) Click **White Marble**.

Use the tooltips as a guide.

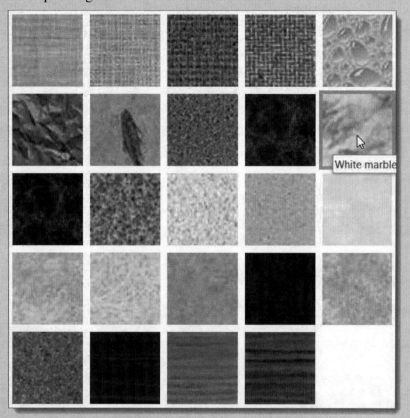

The White Marble background texture is applied. However, it doesn't appear to aid readability of the text, and it looks rather hideous. You'd better fix that!

Do This	How & Why
13. Click the **Reset Background** button.	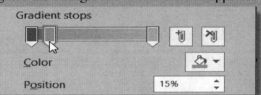
	The slide background reverts to its original gradient fill. However, the "Hide background graphics" option remains checked. In this context, "resetting" refers to background color and texture but does not affect certain additional options.
14. Drag the Gradient stops central slider to the left, until the value in the position box reads **15%**.	To lighten the background where the text appears. The text appears considerably more readable. Perhaps you can display the background graphics after all.

15. Uncheck **Hide background graphics**.

The graphics don't seem to detract from the overall look of the page, and the logo seems necessary on this last slide.

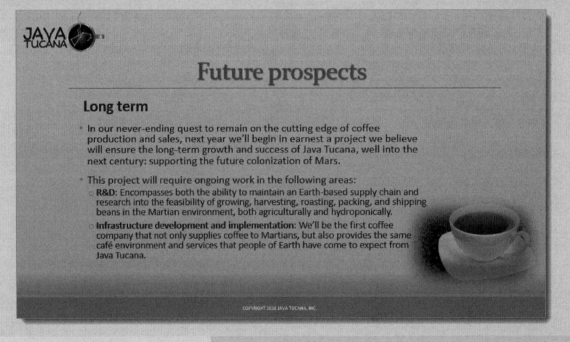

16. Save and close the file.

Assessment: Formatting slides and text

1. Where can you change text styles so that all slides in a presentation will have identically formatted text.
   - On the Slide Title layout, in Slide Master view.
   - On the slide text, in Master view.
   - On the slide master.
   - On the Text Master, in Slide Master view.

2. True or false? You can change the text style of a slide by unchecking Slide Master Layout option in Slide Master view.
   - True
   - False

3. How can you create a numbered list that doesn't begin with the numeral 1?
   - Select the appropriate numbered list style in the Numbering gallery.
   - Specify the starting number of the list on the Numbering tab of the Bullets and Numbering window.
   - In the Bullets and Numbering pane, uncheck the Start at 1 option.
   - In the Numbering window, select the Customize option.

4. True or false? If you've made all your changes to a slide background, including hiding the background graphics, you can restore the graphics by clicking Reset Background.
   - True
   - False

Summary: Formatting

You should now know how to:

- Apply and modify slide masters, headers and footers, and layouts
- Modify text styles of all or individual slides, create bulleted and numbered lists, display gridlines, and modify backgrounds of all or individual slides

Synthesis: Formatting

1. Open `JT Formatting Assessment.pptx`, and save it as `My JT Formatting Assessment.pptx`.
2. Format the two lines of text under the title as a numbered list.
3. On slides 2 through 9, make all the text items (other than introductory phrases) bulleted lists.
4. Apply a theme to the whole presentation.
5. Add a new title slide to begin the presentation, and assign it the Title Slide layout.
6. Give the title slide the title `Java Tucana`. Subtitle it `Only the Best`.
7. Insert footer information.
    a) Edit the copyright statement to read `Copyright 2016 Java Tucana`. Then move it to the lower-left corner of the slide and resize it, as necessary. If you like, display gridlines as a visual reference.
    b) Select a date format to display.
    c) Display slide numbers.
    d) Have the footer display on all slides except for the title slide.
8. Change any (or all) master text styles to affect all the slides in the presentation.
9. Format the title slide text styles to make them unique.
10. Choose at least one other slide, and make its text style(s) different from all the others.
11. Apply a single background to all the slides in the presentation. Apply any formatting—including colors, textures, and other effects—that you like.
12. Make the title slide background unique, and suppress the background images on it.
13. Create another background for the slides that begins each major section. They can either all be the same or completely different from one another. Apply any formatting you like. Feel free to include one or more images, from either a file or downloaded from the Web.
14. Save and close the presentation.

Chapter 4: Working with shapes and images

You will learn how to:

- Create and format shapes
- Insert and work with images

Module A: Creating and formatting shapes

In PowerPoint, you can create shapes that provide visual impact and can help to convey information. There are many tools for drawing and working with basic shapes, and you can change shapes, move them, resize them, and even layer them as you wish.

You will learn how to:

- Draw, modify, and layer shapes on your slides

About shapes

PowerPoint provides some powerful tools that allow you to create and work with shapes on your slides. The easiest way to add a shape to a slide is by using the Shapes gallery. To open the Shapes gallery, on the Insert tab, in the Illustrations group, click **Shapes**.

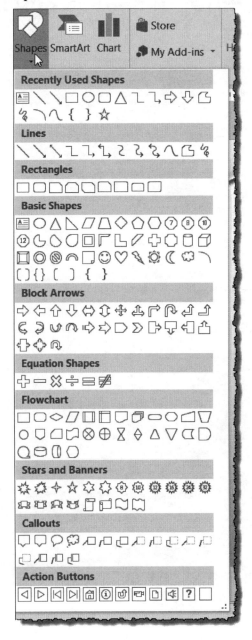

The Shapes gallery is arranged by shape type, making it easier for you to select the shape you want.

- *Recently Used Shapes*: Each time you create/draw a new shape, that shape subsequently appears here. Up to 24 shapes display here; after that, each new shape replaces the oldest one.
- *Lines*: Every type of line, from completely straight to free form.
- *Rectangles*: Every type of "rectangle," even those with one or more corners "cut off."
- *Basic Shapes*: A potpourri of common shapes of various types.
- *Block Arrows*: Straight and curved "hollow" arrows.
- *Equation Shapes*: Used for simple arithmetic.
- *Flowchart*: Used for creating flowcharts.
- *Stars and Banners*: Used primarily for grabbing attention.
- *Callouts*: Speech and text balloons like those used in comics.
- *Action Buttons*: Used primarily for slideshow navigation.

Click a shape in the gallery to select it. Once you've clicked a shape, click to place the shape on the slide. You then "draw" the shape from that point. However, keep in mind that the techniques for drawing shapes vary slightly by type. For example, drawing a straight line is different than drawing a circle or polygon.

Even after you've selected and placed a shape on a slide, you can change it to another shape. To do so, first select the shape you wish to replace, then display the Drawing Tools Format tab. In the Insert Shapes group, click **Edit Shape** to open a menu, and select **Change Shape**, then select the new shape. The selected shape is placed at the position of the one it replaces.

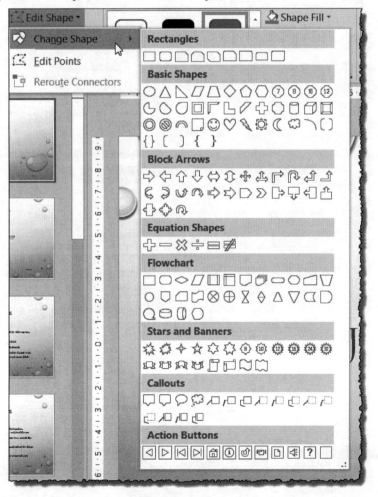

Once you create any open shape, it can serve as a text box as well, in which you can enter text. The effect is the same as clicking **Text Box**. Either way, you drag it to define its area.

Drawing shapes

In PowerPoint, *shapes* are lines—including straight and freehand ones—and open shapes, such as circles, ovals, polygons, and so on.

 MOS PowerPoint Exam Objective(s): 2.2.1, 2.2.2

1. Click **Shapes**.

    On the Insert tab, in the Illustrations group.

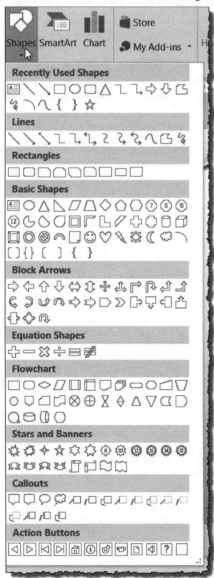

2. Select a shape.
   Click the shape to select it.

3. Click on the slide to place a point of origin for the shape, and drag to a destination point.
   To define the length of the line or the area to contain the open shape. When you click, press and hold the mouse button, so that you're ready to drag. To draw a perfectly straight line, press and hold the **Shift** key before you drag. Dragging up/down or left/right results in a vertical or horizontal line, respectively. However, if you press **Shift** and drag on a diagonal, the straight line is drawn at a 45-degree angle.

 Note: You can insert text within (or over) a shape. Once your shape is drawn, on the Insert tab (or the Drawing Tools Format tab), click **Text Box**. Then drag inside (or over) the shape to define the text box, and type the text.

Curved shapes

If you select the Curve shape from the Line group in the Shapes gallery, you can specify exactly how many curves you'd like in the shape and exactly where you'd like those curves placed along its length.

First, select the **Curve** shape.

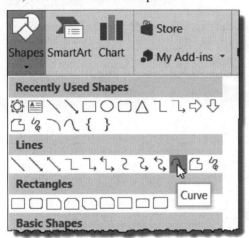

Next, click to place the origin point of the curve. (In this case, you don't press and hold, as there's no need to drag to draw the shape.) Then, click anywhere else that you want the next (and subsequent) curves to appear. To end the shape, double-click a destination point. If you place the destination point at the point of origin, the shape becomes a closed loop.

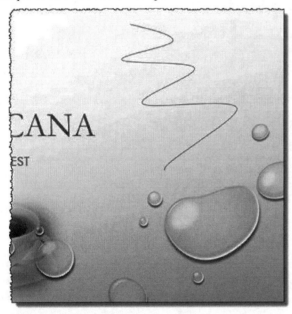

Useful tools for working with shapes

Besides the rulers and gridlines, another very useful tool for helping you to position, size, and align shapes (as well as other slide elements) is PowerPoint's guides. The *guides* are horizontal and vertical crosshairs that meet at the exact center of a slide. Thus, for a visual reference, you can use either crosshair as a center line, or the crosshairs formed by both. Rulers, gridlines, and guides displayed in conjunction can be powerful aids in helping you create well-designed slides.

To display the guides, on the View tab, in the Show group, click **Guides**.

The guides align at the zero points on their respective horizontal and vertical rulers. Whenever you work with drawn shapes, PowerPoint zero-centers the rulers.

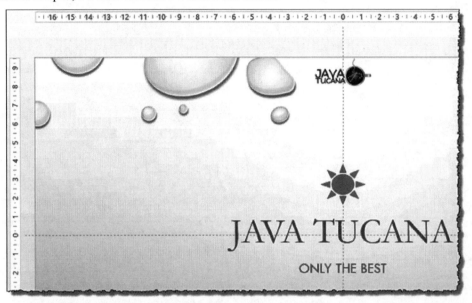

 Note: Once you click on a text object, the rulers measure horizontal and vertical distance and denote tab stops, margins, and so on. Also, if you wish to change the position of one or both guides—and thus were they intersect—just drag them to the new location. For example, this can be useful to center an object on a point that isn't the center of the slide.

For further control of gridlines and guides, click ▣ (the launcher) in the View tab's Show group. This opens the Grid and Guides window. Here, you can adjust features such as grid spacing, and you can specify exactly what displays. The **Snap objects to grid** option is useful when you want to make sure objects are perfectly aligned to the grid: as you move an object close to the grid, the object "snaps" to the gridline as if connected to it by a rubber band.

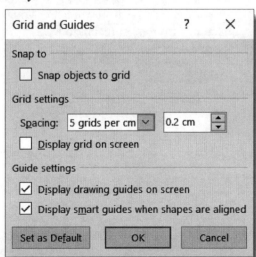

The *zoom slider*, near the right edge of the status bar, can be extremely useful, particularly in helping you size and align smaller shapes at precise locations on your slides. Drag the slider to the right to zoom in or to the left to zoom out. The value displayed is the percentage of zoom. A value of 100% is normal size. Thus, for example, 50% would be half the normal size, and 300% would be three times the normal size.

In the Drawing Tools Format tab's Arrange group, the **Align** button contains many options for aligning a shape (or any object) on a slide.

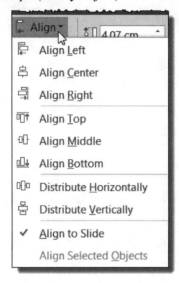

- *Align Left*, *Align Center*, and *Align Right* are used to position shapes (objects) horizontally.
- *Align Top*, *Align Middle*, and *Align Bottom* are used to position them vertically.
- *Distribute Horizontally* and *Distribute Vertically* are for evenly spacing selected shapes (objects) in their respective directions. *Align to Slide* is selected by default; however, selecting multiple shapes activates the *Align Selected Objects* option. The two outermost shapes in the selection determine the area of distribution.

A very important tool in the presentation design arsenal is the **Undo** command, available on the Quick Access toolbar or by pressing **Ctrl+Z**. Even if you're not fond of keyboard shortcuts, it's highly recommended that you remember this one, as it comes in very handy—and not just in PowerPoint.

To undo your last action, click on the Quick Access toolbar, or press **Ctrl+Z**. To display a list of your most recent actions, click the arrow at the right of the button. A list of actions, from most recent to least recent, is displayed. Thus, you can undo your most recent action or multiple ones.

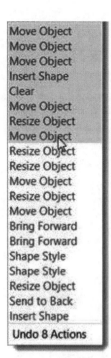

 Note: When you undo multiple actions, you can't "skip over" actions in the list. Thus, using this method, selecting the fifteenth most recent action also "undoes" the 14 actions that followed it.

Resizing shapes

When you select a shape, resizing handles become visible. These handles work the same way as those on text box borders. In addition, shapes display a special handle that allows you to change the shape symmetrically.

 MOS PowerPoint Exam Objective(s): 2.2.3

1. Click the shape you wish to resize.
   To select it and display its resizing handles.

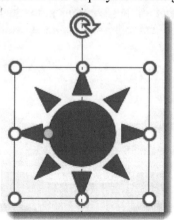

2. Drag the resizing handles as you would to resize a text box.
3. Drag the special yellow sizing handle toward the center of the shape.
   The shape's proportions are altered symmetrically.

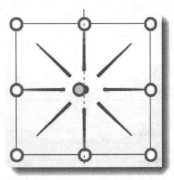

4. Drag the yellow handle back out past its original position, to the outer edge of the shape.

The shape's proportions are again altered, but this time its central area is enlarged and its outer edge is diminished in size.

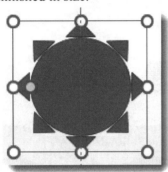

Shape styles

 MOS PowerPoint Exam Objective(s): 2.2.4, 2.2.5

You can format shape styles using the Shape Styles group on the Drawing Tools Format tab. Another—and perhaps more powerful—way is via the Format Shape pane, which you open by clicking the Shape Styles group (launcher) button. Either way, you have the choice of setting fill options, outlines, and shape effects, including 3-D, reflections, and shadows. Besides being able to set all these options individually, PowerPoint provides many different kinds of presets that group these effects to good advantage, which can take some guesswork out of the process, particularly for non-artists.

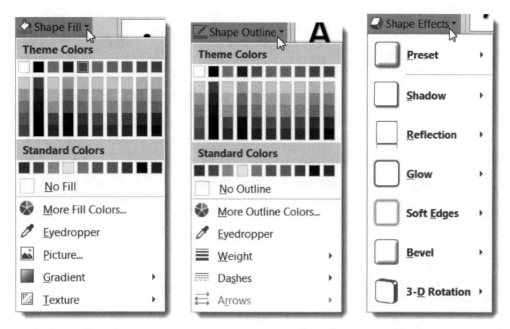

- *Shape Fill* is the color, texture, or pattern you can use to fill a closed shape. Use these options in the same way you would when working with slide backgrounds. Many of the same tools apply to both.
- *Shape Outline* is the outline, or border, of a shape, or, if the shape is a line, the appearance of the line.
- *Shape Effects* allows you to apply effects such as shadows, reflections, and 3-D.

The Format Shape pane provides all these options as well, but they're combined in one location and are more easily fine-tuned. Plus, you have access to precise Size & Properties options.

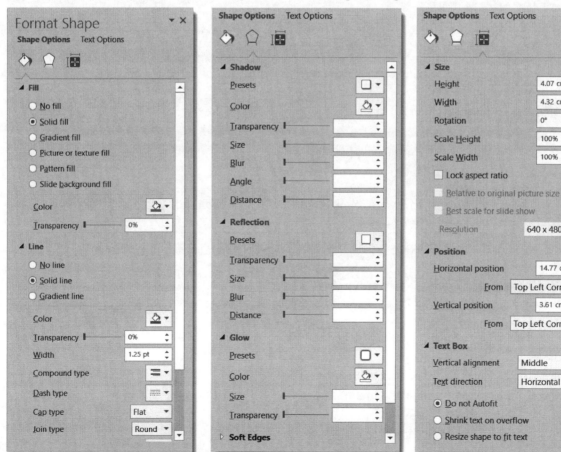

Layering, aligning, and grouping shapes

It's possible to add many different shapes, text boxes, and other objects to a slide. But when you do so, you run the risk of them running into each other in ways that are neither pleasant nor helpful. Fortunately, you can control this slide "traffic" by working with objects as *layers*.

When you add a shape to a slide, it's considered one object layer. If you add another object, whether or not the objects overlap to any extent, the new object is treated as another layer laid on top of the first one, and so on. Thus, you run the risk of having objects that you added earlier covered up, at least to some extent, by those added later. This is especially important when objects added later have an opaque fill color, for example.

Fortunately, PowerPoint allows you to endlessly shuffle the stacking order of layers to your heart's content. You can also align slide layers to position them where you want. Once you've finished working with the layers, you can then group them, so that you can then move the group of layers without altering their relative positions and alignment.

 MOS PowerPoint Exam Objective(s): 2.4.1, 2.4.2, 2.4.3, 2.4.4

1. Select an object layer that you wish to move among the stack.
   Click the object. Its layer is automatically selected.

2. Move the layer to the front (top) or back (bottom) of the stack.
   Using the tools in the Drawing Tools Format tab's Arrange group.

   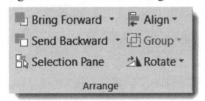

   - To move the layer one layer forward, click **Bring Forward**. Each time you use this command, it brings the object forward one layer.
   - To move the layer to the front, click the arrow next to the Bring Forward tool, and select **Bring to Front** from the menu.

   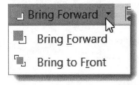

   - To move the layer one layer backward, click **Send Backward**. Each time you use this command, it sends the object back one layer.
   - To move the layer to the back, click the arrow next to the Send Backward tool, and select **Send to Back** from the menu.

   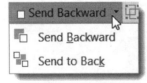

3. To align objects, select the objects, and then click **Align**.
   Use **Ctrl** to select multiple objects. On the Drawing Tools Format tab or Picture Tools Format tab, depending on the objects selected.

   A list of alignment options is displayed.

4. Select an alignment option.

5. To group objects, select them, and then click **Group**.

   To display a list of Group options. Before the objects are grouped, the Group option is the only one available.

6. Click **Group**.

   In the list of Group options.

Exercise: Working with shapes

In this exercise, you'll create and work with shapes.

Do This	How & Why
1. Open `JT Shapes.pptx`, and save it as `My JT Shapes.pptx`.	In the `Working with shapes and images` data folder.
2. Make sure that rulers, gridlines, and guides are displayed.	All three options are available on the View tab, in the Show group. Make sure that each is checked. 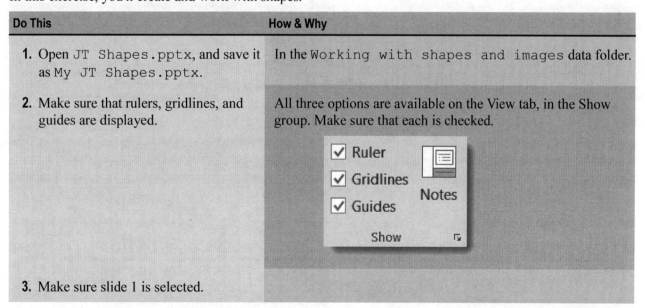
3. Make sure slide 1 is selected.	

Do This	How & Why
4. Select the **Line** tool from the Shapes gallery.	In the Insert tab's Illustrations group. 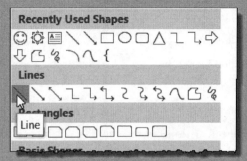 The mouse pointer becomes a crosshair. 
5. Create a perfectly horizontal line, and center it vertically between the lines of text, and horizontally using the vertical guide.	
a) Press and hold **Shift**, and about midway between "JAVA TUCANA" and "ONLY THE BEST," and left of the vertical guide, click to place the mouse pointer, and drag to the right, roughly past the vertical guide.	
b) Click to set a destination point.	A straight, horizontal line appears.
c) Drag to center it between the lines of text.	As you drag the line up and down, at a certain position, fine horizontal guides on either side of the line indicate that it's perfectly centered between the lines of text.
d) Now, carefully center the line horizontally as well.	

The guides for centering vertically appear The horizontal guides (for centering vertically) appear above and below the line, and the vertical center guide (for centering horizontally) becomes bolder, indicating that the line is properly centered.

Do This	How & Why
e) If necessary, resize the line to make it roughly the size shown in the figure.	Use the sizing handles. Afterward, double-check to make sure it's still centered, and adjust it, as necessary.
6. Apply a shape outline to the line.	
a) If necessary, click to select the line.	
b) Click **Shape Outline**.	On the Drawing Tool Format tab, in the Shape Styles group.
c) Select a Weight of **1 pt**.	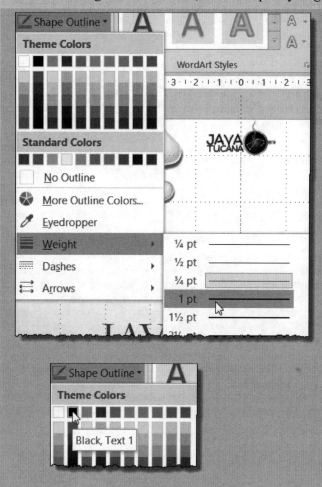
d) Click Shape Outline, and apply the color named **Black, Text 1**.	
7. Place a roughly vertical, curved shape at both ends of "JAVA TUCANA."	

Do This	How & Why
a) Select the Curve shape from the Shapes gallery.	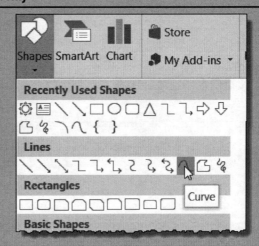
b) Click to place its origin point. Then click a few points along the way to create a roughly vertical wave shape. Double-click to place a destination point and complete the shape.	
c) Repeat steps 7a and 7b to create a similar curved shape at the other end of the text.	
d) Move the curves, as necessary, to roughly match the figure. 	
8. Select both curves.	Select one curve, then press and hold **Ctrl**, and click to select the other curve.

Do This	How & Why

9. Apply the **Green, 5 pt glow, Accent color 2** shape effect.

Click the **Shape Effects** tool in the Shape Styles group to open the Glow gallery.

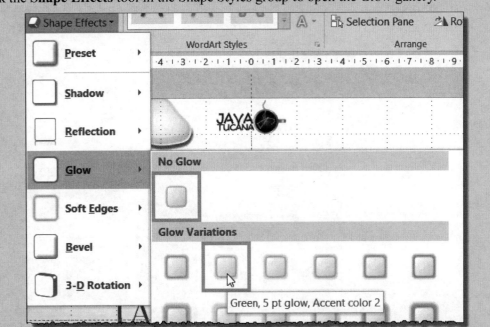

10. Add an open shape on the slide, enclosing the existing shapes and text.

Typical open shapes include rectangles, ovals, and other geometric shapes. The shape is displayed filled by default, and it now covers all the other work you've done! Don't worry, you'll fix this shortly.

Do This	How & Why
11. First, apply the **Recycled paper** fill texture to the new shape.	Click **Shape Fill**, point to Texture, and use the tooltip to find and click **Recycled paper**. 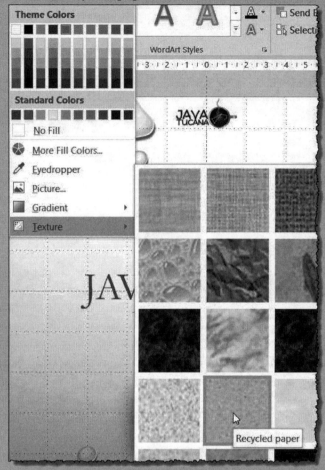 The fill texture is applied to the shape, but you still can't see what's behind it.
12. Send the front layer back one layer. a) If necessary, select the textured shape.	

Do This	How & Why
b) Click **Send Backward**.	To send the front layer back one layer. 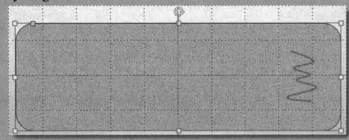 Not exactly the result you'd like! Only the curve last added appears in front now. The other shapes all remain hidden behind the filled shape. It's clearly time for some extreme layering.
13. This time, send the filled shape to the back of the stack.	
a) Click the arrow next to Send Backward.	To open the Send Backward options.
b) Click **Send to Back**.	 Now, all your new shapes and the text are visible and appear to sit on the textured surface of the back layer.
14. Remove the shape outline.	Use the figure as a guide. 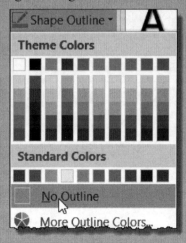

Chapter 4: Working with shapes and images / Module A: Creating and formatting shapes

Do This	How & Why
15. Apply the **Preset 3** shape effect.	Use the figure as a guide.
16. Deselect the shapes, then hide the gridlines and guides. Refer to step 2 for some hints. Observe the completed slide.	
17. Save and close the file.	

Assessment: Creating and formatting shapes

1. True or false? The Shapes gallery allows you to create multiple shape layers at once.

    - True
    - False

2. Which of the following statements about creating curved shapes is true?

    - To create each curve in a single curved shape, click and drag in a rounded manner to avoid sharp angles.
    - It's important to click at the destination point to complete the shape.
    - Double-click at the destination point to complete the shape.
    - You're allowed up to 24 curves in a single curved shape.

3. True or false? Pressing and holding the Shift key while drawing a line allows you to create perfectly straight diagonals.

    - True
    - False

4. Which of the following statements about shape layers is true?

    - To bring the backmost layer to the front, you must click Bring to Front multiple times, especially if there are several layers or more.
    - In a shape group of five layers, if the third layer contains important text, and all other layers are opaque, the text layer could be brought to the front to render it readable.
    - In a shape group of five layers, if the third layer contains important text, and all other layers are opaque, the text on the third layer could be formatted as bold to make it show through the other layers.
    - Always send the front-most layer to the back of the stack if it obscures the layer behind it.

Module B: Working with images

Just as with shapes, you can enhance your presentation by inserting images on your slides. Because PowerPoint treats images as objects, you can modify them, add effects, and layer them to achieve your aims.

You will learn how to:

- Insert, resize, crop, add effects to, and add styles to images

About images

Images can be a great way to enhance and clarify your presentations. An *image* can be a photograph or other graphic represented as a digital file, including scanned art. There are two main types of image files that can be used in PowerPoint: bitmap images and vector graphics.

- A *bitmap* image is composed of millions of tiny dots, or *pixels*, that taken together form an image, like photos in a printed newspaper or magazine. Bitmap images such as photographs and scanned images are commonly used on web pages. The quality of a bitmap image is determined by two factors: its resolution and its size. *Resolution* refers to how many pixels per unit area the image contains—the higher the value, the greater the resolution. This value is variously represented, but one common way is as pixels per inch (ppi). A high-resolution bitmap image will reproduce well when enlarged. However, it does so at the cost of file *size*. Thus, multiple high-resolution bitmap files in a single presentation can result in a huge file. On the other hand, if the image won't be greatly enlarged, and it covers only a small area, its file size need not be overly large. Some common bitmap image file extensions used in PowerPoint presentations are .bmp, .gif, .jpeg, and .png.

- A *vector* graphic is a high-quality image file. It can be as simple as a line drawn using a Microsoft application, or an elaborate graphic drawn using a specialized application such as Adobe Illustrator. In a vector file, information about the precise geometry of every shape contained in the image is encoded with it. The result is a high-resolution image, regardless of size. Thus, a vector graphic can be reduced or enlarged without loss of image quality. Some common vector graphic file extensions used in PowerPoint presentations are .cdr, .cgm, .drw, and .eps.

Once you import an image, you can modify and work with it in countless ways, using many of the same tools used to work with shapes and other objects.

Inserting images from a local file

 MOS PowerPoint Exam Objective(s): 2.3.1

You can insert images from local files via the Insert Picture window.

1. Select a destination for the image.

    You can insert images onto individual slides. However, if you wish to display the exact same image on every slide, you can select the slide master as the destination. There, you can also set it as a background image.

2. Click **Pictures**.

    On the Insert tab, in the Images group.

    The Insert Picture window opens.

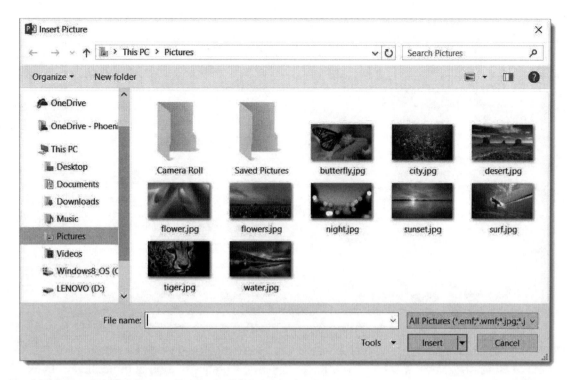

3. Navigate to the location of the image file you wish to insert.
4. Select the file, and click **Insert**.

Inserting online images

A whole world of images is available from online sources. You use the Insert Pictures window to locate online images.

 MOS PowerPoint Exam Objective(s): 1.2.4

1. Select a destination for your online image.
    You can insert images onto individual slides. However, if you wish to display the exact same image on every slide, you can select the slide master as the destination.
2. Click **Online Pictures**.
    On the Insert tab, in the Images group.

    The Insert Pictures window opens.

3. Click in the Search Bing box, and type a search word or string. Then press **Enter**.

   Next to Bing Image Search. Unless you have a specific web destination in mind, this is an excellent portal for image searches. When typing a search string or keyword, try to be as precise as possible. For example, if you're looking for images of coffee beans, that's an excellent search string to type. Typing "beverage" or "hot drink" would result in too broad a search.

   The Bing Image Search results are displayed in the window. Often, when searching for online images, a warning message like the one shown in the figure is displayed. This is a reminder to be careful about downloading and using images that might be protected by copyright. It can be alright to download copyrighted images for your own private use, but it's often better to be safe and not use them at all, unless you request and receive permission from the copyright owner. You can search specifically for images available in the public domain. In the figure, the *Show all web results* option displays all images, regardless of their copyright status.

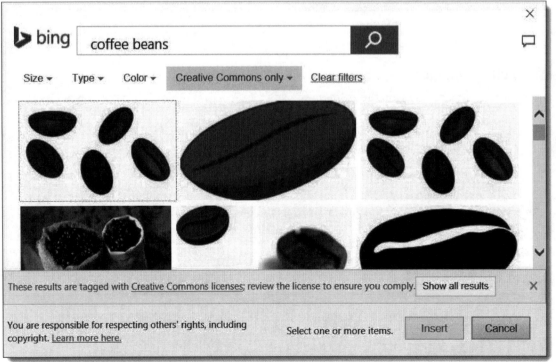

4. Scroll through the images displayed, and hover over images to view their size information.

   This is a quick way to glean information about a specific image. For example, the tooltip in this image lets you know that it's a vector graphic.

5. Select the image you wish to insert, and click **Insert**.

   To select multiple images, click each image's checkbox, which appears in the upper-left corner when you hover over it. Then click **Insert**.

   Depending on the size of the inserted image, it can cover the larger part of a slide, which means that some adjustments are usually necessary before the image appears exactly as you want it.

    Note: To use an inserted image as a background image for all slides in a presentation, first open Slide Master view, and select the slide master. Then insert the image onto the slide master, resize and position it as needed, display the Send Backward options, and click **Send to Back**.

Sizing and moving images

In PowerPoint, text boxes, shapes, and images are all considered objects. As such, many of the same controls are available to all types of objects. Thus, sizing and moving images works in the same way as with other objects.

 MOS PowerPoint Exam Objective(s): 2.3.2

1. Select the image.

   Image handles appear on the image border. For rectangular images, handles appear on each side and at the corners.

2. Resize the image.

   - Drag a handle on any side of the image to increase/decrease its size in that dimension. However, keep in mind that doing so distorts its *aspect ratio*—the ratio of width to height.

   - Drag a corner handle to increase/decrease the size of the image diagonally. Doing so retains the original aspect ratio.

   - Press and hold **Ctrl** and drag a handle to make the above changes, but with the object centered at the same point on the slide. So, if you've already picked the perfect position for your masterpiece and don't wish to move it, using Ctrl resizes the object while keeping it centered in the same spot.

   Sometimes, however, you might need to move the image even after you've carefully resized it.

3. Drag the image where you'd like it to appear on the slide.

Whether an image is selected or not, you can still move it. Images are a bit different than some other objects, in that when an image is selected, you don't have to carefully hover over the border to see the four-headed arrow. Instead, hovering anywhere over the image makes it visible.

Cropping images

When you select an image, the Picture Tools Format tab becomes available. It contains many powerful tools for working with images. The tools in the Size group are the ones used for cropping and sizing.

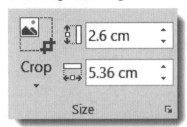

 MOS PowerPoint Exam Objective(s): 2.3.2

1. Select the image to be cropped.

    The Picture Tools Format tab is displayed.

2. Click the **Crop** tool.

    Not the downward-pointing arrow below it.

    Next to each sizing handle, a cropping handle appears.

3. Drag any crop handle to crop the image as desired.

You can use cropping handles in much the same way you use sizing handles. However, when cropping, you're actually removing a portion of the image, not resizing it.

Plainly visible within the cropping handles is the area of the image left intact. Faintly visible is the image area from which the image itself was cropped. This provides a helpful aid to seeing what's been cropped from the image.

4. Deactivate the Crop tool.

Clip **Crop** again, or press **Esc**.

The cropping handles are removed, and the image area that held the removed part of the image is now also removed.

5. If necessary, move the image to its original location, prior to cropping.

Applying styles and effects

The Picture Tools Format tab provides you with many powerful tools for changing the appearance of images. To apply styles to an image, use the tools in the Picture Styles group. Here, you can apply all the same kinds of stylistic effects to your image as you would to shapes, including shadows, reflections, borders, and 3-D effects.

MOS PowerPoint Exam Objective(s): 2.3.3

The preset styles in the Picture Styles gallery provide a great way to quickly apply combinations of effects. Even if you end up customizing your formatting, a preset can provide a great starting point from which to orient yourself in terms of formatting an image in the most meaningful way. However, keep in mind that when applying effects to images, more is often not better. At its best, overindulgence distracts viewers from the point of a slide; at its worst, it could undermine a whole presentation.

1. Select the image, if necessary.

   The Picture Tools Format tab is displayed. Let's take a look at all the style presets.

2. Display the full Picture Styles gallery.

   In the lower right of the Picture Styles gallery, click the **More** button.

   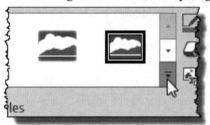

   The full Picture Styles gallery opens.

   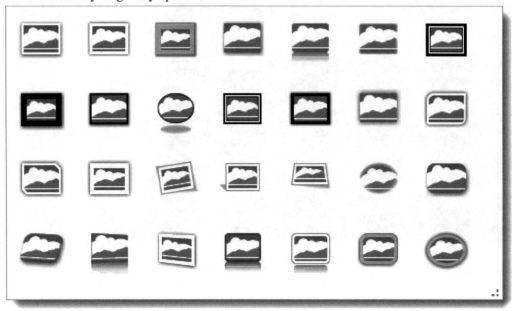

3. Hover over each preset. Observe the image as you do so.

   The image previews the effect of applying each preset.

4. Select a preset.

   The preset style is applied to the image.

5. Click **Picture Effects**.

   In the Picture Styles group.

   The Picture Effects gallery opens, displaying many of the same effects options available when working with shapes and other objects.

   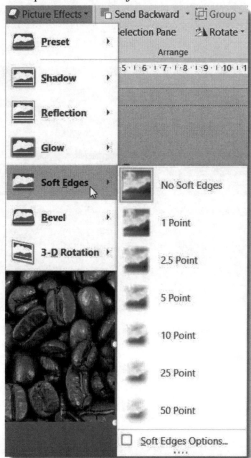

6. Use the Picture Effects tool to apply an effect.

In case you come to a point where you realize that you've seriously ruined a precious image you're working on, you can always choose from the Reset Picture options in the Adjust group of the Picture Tools Format tab. Clicking the **Reset Picture** button itself removes any formatting, such as styles and effects, that you've applied. However, to remove all formatting and sizing and return the image to its original, pristine condition, click the arrow next to Reset Picture, and click **Reset Picture & Size**.

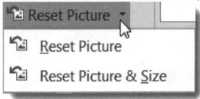

Exercise: Working with images

In this exercise, you'll insert, adjust, and work with images.

Do This	How & Why
1. Open JT Images.pptx, and save it as My JT Images.pptx.	From the Working with shapes and images data folder.
2. Observe the slides in this short presentation.	They are all lacking a logo and at least one other image.
3. Open Slide Master view, and select the slide master.	On the View tab, click **Slide Master**. Navigate up to the slide master.
4. Insert the Java Tucana logo onto the slide master.	

Do This	How & Why
a) Click **Pictures**. On the Insert tab.  The **Insert Picture** window opens. 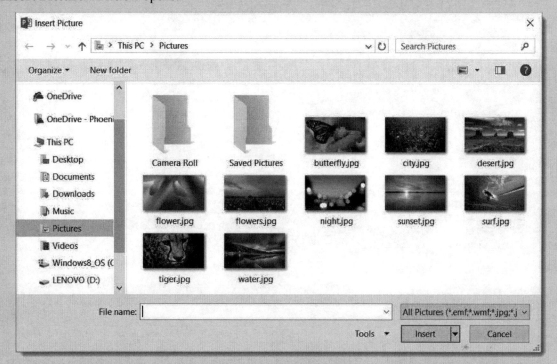 b) Navigate to the `Working with shapes and images` data folder.	
c) Select **JT Logo - Trans Back.png**, and click **Insert**.	The Java Tucana logo appears on the master slide.
5. Size and position the logo to match the figure. Try to maintain the original aspect ratio of the image.	Use the sizing handles to resize it. One way to maintain the aspect ratio is to drag a corner handle, rather than a side handle. 

Do This	How & Why
6. Insert the **coffee cup.jpg** image onto the slide master.	Use step 4 as a guide.
7. Crop the image to match the figure.	
a) On the Picture Tools Format tab, click **Crop**.	The cropping handles are displayed at the image border.
b) Drag the cropping handles to roughly match the figure. 	
c) Click **Crop** or press **Esc**.	To complete the cropping.
8. View all the presets in the Picture Styles gallery.	Click the **More** button. 
9. Select a preset style from the gallery.	
10. Apply any other effects to the image.	Remember that you can always click **Reset Picture** or **Reset Picture & Size** to start over. Likewise, **Undo** is especially good to use for undoing your most recent artistic transgressions.
11. Position the image on the slide where you think it should go, then set it as the back layer.	To ensure that it doesn't cover any other slide objects. Click **Send to Back**.
12. Return to Normal view, and navigate through the presentation to observe your handiwork.	
13. Save and close the file.	

Assessment: Working with images

1. Which of the following statement is true when sizing images?

    - Dragging a corner sizing handle is one way to preserve an image's aspect ratio.
    - Pressing and holding Ctrl before moving a sizing handle maintains an image's aspect ratio.
    - Dragging a corner sizing handle keeps the image centered in its original position.
    - Pressing and holding Ctrl and moving any sizing handle is the only way to preserve image resolution while enlarging or reducing it.

2. True or false? When repositioning an image, care must be taken not to slide the image between object layers.

    - True
    - False

3. What happens to the image area after cropping is completed?

    - It's reduced to the newly cropped image size.
    - Nothing happens; the original image area border retains its position.
    - The cropped image expands to fill it.
    - Its center remains anchored to the same point on the slide.

4. Even after you've applied a preset style from the Picture Styles gallery, you can continue to apply individual effects to images.

    - True
    - False

Summary: Working with shapes and images

You should now know how to:

- Draw straight lines and freehand curves; create open shapes; and resize, apply styles to, and layer shapes
- Insert images from local and online sources; use them as slide backgrounds; size, reposition, and crop them; and apply styles to them

Synthesis: Working with shapes and images

1. Open `JT Shapes-Images Synthesis.pptx`, and save it as `My JT Shapes-Images Synthesis.pptx`.
   From the `Working with shapes and images` data folder.
2. Ensure that rulers, gridlines, and guides are all displayed; and use the zoom tool, as necessary.
3. Draw three types of straight lines in the presentation: horizontal, vertical, and diagonal. Make at least one of them a feature on all slides of the presentation. Make at least one of the three a feature of only one slide.
4. Create one shape with multiple curves that's displayed on all slides.
5. Create an open shape that contains a text object.
6. Carefully size and position the shapes. Use the Align feature to place shapes, where appropriate.
7. Apply styles to the shapes.
8. Layer the shapes, where appropriate, so that all layers are visible.
9. Insert the `JT Logo - Trans Back.png` image file to display on every slide.
   From the data folder.
10. Size and position it in a good spot, so that it doesn't cover up any essential elements on any slide.
11. Apply any effects to the logo that will keep it clearly readable.
12. Insert the `coffee cup.jpg` file so that it's also a feature of every slide, and crop it to show only the part of the image that you want.
13. Apply a style to it, and add any effects that you like.
14. Set it as the background image for all slides in the presentation.
15. Return to Normal view, then navigate the presentation to observe the results.
16. Save and close the presentation.

Chapter 5: Working with charts and tables

You will learn how to:

- Create and modify charts
- Create and format tables

Module A: Working with charts

PowerPoint allows you to create charts on your slides. Charts are simply a pictorial representation of your data. Sometimes, a picture really does say a thousand words or, more accurately, conveys what a thousand numbers can't.

You will learn how to:

- Create and modify charts in your presentations

About charts

A *chart* shows you, in one of many ways, pictures of *series* of numbers. In a *pie chart*, for example, a series of numbers appears as slices of a pie that represents a whole.

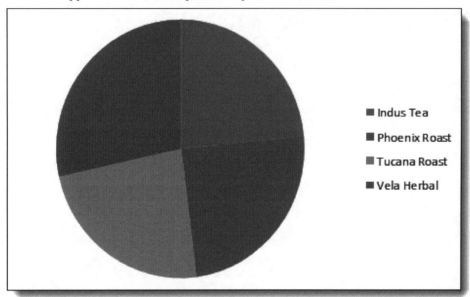

In a *line chart*, on the other hand, each series is a line, with points representing each individual value.

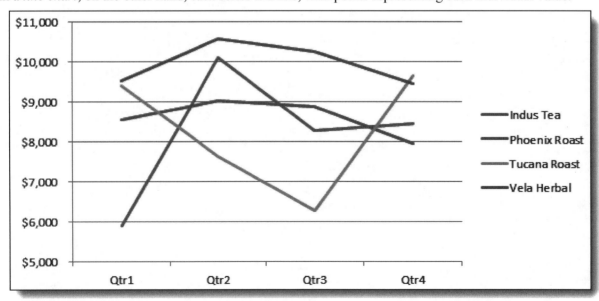

PowerPoint makes it easy to create simple charts like these. But you also have the power to make complex charts that compare different kinds of data, combine different chart types, and highlight the point you want to make.

Chart types

PowerPoint offers many chart types that you can use for representing various kinds of data, and thus make various points to an audience. Within each type, there are also many sub-types.

- *Column charts* show data as columns, either single columns for each value, or stacked to show how individual values relate to totals for a particular category. They are useful for showing magnitude in an obvious way.
- *Line charts* show series of values as points along a line. They are great for showing trends.
- *Pie charts* show how values relate to a whole. The data you select for a pie chart should have only one series of values.
- *Bar charts* are really the same as column charts, with the bars running horizontally (as opposed to columns, which run vertically).
- *Area charts* combine line charts and columns by filling in the areas below the lines.
- *X Y (scatter) charts* show coordinates, and are useful for looking at how two related variables are distributed.

PowerPoint also has a few other chart types that are useful for other types of data.

Adding a chart to a presentation

In PowerPoint, there are a few ways to add a chart to your presentation. Whatever method you choose, it's easiest to do so by first adding a new slide to your presentation to serve as the chart's destination.

 MOS PowerPoint Exam Objective(s): 3.2.1

1. Add a new slide to your presentation.

    - On the Home tab, click the upper part of the **New Slide** button.

    - Click the lower part of the New Slide button to display layout options, and select a layout that includes a Content area.

    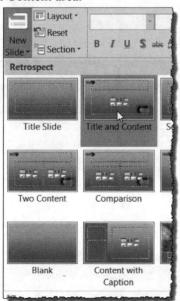

2. Click the **Insert Chart** icon.

   In the content placeholder of the new slide. Or, on the Insert tab, in the Illustrations group, click **Chart**.

The Insert Chart window opens. The left pane of the All Charts tab displays all the main chart types that are available in PowerPoint. Selecting one displays a series of sub-types across the top of the tab, to help you refine your chart selection. The larger area previews the appearance of the select chart type and sub-type. The Recent option displays recently used chart types, and Templates displays any saved chart templates.

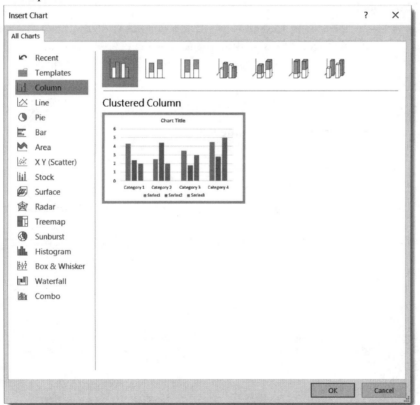

3. Select a main chart type.

   In the left pane.

4. Select a sub-type, if you wish.

   In the upper pane, to further refine your selection.

5. Click **OK**.

   The new chart appears on the slide. The chart's selected, and above it an Excel spreadsheet contains data placeholders in cells, columns, and rows.

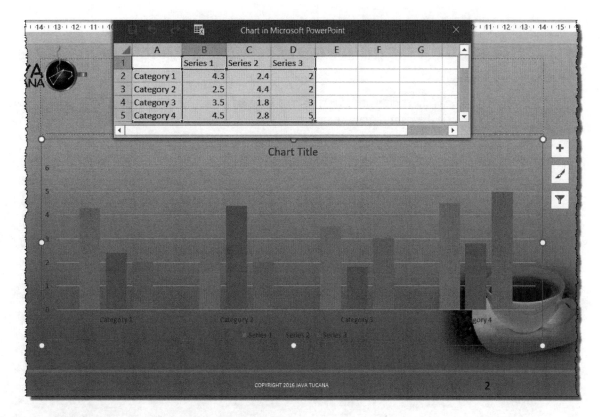

6. Enter the data that you intend the chart to represent.
   In the spreadsheet cells.

   As you enter data, the chart changes to reflect them.

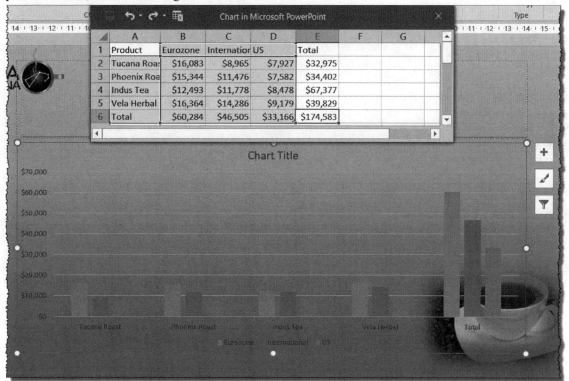

Note: When you add a chart to a slide that already contains other objects, use your knowledge of moving, resizing, aligning, and layering them to achieve the look you want, and to make sure that everything that should be seen can be seen.

7. Close the Excel spreadsheet.

When you've finished entering data and want to get a better look at the chart, click in the spreadsheet window.

 Note: The spreadsheet data are saved as part of your presentation, so even though you close the spreadsheet, the data remain intact. Just remember to save your presentation.

8. Add a chart title.
    Click in the Chart Title text box, and enter a title for your chart.

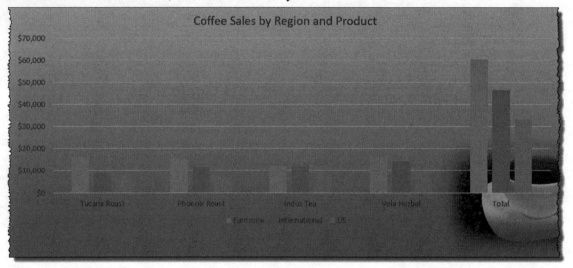

Changing the chart type

After you set the type of a chart, you can very easily change its layout and style.

 MOS PowerPoint Exam Objective(s): 3.2.3

1. Select the chart.
2. On the Chart Tools Design tab, click **Change Chart Type**.
   To display the Change Chart Type window.

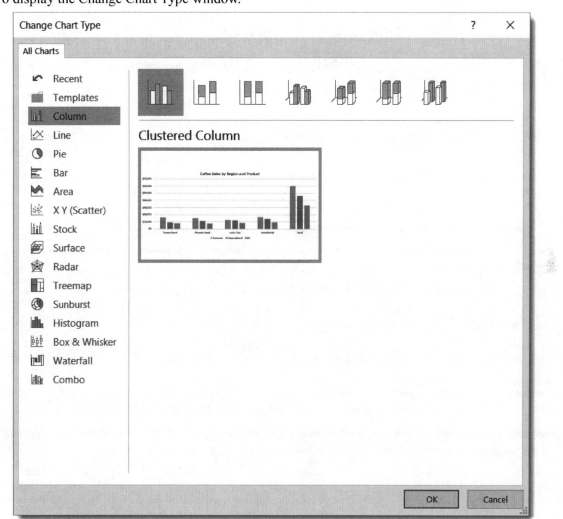

3. Select a type on the left, then a sub-type, and click **OK**.
   You can get a preview of what your data will look like in a particular chart type by hovering over it.

The chart type changes, and now the Chart Tools Design tab gives you many options for layout and style that are specific to the new type. Simply click **Quick Layout** and choose an option, or select a style to see what it will look like.

Chart elements

Charts come from the data you select when you make them. And each element of the chart represents either something in that data or something you can add to the chart and control.

MOS PowerPoint Exam Objective(s): 3.2.4

Figure 1: Chart elements

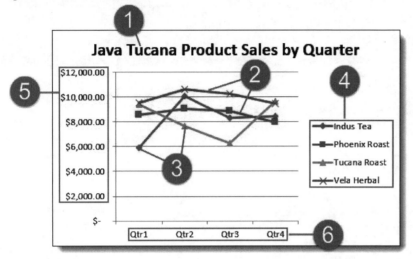

1. The *chart title* is usually something you will add to the chart, rather than something that comes from the selected data.

2. *Data series* are the series of values that show up in lines, columns, or other ways in your charts.

3. *Data points* represent the individual values within data series.

4. The *legend* identifies the data series in the chart.

5. The *value axis* shows the scale for what the chart is measuring. You can exercise enormous control over how the value axis appears and works. It is often plotted vertically, as in this example, but it does not have to be.

6. The *category axis* shows the categories of information within the data series. It is usually the horizontal axis, but not always.

Changing the chart layout

A chart's *layout* is the arrangement of its elements. PowerPoint makes it very easy to change the chart layout.

MOS PowerPoint Exam Objective(s): 3.3.5

1. Select the chart.
2. On the Chart Tools Design tab, click **Quick Layout**.
   In the Chart Layouts group.
   The Quick Layout gallery opens.

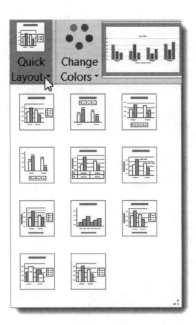

3. Hover over each layout in the gallery, and observe your chart.
   The chart previews each layout as you hover over it.
4. Select a layout from the gallery.
   Click to select it.
   The chart is updated with the new layout.
5. Click the **Chart Elements** button.
   To the right of the selected chart. To further refine your layout selection.

A checklist of Chart Elements options is display. Check an option to have it displayed with the chart; uncheck to hide it.

Applying chart styles

PowerPoint provides many different chart styles that you can apply to your charts. A chart *style* is a preset combination of color and other formatting options.

  MOS PowerPoint Exam Objective(s): 3.2.5

1. Select the chart.
2. On the Chart Tools Design tab, select a style preset from the Chart Styles gallery.
   You can display all the gallery options at once by clicking the gallery's **More** button.

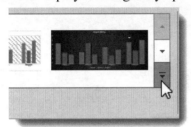

The full Chart Styles gallery displays all the styles appropriate to the current chart type.

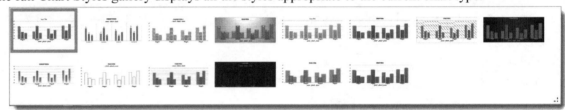

3. Select a style from the gallery.
   The new style is applied to the chart.

Inserting an Excel chart

PowerPoint makes it easy to import an Excel chart into PowerPoint.

  MOS PowerPoint Exam Objective(s): 3.2.2

1. Copy the Excel chart.
   Excel is running, and the workbook containing the chart is open. On the Home tab, in the Clipboard group, click the **Copy** button; or press **Ctrl+C**.

   The chart is copied to the Clipboard.
2. Switch to PowerPoint, and select the destination slide.
3. Paste the chart onto the slide.
   Click **Paste**, or press **Ctrl+V**.

   The Excel chart appears on the slide, and a Paste Options button appears at the lower-right corner of the chart.
4. Click the **Paste Options** button.

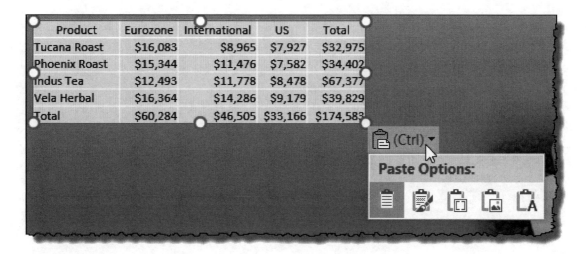

5. Select a Paste option.

Paste icon	Function
	Use Destination Styles pastes the raw data using the destination styles and becomes a PowerPoint table in the current presentation format. This is the default option.
	Keep Source Formatting retains source formatting to copy the data to PowerPoint.
	Embed uses the destination theme and links data to the workbook. Any subsequent data changes are made in Excel.
	Picture uses only the chart image, which can't be updated in either PowerPoint or Excel.
	Keep Text Only pastes the text as a single text box.

Editing chart data

Once you've created a chart with embedded or linked data, you can update the data whenever you like. When you do so, the chart automatically updates as well.

1. Select the chart containing data you wish to edit, then choose an Edit Data option.
   On the Chart Tools Design tab, in the Data group.

   - To edit the data in PowerPoint, click **Edit Data**. An Excel spreadsheet containing the data opens above the chart.

- To edit the data in Excel, click the lower part of the Edit Data button, and select **Edit Data in Excel**. The original workbook opens in Excel.

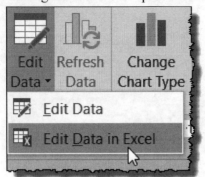

2. Edit the data, as necessary.

    To change the value in a spreadsheet cell, click the cell, type the new value, and press **Enter**. The chart itself updates automatically after you enter the new value.

     Note: If source values are changed in their Excel workbook, you can update the corresponding chart within PowerPoint by selecting the chart, then clicking **Refresh Data** on the Chart Tools Design tab.

Exercise: Working with charts

You'll create a chart, change its type and layout, apply styles, and import a chart directly from Excel.

Do This	How & Why
1. Open **JT Charts.pptx**, and save it as `My JT Charts.pptx`.	From the `Working with charts and tables` data folder.

2. Navigate to and observe slide 2.

It contains a table that's an embedded Excel spreadsheet.

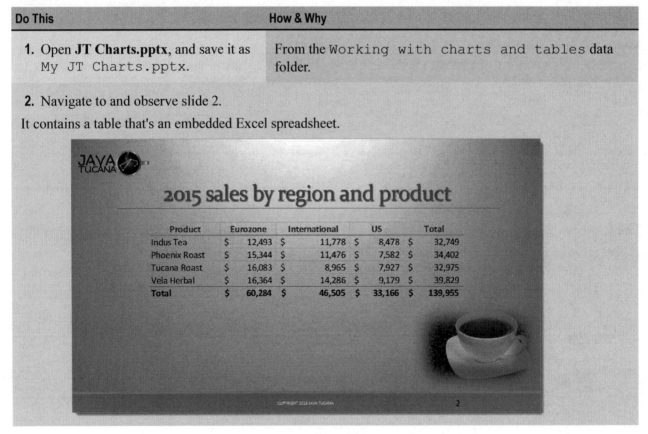

Do This	How & Why
3. Double-click the table.	

The PowerPoint window shudders, then mutates into a hybrid PowerPoint-Excel window, giving you access to many of Excel's powerful commands and options. In the Excel table, the data are already selected.

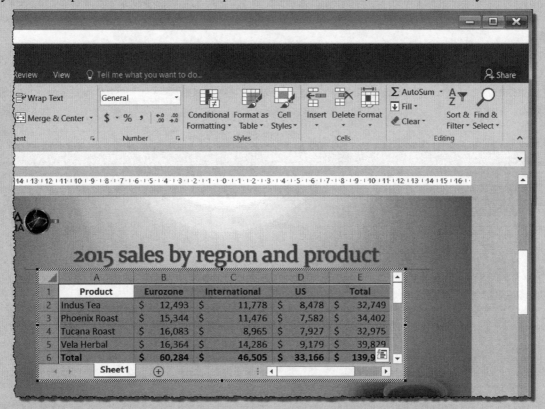

Do This	How & Why
4. Copy the selected table data to the Clipboard.	Click **Copy** or press **Ctrl+C**.
5. Press **Esc** *twice* to return to the PowerPoint presentation.	The first press deselects the data, the second closes the hybrid view and returns to PowerPoint.
6. Add a new slide to the presentation.	With slide 2 still selected, on the Home tab, click **New Slide**. A new, blank slide 3 appears.

Do This	How & Why
7. On slide 3, in the Content placeholder, click the **Insert Chart** icon. 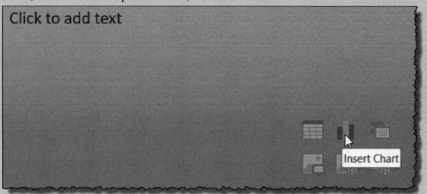 The Insert Chart window opens. 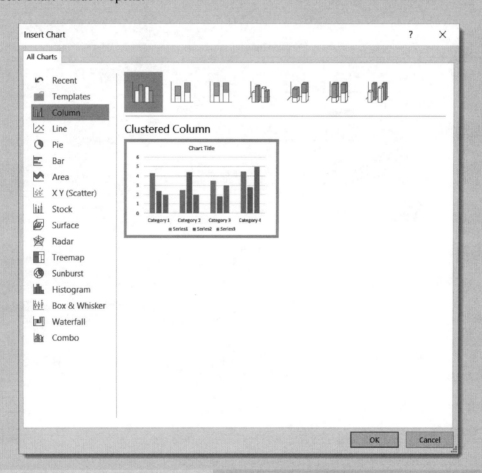	
8. Navigate to view some of the available chart types and sub-types, and observe the results in the displayed preview.	
9. Click the **Column** chart type, click **Clustered Column**, and click **OK**.	The leftmost Column sub-type. The chart appears on the slide with the Excel spreadsheet above it, but it contains only placeholder data.

Do This	How & Why
10. On the spreadsheet, click in cell A1, and paste the contents of the Clipboard.	Click **Paste** or press **Ctrl+V**. The spreadsheet is populated with the pasted data, and the chart updates to illustrate the data. 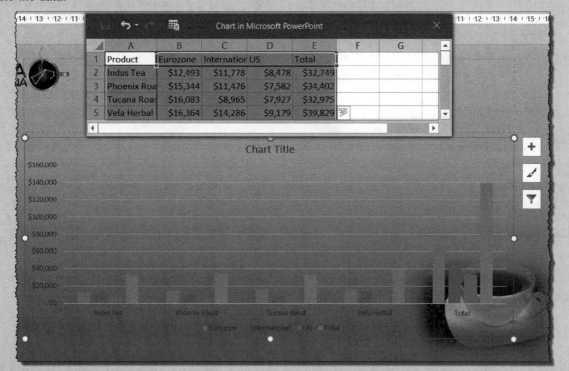 **Note:** If a warning message displays regarding pasting formulas, click **OK** to close it.
11. Close the spreadsheet.	Click the  button.
12. If necessary, select the chart on slide 3.	
13. On the Chart Tools Design tab, click **Change Chart Type**.	 The Change Chart Type window opens. This is essentially the Insert Chart window renamed.
14. Select a different chart type and sub-type, then click on **OK**.	The same data are illustrated in a different way. With some chart types, certain chart features aren't included by default, while others are.

Do This	How & Why
15. Click **Quick Layout**, and hover over the different layouts available. As you do so, observe the results on the chart.	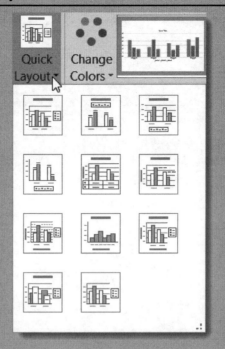
16. Select a layout from the gallery, and observe your results.	
17. Click the **Chart Elements** button.	
18. In the Chart Element options checklist, uncheck the **Chart Title** option, and include/exclude other elements.	Try to keep the important options checked. However, you can always go back and change what's displayed, should things not work out as you intend. You won't need the Chart Title option, as you'll use the Title area of the slide instead.
19. Apply a chart style of your choice.	Select a style from the Chart Styles gallery on the Chart Tools Design tab. You can use the More button to display all styles at once. 
20. Edit the chart data. a) Click **Edit Data**.	 The Excel spreadsheet containing the data opens.

Do This	How & Why
b) Change a few values in the spreadsheet, and observe the chart as you do so.	The chart reflects each change in the data.
21. When you're finished changing data, close the spreadsheet and observe the completed chart.	
22. In the slide Title placeholder area, type 2015 sales by region and product.	
23. Save and close the presentation.	

Assessment: Working with charts

1. True or false? When charting your data, once you've decided on a chart type, if you decide to change the type later, you can only pick one from the same type.

    - True
    - False

2. Which statement about chart elements is correct?

    - The chart title is usually something you add to the chart, rather than something that comes from the selected data.
    - A data series is the collection of chart data used in a single presentation.
    - A chart legend tells the story behind the data.
    - The category axis shows the types of data you can use for a specific type of chart.

3. True or false? When you edit the data in an embedded Excel spreadsheet in PowerPoint, the resulting chart is updated automatically.

    - True
    - False

Module B: Working with tables

In the same way that a picture can be worth a thousand words, displaying values can be a powerful way to deliver information. One great way to do this in a presentation is to display values in a table.

You will learn how to:

- Create and work with tables in your presentation

About tables

A table is a series of rows and columns of data. A *cell* is the intersection of a row and column. Each cell in a table contains a singular data item, consisting of either text, numbers (quantities, currency amounts, dates, and measurements), or formulas to perform calculations.

Expense	Year1	Year2	Year3	Year4	Year5
Rent	24000	24000	24000	25200	25200
Remodeling	12000	2000	2000	2000	2000
Legal	5000	500	500	500	500
Equipment	9000	1000	10	2000	1000
Supplies	12000	13200	0	16000	17600
Advertising	4000	1000	1200	1400	1600
Payroll	60000	65000	80000	90000	100000
Miscellaneous	10000	11000	12000	13000	14000
Totals:	$136,000	$117,700	$135,200	$150,100	$161,900

① *Text*, which you use to label information. Here, the text identifies what is in the rows (categories of expenses) and the columns (yearly figures).

② *Numbers*, which can be of various kinds (quantities, currency amounts, dates, and measurements). Here, the numbers represent dollar amounts in the budget.

The other important thing you can enter in tables is formulas. The totals in this figure are calculated using formulas. Of course, the types of tables you might use in PowerPoint can be much less or much more complicated.

Creating tables

In PowerPoint, there are a few different ways to create a table. One way is to use the Insert Table icon in a Content placeholder. Another way is to use the Table button on the Insert tab, from which you can use a grid to specify your table's dimensions, draw a table using Draw Table, or create an Excel spreadsheet. However, the simplest and most direct of these methods is to use the Insert Table icon.

Inserting a table

To use the Insert Table icon in a Content placeholder, it's easiest to do so on a fresh slide.

 MOS PowerPoint Exam Objective(s): 3.1.1, 3.1.2

1. On a new slide, click the **Insert Table** icon.
   In the Content placeholder.

   The Insert Table window opens. Here, you set the number of columns and rows you want in your table.

   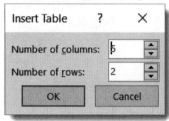

2. Specify the number of columns and rows in their respective boxes.
   You can select the value in each box, and type a value directly, or you can use the ▲ (increment) and ▼ (decrement) buttons to change the values. Be sure to account for a header row (for column headings).

3. Click **OK**.
   The table is inserted onto the slide. Notice that the top row is shaded. PowerPoint assumes the top row of the table will contain column headings and thus sets it off from the rest of the table.

   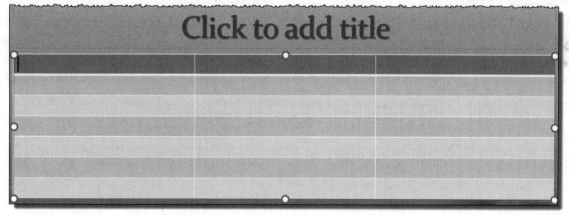

    Note: Even after you've created a table, you might need to add/delete rows and/or columns to your table. To do so, use the tools in the Rows & Columns group on the Table Tools Layout tab.

   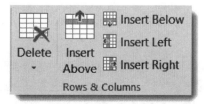

Entering data

Entering and editing data is most of what you do in a table. There are many kinds of data: numbers, text, dates, and formulas, for example. But the basics of entering data are always the same.

1. Select the cell where you want to enter data.
2. Type the data you want to enter.
3. Press **Enter**.

    If you're entering data in a PowerPoint table using an Excel spreadsheet and the formula bar is visible, you can press **Enter** or click the Enter box (the check mark) on the formula bar.

Applying styles

  MOS PowerPoint Exam Objective(s): 3.1.3

PowerPoint's Table Tools Design tab offers many options for applying styles and formatting to your tables. And don't forget, you can also use the many formatting options on the Home tab. For more structural changes to your tables, there's the Table Tools Layout tab.

You can apply style and formatting options to a table either before or after you've entered the table data. However, whenever possible, it makes sense to have at least some of your data in place before you experiment with styles and formats. With the data in place, it's often much easier to get a sense of how particular data should be emphasized, for example.

When considering style and formatting options, it's a good idea first to apply a preset style from the Table Styles gallery to your table, and then to make any additional "minor" changes using some of those other style and formatting tools.

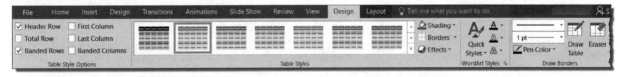

1. Select the table.

    When you select or click in a table, the Table Tools Design and Layout tabs become available, and the Design tab is displayed.

2. Display the full Tables Styles gallery, and observe the available gallery styles.

    Click the gallery's **More** button.

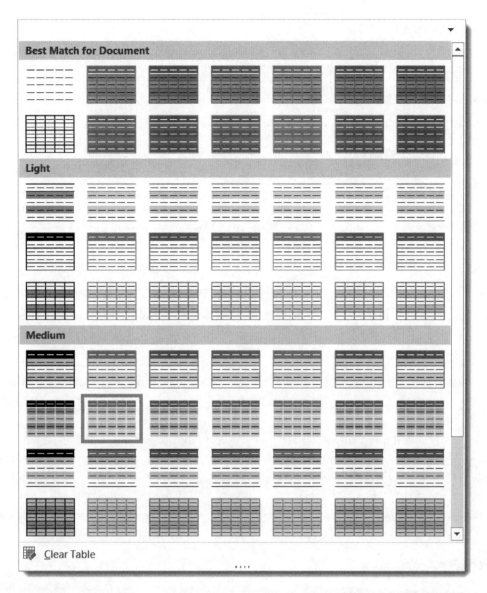

3. Hover over the different styles available, and notice the effect on your table.
4. Click a style from the gallery.
   To select it.
   The table is updated to the new style.
5. Apply any additional style or formatting elements you like.
   Use the tools in the Table Style Options group, the Draw Borders group, or any others.

The Table Style Options group

The Table Style Options Group, located on the Table Tools Design tab, contains important style options for working with tables. Check an option to turn it on; uncheck it to turn it off.

- *Header Row*: Applies a special format to the first row of a table, which normally contains column headings.
- *Total Row*: Applies a special format to the last row of a table, which often contains column totals.
- *Banded Rows*: Applies shading effects to alternating rows, making larger tables easier to scan.
- *First Column*: Applies a special format to the first column, which normally contains row headings.
- *Last Column*: Applies a special format to the last column, which sometimes contains row totals or subtotals.
- *Banded Columns*: Applies shading effects to alternating columns, making larger tables easier to scan.

Importing tables

You can import tables from other applications to use in your PowerPoint presentations. It's important to know that a table, a chart, a PDF document, or any such product of an external application is referred to as an *object* in PowerPoint. As always, when adding an object to a presentation, it's always good to start with a new slide, or at least one with an empty Content placeholder.

Once you've imported your table object, you can apply additional styles and formatting options using the tools on the Drawing Tools Format tab.

MOS PowerPoint Exam Objective(s): 3.1.4

1. Select the destination slide for the table.
2. Click **Object**.
   In the Insert tab's Text group.

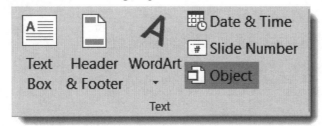

   The Insert Object window opens.
3. Select **Create from file**.
   The object that you create using this option embeds the external object in PowerPoint and links it to its source application.

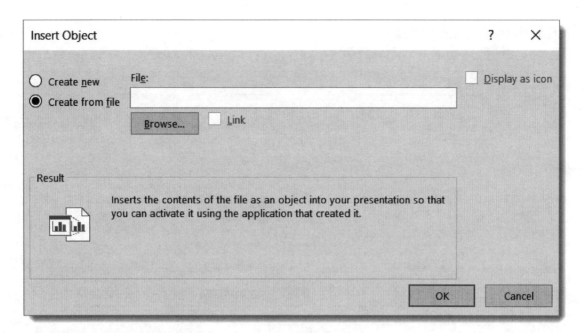

4. Click **Browse**, navigate to the source file, and click **Insert**.

   Checking the **Link** option allows you to maintain an active connection to the original Excel data: updating the original updates its linked slide object. However, because using this option results in only a picture of the data being pasted onto the slide, you can't apply many of PowerPoint's formatting and effects options to it. Also, you can only link to files saved in Excel 2013 or later.

   The imported table object is inserted onto the slide.

   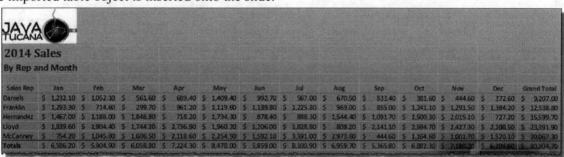

5. Double-click the imported object.

   The object opens in its source application for further editing, and so on.

6. When you're done editing the object in its source application, save your changes.

   The object is automatically updated in PowerPoint.

Exercise: Working with tables

You'll create a table, apply styles and formatting, and import an Excel spreadsheet as a table object.

Do This	How & Why
1. Open **JT Tables.pptx**, and save it as `My JT Tables.pptx`.	From the `Working with charts and tables` data folder.
2. Insert a table on slide 2.	This slide is blank.
a) Select slide 2.	
b) On the new slide, click the **Insert Table** icon.	The **Insert Table** window opens.
c) In the "Number of columns" box, enter **3**.	Type the value in the box, or use the decrement button.
a) In the "Number of rows" box, enter **7**.	Type the value in the box, or use the increment button.

b) Click **OK**.

The table is inserted onto the slide.

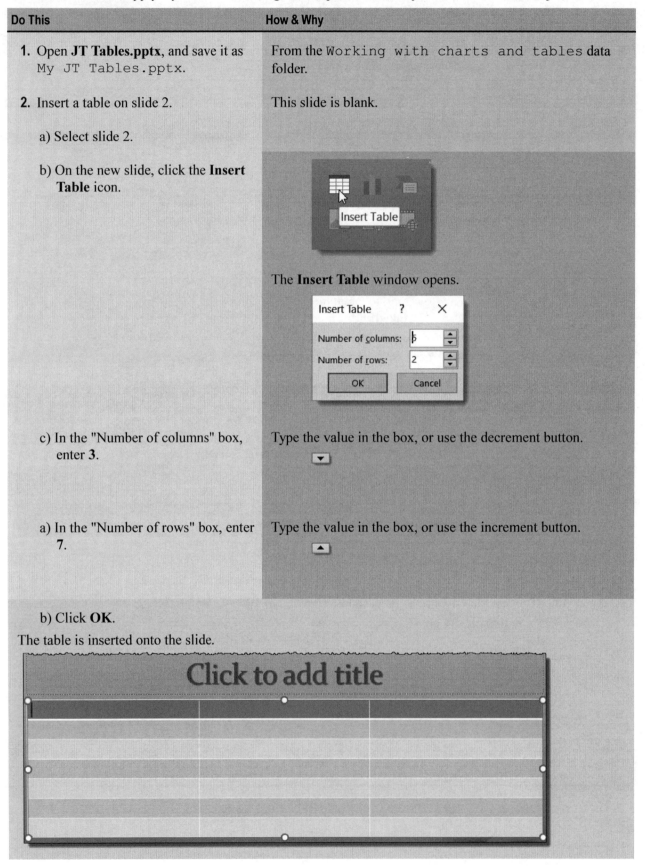

Do This	How & Why
3. Enter the table data shown in the figure below. Click in each cell and type the data. You can also use the **Tab** key to move to the next cell, and **Shift**+**Tab** to move to the previous cell. 	Rank	Country	Millions of tons
---	---	---
1	Brazil	3.0
2	Vietnam	1.5
3	Indonesia	0.7
4	Colombia	0.7
5	India	0.3
	World	8.9		
4. Open the Table Styles gallery, and hover over the various presets until you arrive at one you like. Then select it to apply the style.	On the Table Tools Design tab. Use the gallery's More button to view the entire gallery.
5. Make sure the **Header Row**, **Total Row**, **Banded Rows**, and **First Column** options are checked.	In the Table Style Options group. 
6. Apply any additional style elements or formatting that you wish.	You can use tools from the Table Tools Design and Layout tabs, as well as the Home tab.
7. Resize the columns to best fit the data by dragging the column borders, then resize that table to nicely fit the slide.	
8. In the slide's Title placeholder, type `The Top Five Green Coffee Producers`.	

Do This	How & Why

9. Deselect the table, and observe your results.

The Top Five Green Coffee Producers

Rank	Country	Millions of tons
1	Brazil	3.0
2	Vietnam	1.5
3	Indonesia	0.7
4	Colombia	0.7
5	India	0.3
	World	8.9

10. Insert a new slide 3.

11. Insert the Excel table object **Sales - Rep and product.xlsx**.

   a) Click **Object**.

On the Insert tab.

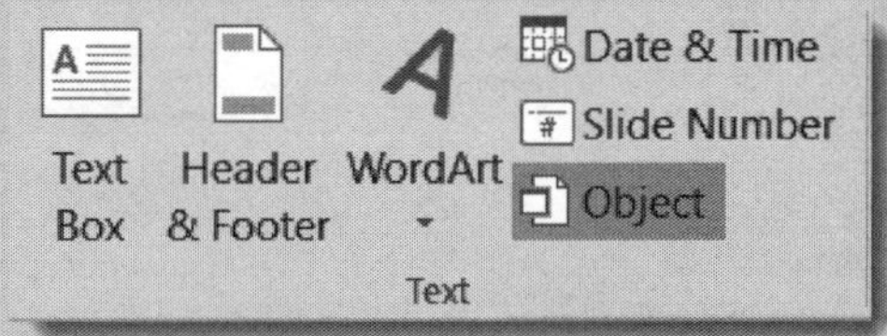

The Insert Object window opens.

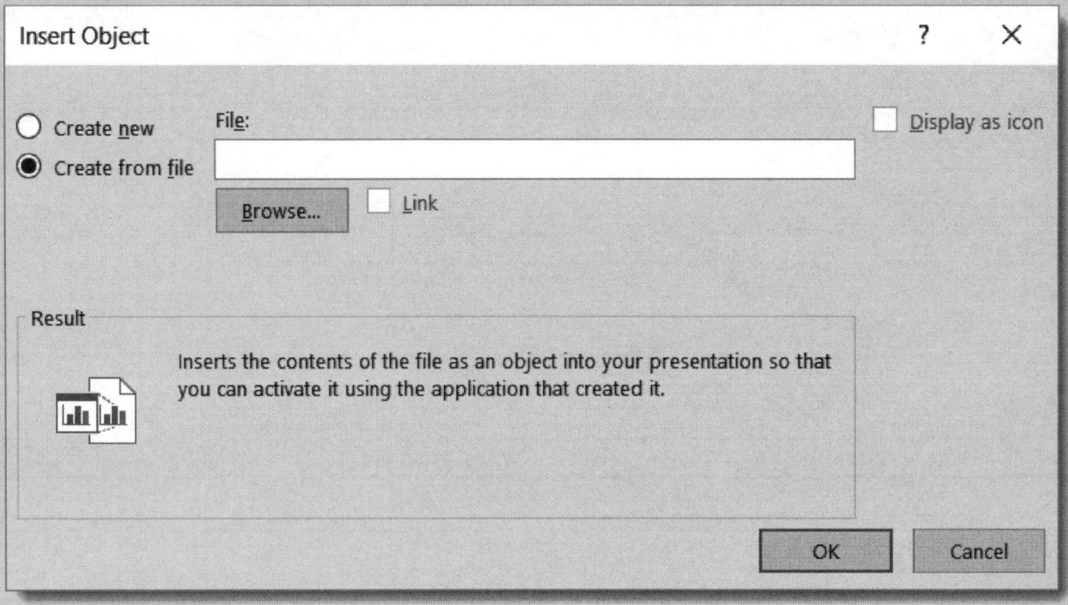

Insert Object

- ○ Create new
- ● Create from file

File:

Browse... ☐ Link

☐ Display as icon

Result: Inserts the contents of the file as an object into your presentation so that you can activate it using the application that created it.

OK   Cancel

Do This	How & Why
b) Click Browse, navigate to the data folder, and select **Sales - Rep and product.xlsx**.	
c) Click **OK**.	

The Excel table object is inserted onto the slide.

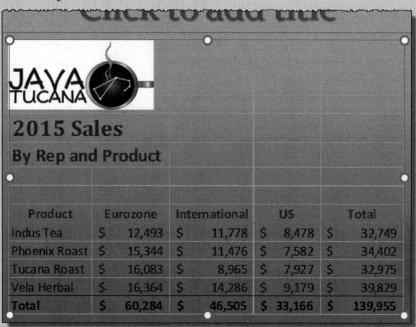

12. Resize the table to fit the slide. Apply any formatting and style elements that you'd like.

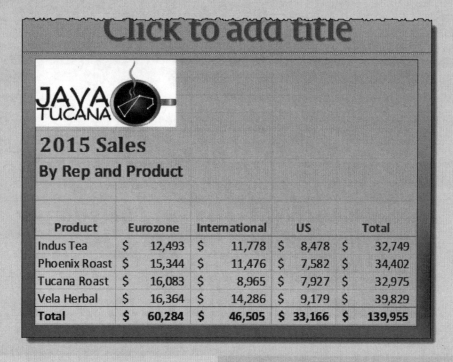

13. Save and close the presentation.

Assessment: Working with tables

1. Which of these answers describes an easy way to create a table in PowerPoint?

    - Use the Table placeholder in the Content field.
    - Use the Table Creation tool on the Layout tab.
    - Use the Insert Table icon in the Content placeholder.
    - Use the Table tool in the Object group.

2. True or false? When formatting a table, it's a good idea to do all the minor formatting first, then select a style preset to apply, then enter the data last.

    - True
    - False

3. Which of these statements about importing Excel tables into PowerPoint is true?

    - Once imported, any additional formatting that you apply to a table must be done in Excel.
    - Once imported, if you need to edit table data, that must be done in Excel.
    - Once imported, the table is actually controlled by PowerPoint.
    - Once imported, the table becomes a Picture and is no longer an independent object.

Summary: Working with charts and tables

You should now know how to:

- Add a chart to a presentation; change its type, size, elements, and layout; apply a style to it; insert an Excel chart; and edit chart data
- Design and insert a table appropriate to the data it will contain, enter table data, apply a style and formatting, and import an Excel table

Synthesis: Working with charts and tables

In this synthesis, you'll add a chart to a presentation, modify its structure, apply styles and formatting, and edit the underlying data. Then you'll create a table using Excel data, resize it, and apply formatting.

1. Open **JT Charts-Tables Assessment.pptx**, and save it as `My JT Charts-Tables Assessment.pptx`.

    From this chapter's data folder.

2. On slide 2, use the Insert Chart icon to select an appropriate chart type, and insert the chart.
3. Open **Chart Data.xlsx**.
4. Select only the table data, including row and column headings, then copy the data.
5. Paste the data into the PowerPoint table on slide 2, using the default Paste option.
6. Close the spreadsheet to see only the chart.
7. Add the title `2015 Sales by Product and Region` to either the slide itself or the chart.
8. Change the chart type, add any chart elements you think should be displayed, and remove any that are unnecessary.
9. Apply a style to the chart, and add any additional formatting you wish.
10. Edit the chart data, and make sure the chart updates to reflect the changes.
11. On slide 3, import the Excel file **Excel Table - Assessment.xlsx** as a table object.
12. Resize the table, as necessary, and apply any formatting you wish, making sure the data are clearly visible on the slide.
13. Save and close the presentation.

Chapter 6: Customization

You will learn how to:

- Apply slide transitions
- Work with additional text features
- Work with printing options
- Create custom slide shows

Module A: Slide transitions

A slide show is by definition relatively static. At its most basic, there's no actual movement until you change slides. However, there are ways to make your presentations far more dynamic. One of these is by applying transitions to the slides in your presentations.

You will learn how to:

- Apply transition effects to all the slides in your presentation
- Apply transition effects to one or more selected slides

About slide transitions

MOS PowerPoint Exam Objective(s): 4.1.2

PowerPoint provides many options for governing *how* your presentation flows from slide to slide, or *slide transitions*. The default way for a slide show to progress is to manually click through the presentation, switching abruptly to the next slide with each click. However, transitions allow you to set the presentation to move through the slides automatically. Perhaps more importantly, you can set the transition effect for individual slides, which is a powerful way to customize your presentation.

The Transitions tab on the ribbon provides the tools you need to create and modify the presentation of your slide show. It's divided into three main groups.

- *Transition to This Slide*: Here, you can select an effect type to transition to the current slide. You can then use Effect Options to modify the effect further.
- *Timing*: Controls the timing of the slide transition effect, as well as how the effect is triggered. Here, you can also select a sound effect to accompany the transition.
- *Preview*: Allows you to preview the effect you've selected for the transition to the current slide.

Applying the same transition to all slides

To apply a transition to all slides in a presentation, it's easiest to do so in Normal view or Slide Sorter view.

MOS PowerPoint Exam Objective(s): 4.1.1, 4.1.2

1. Select a slide.
   You can select any number of slides, but there's no need to do so.
2. On the Transitions tab, select a transition.

   From the Transition to This Slide gallery. To display the entire gallery, click its More button ( ).

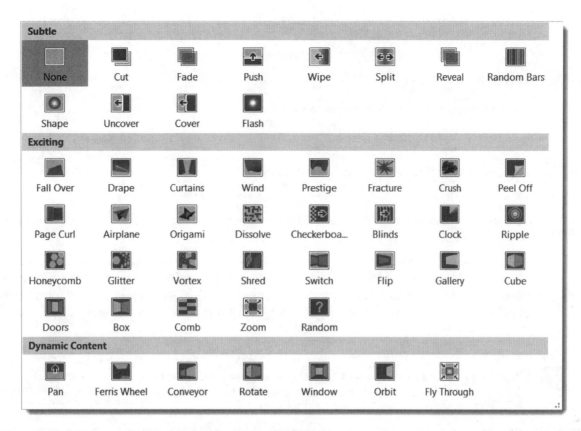

3. Select a transition preset, and observe the selected slide(s).

   The transition is applied, and the effect is previewed on the slide(s). To replay the effect, click the **Play Animations** icon in the Slide pane (or in Slide Sorter view). This icon appears next to a slide to which a transition (and/or animation) is applied, thus allowing you to replay the effect at any time.

4. Apply an effect option.

   a) Click **Effect Options**.

      The effect options are displayed. They serve as a subset of the transition preset selected. Thus, the number and types of options vary with each transition preset selected.

   b) Select an effect option.

      Each time you select a new transition feature, the effect is previewed on the selected slide(s).

5. Set any timing options.

   In the Timing group.

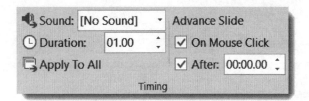

- *Sound*: Select a sound to play at the transition. The list of sounds provided is quite long, but should you wish to use your own custom sound, choose Other Sound, which lets you navigate to and load the sound file of your choice to apply to the transition.
- *Duration*: Set the length of time in seconds that the transition effect takes to complete.
- *Apply To All*: Applies all current transition effects to all slides in the presentation. For this reason, it's best to use this option after you've fine-tuned the transition.
- The Advance Slide area contains two options: *On Mouse Click* advances to the next slide only when you click. Set a value in the *After* box to have the slide automatically advance after that time elapses. Clicking both options creates a "whichever-comes-first" situation, so that you can still advance by clicking, but if you haven't clicked by the time the After value has elapsed, the transition will occur.

6. Click **Apply To All**.

    The transition effects are applied to all slides in the presentation.

    Note: It's important to remember that after you've applied transition effects to slides, if you decide to add or remove any options and you wish to apply those changes to all (or multiple) slides, click **Apply To All** (or select multiple slides before making the changes).

Applying transitions to individual slides

Apply transition effects to selected slides in Normal view or Slide Sorter view. If you're selecting many slides, however, Slide Sorter view is probably the better choice.

 MOS PowerPoint Exam Objective(s): 4.1.2

1. Open Slide Sorter view.

    On the taskbar, click .

2. Select a transition preset from the gallery.

    On the Transitions tab, in the Transition to This Slide group.

3. Apply any additional transition effects.

4. Click the **Preview** tool.

    This is another way to preview the transition. If you've applied the transition to multiple slides, it previews all of them.

Exercise: Setting slide transitions

You'll apply slide transitions in a presentation.

Do This	How & Why
1. Open **JT Transitions.pptx**, and save it as `My JT Transitions.pptx`.	From the `Customization` data folder.
2. Navigate the presentation.	It consists of a few sections of information about Java Tucana.
3. Apply transition effects to slides 1–3, 6, and 18, all of which begin sections of the presentation.	
a) Switch to Slide Sorter view.	Click [icon].
b) Select slides 1, 2, 3, 6, and 18.	Press and hold **Ctrl** to make multiple selections.
c) On the Transitions tab, display all the Transition to This Slide gallery presets.	Click [icon]. The gallery opens.
d) Try clicking various presets from each category, and observe their effects as they're applied sequentially through the selected slides.	To replay the effect for a single slide, click its **Play Animation** icon. To replay it for all slides in sequence, click **Preview**.
e) With the slides still selected, use the **Effects Options** tool to fine-tune the transition.	Select an effect option from the list displayed for your transition preset.

Do This	How & Why
4. Set any Timing group options you'd like to use.	*Except* for Apply to All. You'll use this option shortly. 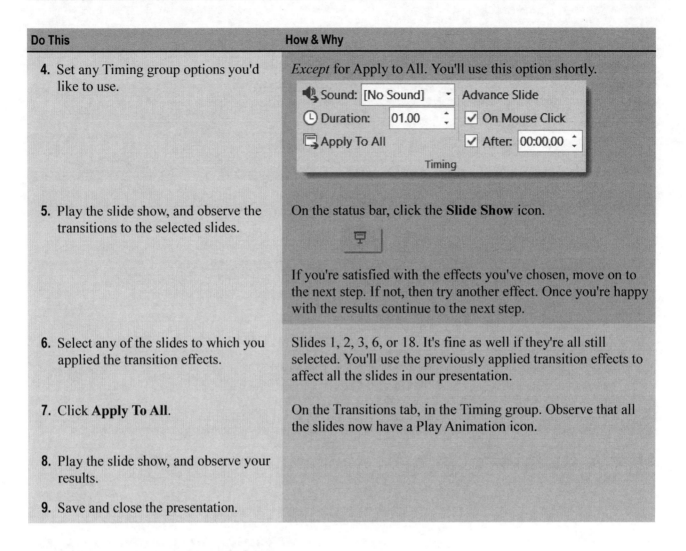
5. Play the slide show, and observe the transitions to the selected slides.	On the status bar, click the **Slide Show** icon. If you're satisfied with the effects you've chosen, move on to the next step. If not, then try another effect. Once you're happy with the results continue to the next step.
6. Select any of the slides to which you applied the transition effects.	Slides 1, 2, 3, 6, or 18. It's fine as well if they're all still selected. You'll use the previously applied transition effects to affect all the slides in our presentation.
7. Click **Apply To All**.	On the Transitions tab, in the Timing group. Observe that all the slides now have a Play Animation icon.
8. Play the slide show, and observe your results.	
9. Save and close the presentation.	

Assessment: Applying transitions between slides

1. True or false? To apply transition effects to all slides in a presentation, there's no need to select all the slides before doing so.

    - True
    - False

2. Which statement about transition effects is *not* true?

    - Transition effects can be previewed by clicking Preview or Play Animation.
    - The Duration option controls the length of time the affected slide is displayed.
    - Available Effect Options are context-sensitive.
    - You can use sounds from your own audio files to signal slide transitions.

3. True or false? In the Timing group, under Advance Slide, you can either check On Mouse Click, or check After and specify a time, but not both.

    - True
    - False

Module B: Additional text options

You can use text from other kinds of documents, created in many different kinds of applications. And there are different ways to add this text to your PowerPoint presentation, depending on the source, the type of file, the contents, and so on.

You will know how to:

- Import and outline from a Word document
- Import a PDF file
- Create WordArt from text

Text from other sources

You can incorporate text from many different kinds of sources into your PowerPoint presentations. Of course, you can always create the text within PowerPoint itself; however, its strength is as a presentation tool, not as a word processor. For this reason alone, a great benefit of using text from other sources is that quite often the source text is already formatted. And why "reinvent the wheel" when you can use the text as is?

A great many types of text documents are supported in PowerPoint. These can range from simple text (.txt) files created in programs such as Notepad or WordPad, to rich-text files (.rtf) or Microsoft Word (.doc, .docx) files. Of course, for small amounts of text from other sources, you often have the option of simply copying source text and pasting it onto a slide. However, certain applications don't allow you to do this very easily or very well. For larger amounts of text, importing the file—or in some case, text from it—can produce much more effective results.

Besides being able to preserve original source text formats, you do, of course, have the option of further customizing the look of text in PowerPoint. And you can do so whether you import the text or create it in PowerPoint. One such way of manipulating text to create more visual interest is to format it as WordArt.

A slide presentation lends itself to bits of information that are easily digested. Thus, when slides contain text, it's best to use elements such as titles, subtitles, bulleted or numbered lists, and so on, allowing them to be scanned fairly quickly. Put another way, slide text is best presented in something resembling outline form. For this reason, one very helpful feature is being able to import text documents (for example, Word documents or text files) in outline form, which can save you the trouble of having to create an outline from scratch in a presentation.

Importing a Word document outline

 MOS PowerPoint Exam Objective(s): 1.1.3

You can import most text documents into PowerPoint. Particularly if the text has been formatted in the source application, resulting in titles, subtitles, and other kinds of headings, PowerPoint can retrieve this text in the form of an outline. When you import it, the outline items are placed on slides, saving you the time of having to create these slides from scratch.

The types of text formats that can be imported are many, and Word documents are, of course, among them. You can import these outlines into a new or existing presentation. The outline slides are added after the slide that was displayed before the import.

1. Click **New Slide > Slides from Outline**.
   Use the lower part of the New Slide tool.

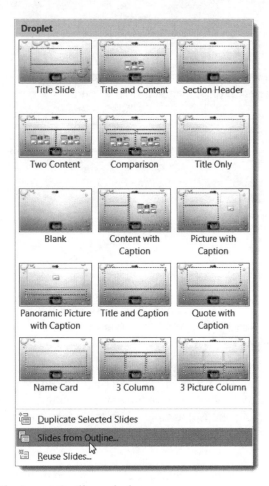

The Insert Outline window opens.

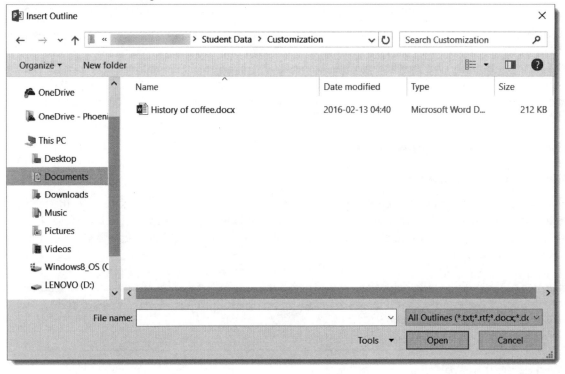

2. Navigate to the desired file, and click **Open**.

An outline of the file's text appears on new slides in the presentation.

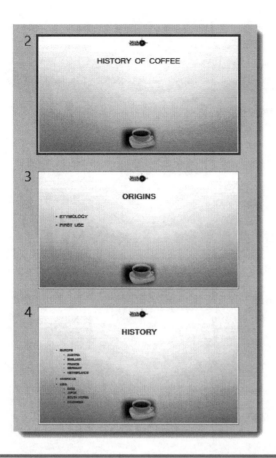

Importing a PDF file

You can import a PDF (portable document format) file into your PowerPoint presentation. Once you have imported a PDF file as an object, you can assign an *action* to it.

1. Import the PDF as an object.

   a) Select the destination slide, and click **Object**.

   b) In the Insert Object window, click **Create from file**, and click **Browse**.

   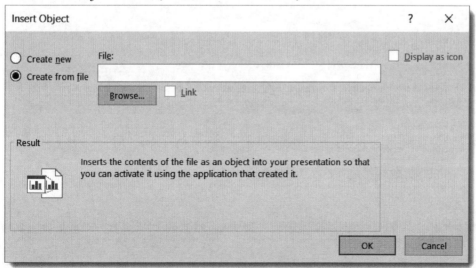

c) Navigate to and select the file, and click **Open**.

d) To display the file as a PDF icon on the slide, click **Display as icon**.
Otherwise, the PDF is displayed as a standard object in a frame with handles, with its opening text visible.

2. Select the object or icon, and click **Action**.
To attach an action to the PDF file object or icon. On the Insert tab, in the Links group.

The Action Settings window opens.

3. Select the desired tab.
   - To cause the action on a mouse click, click the **Mouse Click** tab.
   - To cause the action on mouse over, click the **Mouse Over** tab.

4. Select **Object action**, and make sure that **Activate Contents** is selected in the list.

5. Click **OK**.
Now, during a slide show, when you click on or mouse over the PDF icon, the PDF file opens.

Creating WordArt from text

You can create WordArt from text and use it in your presentations. *WordArt* is a feature that was once available only in Microsoft Word (hence the name), but it's now available in other Office applications, including PowerPoint.

MOS PowerPoint Exam Objective(s): 2.1.3

1. Select the text to be formatted.
2. Display the WordArt Styles group.
   On the Drawing Tools Format tab. This group contains a gallery of WordArt style presets, as well as other formatting options and effects.

3. Select a WordArt style preset from the gallery.
4. Apply any additional formatting and effects from the Text Fill, Text Outline, and/or Text Effects options.

Exercise: Using text from other sources

In this exercise, you'll import a document outline and a PDF file, and then you'll format text as WordArt.

Do This	How & Why
1. Create a new presentation.	Click **File > New > Blank Presentation**.
2. Display the New Slide options.	Click the lower part of the New Slide tool.
3. Click **Slides from Outline**. The Insert Outline window opens.	

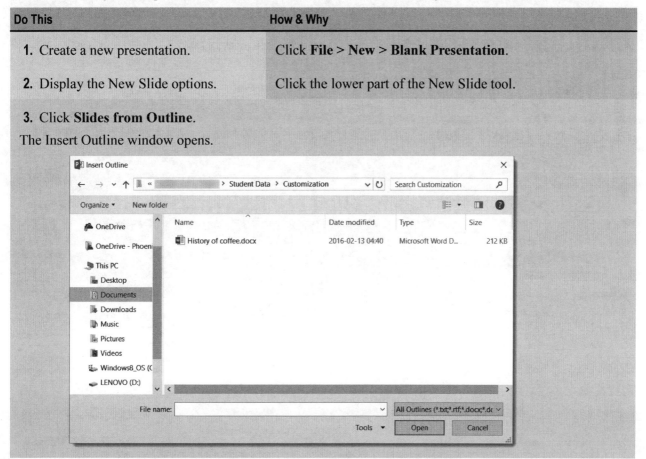

Do This	How & Why
4. Navigate to and open **History of coffee.docx**, and observe the results.	From the data folder. Select the file, and click **Open**. 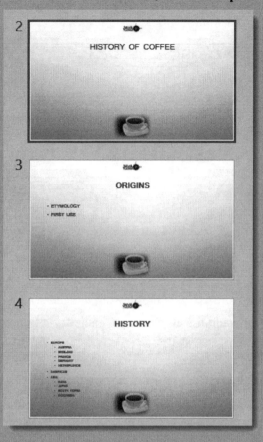
5. Add a new slide to the end of the presentation.	
a) Click just below the last slide in the Slide pane.	A horizontal I-beam insertion point appears there. 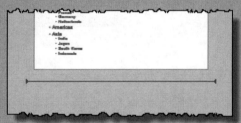
b) Click **New Slide**.	This is an alternative to first selecting a slide, and it's especially useful when you want to add a new slide 1 to the presentation. You can also use this technique in Slide Sorter view. The new slide appears at the end of the presentation.

Do This	How & Why
6. Onto the new slide, import the **History of coffee.pdf** file as an object.	The PDF icon appears on the slide. 
a) Click **Object**.	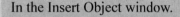
b) In the Insert Object window, click **Create from file**, and click **Browse**.	
c) Navigate to and select the file, and click **Open**.	
d) Click **Display as icon**.	In the Insert Object window.
7. With the PDF icon still selected, click **Action**.	On the Insert tab, in the Links group. To assign an action to the PDF icon. The Action Settings window opens.
8. On the Mouse Over tab, click **Object action**, and ensure that **Activate Contents** is selected.	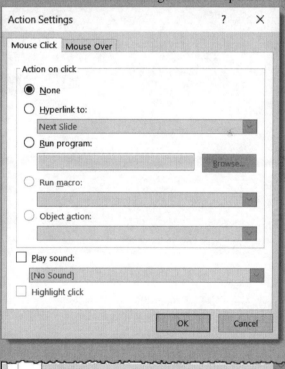
9. Click **OK**.	Nothing appears to change, but this mouse-over setting only applies during a slide show. You'll get to test this shortly.

Do This	How & Why
10. On slide 2, select the "History of coffee" heading.	
11. Display the full WordArt Styles gallery.	On the Drawing Tools Format tab. 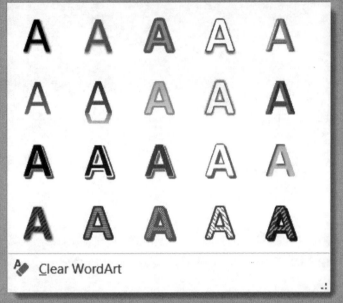
12. Select a preset from the gallery.	
13. Apply any additional formatting and effects from the WordArt Styles group options.	
14. Save the file.	
15. Run the slide show, and be sure to hover the mouse over the PDF icon on the last slide.	
16. After running the slide show, make any additional change you wish, then save and close the presentation.	

Assessment: Using text from other sources

1. Which of these statements is true about importing a document in outline form?

    - It must be a Word file.
    - The source document can't be a normal text document; it must be written as an outline.
    - When imported, the source document is displayed one document page per slide.
    - Click Slides from Outline in the New Slide options to do so.

2. True or false? When importing a PDF file, you use the "Create from file" option in the Insert Object window.

    - True
    - False

3. Which statement about WordArt styles is true?

    - WordArt styles are complementary effects combined as individual presets.
    - To view the effects of WordArt styles, you must view the embedded object in Word.
    - You must set the Text Fill, Text Outline, and Text Effects options before applying a WordArt style preset.
    - To apply WordArt formatting in PowerPoint, Word must also be running.

Module C: Printing

Normally, the ultimate endpoint of the PowerPoint presentation trajectory is a slide show. However, at any time, and for different reasons, you might need to print any part of—or even all of—your presentations. To do so, you might also need to adjust PowerPoint Print Options.

You will learn how to:

- Preview your presentation before printing
- Work with Print Options
- Adjust Print settings to print handouts, notes, and individual slides
- Add the Quick Print tool to the ribbon
- Add the Quick Print tool to the Quick Access toolbar
- Print your presentation

Printing in PowerPoint

In order to print, you need a couple of things.

- Access to a printer, either by a local connection to your computer or through a network
- A printer driver for the printer you want to use

Generally, these things are set up for you at your workplace. After they are set up, printing in PowerPoint can be relatively straightforward. But you might find that a default printout doesn't give you what you want. There are also many available ways to specify your print job and many options for doing so.

The good news is that you can customize PowerPoint to better suit the way you work and your printing requirements. For this reason, you should preview your worksheets before you print them.

- *Print Preview*: In Backstage view. Whenever you intend to print, it's a good idea to preview your printout. In doing so, you might find some things to tweak in your presentation before taking the time (and using the paper) to print. You can preview all or any part of your presentation.
- *Print Options*: Also in Backstage view, this is where you set default options to control how PowerPoint prints in general.
- *Print settings*: On the Print Preview screen, you have access to settings for controlling each print job, including exactly what presentation components you wish to print. These include one or more slides, notes, handouts, or the entire presentation.
- *Quick Print*: As its name implies, this is the quickest way to print. Unfortunately, it's not available by default, but you can customize both the Quick Access toolbar and the ribbon to accommodate it.

Previewing your printout

In Backstage view, you can see a preview of how your worksheet will look when printed.

1. Click **File**, then click **Print**.

    To display the Print screen in Backstage view. Here, you can change print settings and see how they'll affect the printout.

    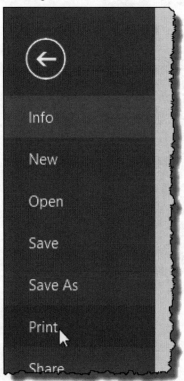

2. Click the preview, and then use the Page Down and Page Up keys to move through the preview.

    You can also use the page navigation functions below the preview. From here, you can print, adjust printer settings, or return to the presentation to make any additional adjustments.

    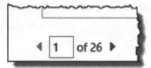

Setting Print Options

Use the Print Options settings in Backstage view to adjust general default printing options in PowerPoint.

 MOS PowerPoint Exam Objective(s): 1.6.4

1. In Backstage view, click Options.
    Click **File > Options**.

    The PowerPoint Options window opens.

2. Click **Advanced**.
    In the left pane.

3. Scroll to display the Print options.
    These settings control printer-handling features such as print quality, resolution, color, and scaling.

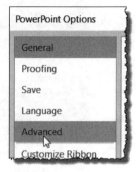

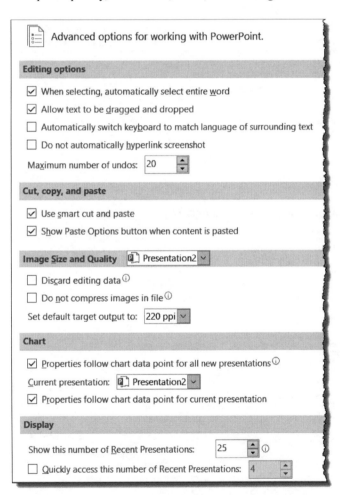

4. Once you've finished adjusting settings, click **OK** to implement your changes, or click **Cancel**.
    Either way, you're returned to the presentation.

Adjusting printer and print settings

You adjust printer and print settings from the Print screen in Backstage view—the same one you use for Print Preview.

 MOS PowerPoint Exam Objective(s): 1.6.1, 1.6.2, 1.6.3, 1.6.4

1. In Backstage view, click **Print**.
2. Make any changes to settings.
   Under Print, to the left of the preview pane.

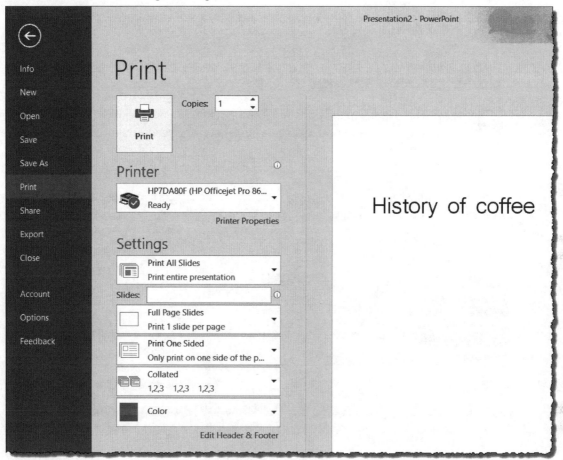

- Under Printer, you can select a different printer from the dropdown list, and click Printer Properties to adjust settings specific to the selected printer.
- In the Copies box, you can specify the number of copies you wish to print.
- Under Settings:
  - The Print All Slides dropdown list contains options for specifying exactly what slides you want to print.

PowerPoint 2016 Level 1

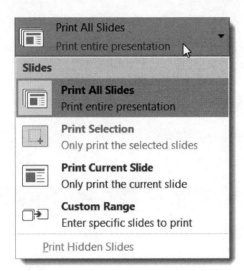

 Note: The options in the remaining dropdown lists depend, in part, on what option is selected here. In some case, other types of options become available, such as printout orientation.

- In the Slides box, you can specify the number(s) of the slide(s) you wish to print. For example, to print slides 6 through 10, you could type `6-10` or `6, 7, 8, 9, 10`.

- The Full Page Slides dropdown list displays options for printing slides, notes pages, and handouts, as well as others.

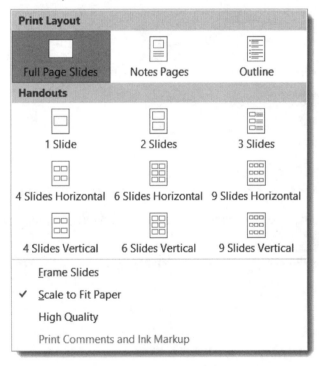

- The Print One Sided dropdown list

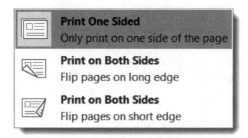

- The Collated dropdown list allows you to specify collated/uncollated printing.

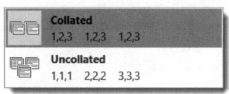

- The Color dropdown list allows you to choose whether you wish to print in color, black and white, or grayscale.

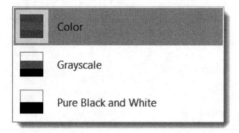

Printing

Once you've set your print option and settings and selected your printer, you need only print.

1. Open the Print screen in Backstage view, if necessary.
2. Click **Print**.

Adding Quick Print to the Quick Access toolbar

The fastest and simplest way to print in PowerPoint is to click the **Quick Print** tool. But this tool isn't available by default. One place you can add the Quick Print tool is on the Quick Access toolbar, which is handy because it's always available in the main PowerPoint window, regardless of what's showing (or hidden) in the ribbon.

1. Click the Quick Access toolbar down arrow.

    The Customize Quick Access Toolbar dropdown list opens.

2. Click **Quick Print**.

    To select it.

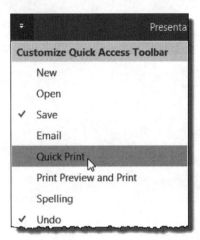

The Quick Print button appears in the toolbar.

Adding Quick Print to the ribbon

Another place to add the Quick Print tool is on the ribbon.

1. In Backstage view, click **Options**, and click **Customize Ribbon**.

   The Customize Ribbon screen is displayed.

2. Under "Choose commands from," in the list of tools, click **Quick Print**.

   You'll need to scroll down to see it.

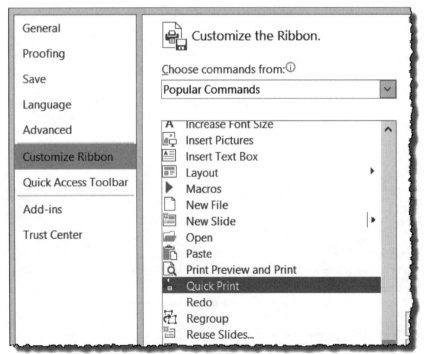

3. In the Customize the Ribbon tabs list, select a destination tab for the Quick Print tool, and click **New Group**.

   Quick Print is considered a "custom" tool in PowerPoint, so it has to be added to a special custom group. However, you can add that custom group to any ribbon tab.

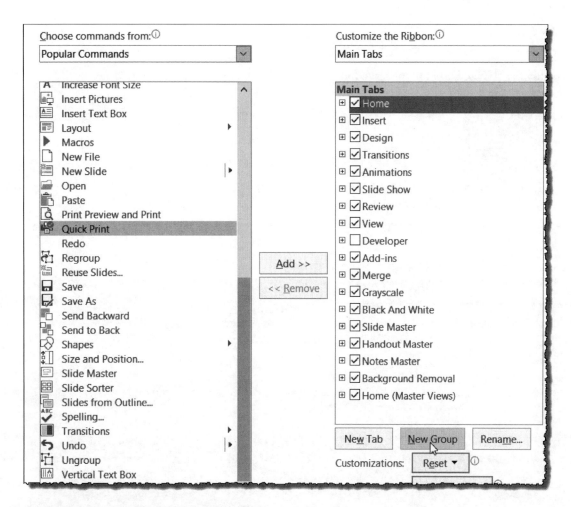

The custom group is added to the selected tab.

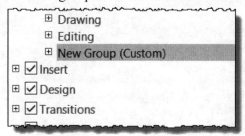

4. To change the position of the new group on its tab, click the up arrow or down arrow.
   To the right of the tabs list.

5. Click **Add**.
   Quick Print and New Group (Custom) should both still be selected.

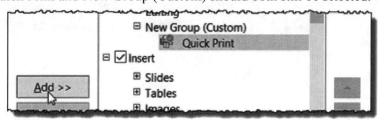

Note: To rename the new group, select **New Group (Custom)**, click **Rename**, and enter a new name.

6. Click **OK**.
   To save your changes.

7. Display the selected tab, and observe the Quick Tool in the new custom group.

Exercise: Exploring preview and print settings

Do This	How & Why
1. Open **JT Printing.pptx**.	In the `Customization` data folder.
2. Click **File**, and click **Print**.	The Print screen is displayed.
3. Navigate through the presentation in the Print Preview area.	Use the navigation area under the preview, or press **PgUp** and **PgDn**.
4. Observe the Print button.	If you click it, the current presentation will print on the current printer immediately, using all current settings. You're not going to do that now.
5. Click **Options**, and click **Advanced**.	In the PowerPoint Options window.
6. Observe the available Print Options.	You won't change any settings here.
7. Click **Cancel**.	
8. Return to the Print screen, and observe the available Print settings options.	Click **File** > **Print**.
9. Explore the available settings in each dropdown list.	
10. Open the Printer dropdown list.	Notice that besides being able to select printers, there are options such as printing to a PDF file and sending your presentation as a fax.
11. Return to the presentation.	You'll add the Quick Print tool to this toolbar.
12. Click the arrow at the right end of the Quick Access toolbar.	The Customize Quick Access Toolbar option are displayed.

Do This	How & Why
13. Click **Quick Print**.	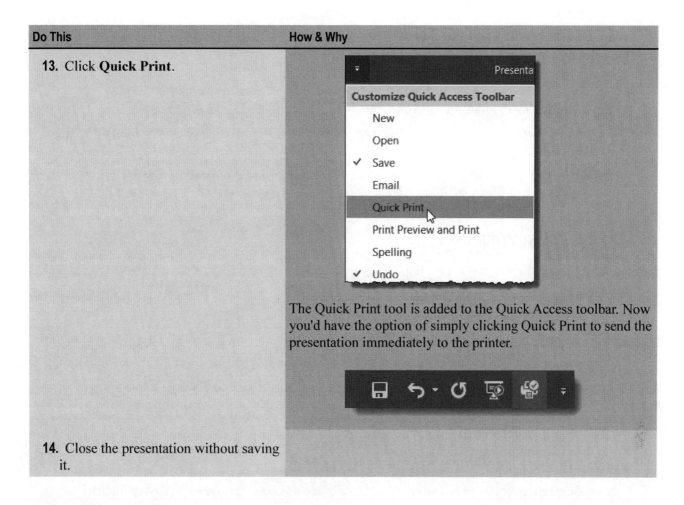 The Quick Print tool is added to the Quick Access toolbar. Now you'd have the option of simply clicking Quick Print to send the presentation immediately to the printer.
14. Close the presentation without saving it.	

Assessment: Previewing and printing

1. True or false? One way to preview your printouts is to use the Preview tool on the View tab.

    - True
    - False

2. Which of these options is *not* contained in the print settings?

    - Double-sided printing
    - Faxing
    - Collating
    - Color

3. True or false? The benefit of having the Quick Print tool in a custom group on the ribbon is that it's always visible.

    - True
    - False

Summary: Customization

You should now know how to:

- Apply transitions and transition effects to all or individual slides in a presentation
- Import text documents as an outline from applications such as Word, import a PDF file, and create WordArt from text
- Preview your printout, set print options, adjust printer and print settings, add the Quick Print tool to the Quick Access toolbar and to the ribbon, and print using either Print or Quick Print

Synthesis: Customization

In this synthesis, you'll apply transitions, import from Word and PDF files, create WordArt from text, preview your printout, set Print Options, adjust print settings, and print the presentation to a PDF file.

1. Open **JT Synthesis.pptx**, and save it as `My JT Synthesis.pptx`.
2. Apply transitions to a slide, and fine-tune the effects until they're exactly as you want them.
3. Apply the same transitions to all the slides in the presentation.
4. At the end of the presentation, import `History of coffee.docx` as a Word outline.
5. At the very end of the presentation, import `History of coffee.pdf` as an icon, setting it to activate content on mouse click.
6. Apply WordArt formatting to selected text in the presentation. Think about adding visual interest without drawing undue attention.
7. Preview the printout of the presentation, then return to the presentation and make any additional formatting changes you like.
8. In Print Options, check the **High quality** option.
9. Open the print settings, select **2 Slides**, **Collated**, **Portrait Orientation**, and **Color**.

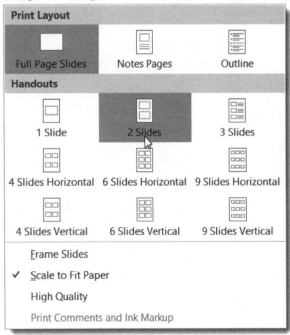

10. In the Printer options, select **Microsoft Print to PDF**.

11. Return to the presentation.
12. Hover over the Quick Print tool.
    It's set to automatically print to a PDF file according to your print settings.
13. Click **Quick Print**.

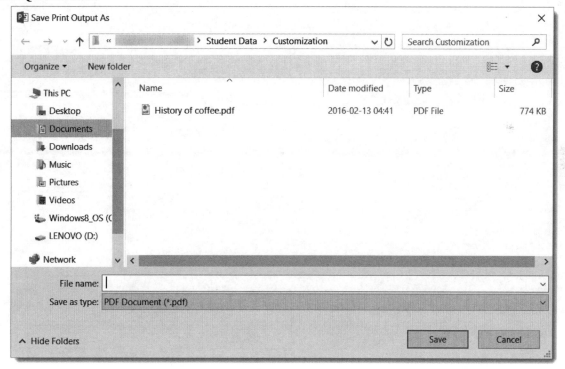

14. Name the file `My JT Printout`, and save it to the data folder.
15. Save and close the presentation.

Chapter 7: Advanced formatting

You will learn how to:

- Create and format SmartArt
- Explore additional formatting options

Module A: Inserting and formatting SmartArt

PowerPoint's SmartArt feature provides a quick way of creating illustrations of slide content, including text and pictures. SmartArt can be used to illustrate lists, whether sequential or unordered, and relationships among items.

You will learn how to:

- Convert lists to SmartArt and format them
- Create and add shapes to SmartArt organization charts

About SmartArt

Adding things like shapes and clipart to your slides can be a way to create some visual appeal in your presentations. But a great way to add visual appeal while better conveying the meaning of slide text is through PowerPoint's SmartArt feature. *SmartArt* mainly uses text to create graphics diagrams that illustrate relationships among items of information.

There are eight classes of SmartArt diagrams available in PowerPoint, each of which also contains many variations. Besides text, some SmartArt diagrams can also contain other objects, such as images. What makes SmartArt very handy is that the individual elements, such as lines and boxes, are drawn for you; you don't have to draw them yourself. They also automatically resize to fit the text or graphic objects that they contain or—in the case of lines—connect.

Types of SmartArt diagrams

Icon and diagram type	Description
List	Displays items in a list. Some list types don't convey any organization or hierarchy. Others can be used to display sequence, such as steps in a procedure.
Process	Displays steps in a linear, sequential fashion.
Cycle	Displays a process that repeats in a continuous loop.
Hierarchy	Displays hierarchical relationships, as in company organizational charts.
Relationship	Displays relationships between/among items. Depending on the number of items and their relationships, these diagrams can be very simple or extremely complex. A good example is the Venn diagram.
Matrix	Displays four items arranged in quadrants, and their relationship to the whole.
Pyramid	Displays proportional, interconnected, hierarchical relationships among items.
Picture	Displays one or more images with related items listed alongside them.

Remember that once you've created a SmartArt graphic object, you can copy and paste it into other Office applications, including Word, Excel, and Outlook. This fact alone makes SmartArt a powerful feature indeed.

The image below shows different kinds of SmartArt applied to text and, in some cases, images. Slides 5–9 all show the same information, but each illustrates it differently.

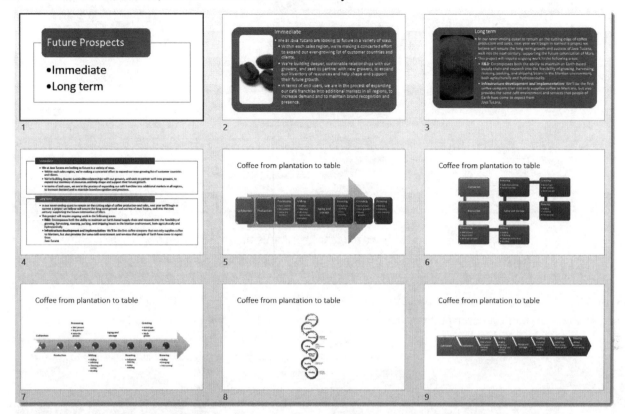

Note that even if a SmartArt design doesn't come with a picture placeholder, you can always add pictures (or other objects) to your design afterwards. To do so, use the tools on the Insert tab, for example, Pictures or Online Pictures. Once you've completed your design, it's a good idea to use **Arrange > Group** on the SmartArt Tools Format tab to make all the elements function as a single object.

Creating SmartArt

One way to employ SmartArt on your slides is to select a SmartArt design, then enter text (and/or other objects) into the placeholders that are created. It's important to keep in mind, however, that doing so can be more cumbersome; for example, as you enter text, you must be careful to do so in the appropriate placeholder. Otherwise, you might not end up with your intended results.

 MOS PowerPoint Exam Objective(s): 3.3.1

1. Select a destination slide.
2. Click **SmartArt**.
   On the Insert tab, in the Illustrations group.

   The Choose a SmartArt Graphic window opens. By default, All is selected in the left pane. In the central pane, all possible SmartArt graphics are displayed, arranged by category.

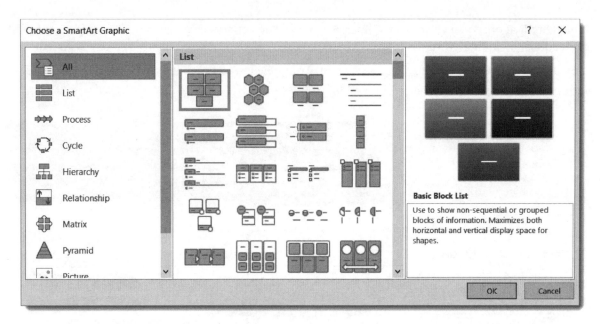

3. In the left pane, select the category of SmartArt that best suits the information you wish to convey.

   A subset of SmartArt graphics is now displayed in the central pane, corresponding to the category selected in the left pane.

4. In the central pane, click to select a SmartArt graphic.

   In the right pane, a description of the selected graphic and its function is displayed.

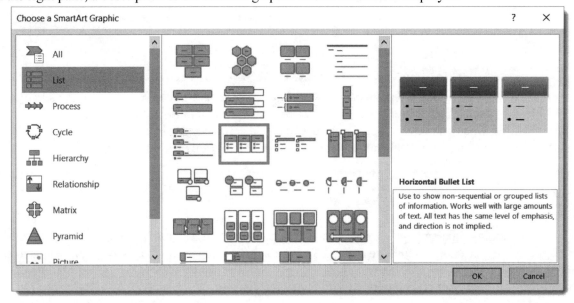

5. Once you've decided on and selected a SmartArt graphic, click **OK**.

   The SmartArt graphic's displayed on the slide and selected. A box for inserting text is provided.

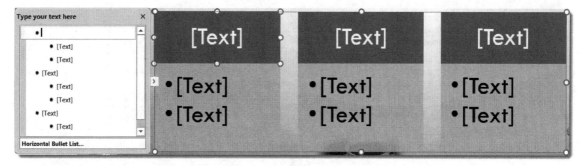

6. Enter your text in the placeholders provided.

   To create additional bullet items, after you've entered text in the last bullet provided, simply press **Enter**. To delete a bullet placeholder, click in it, and press **Backspace**.

7. To view the result, click outside the SmartArt.

   To deselect it.

8. To edit SmartArt text, click on the text you wish to change.

   The SmartArt is once again selected, and text-entry placeholders display its current text.

9. Select the text, and edit as necessary.

Converting lists to SmartArt

You've already learned how to create a SmartArt list from scratch. However, a more efficient method for creating SmartArt lists is to convert an existing list to SmartArt. Even if you're creating a list from scratch, doing so by first typing a list on a slide and then converting it to SmartArt tends to be much faster. As you hover over designs in the SmartArt gallery, your text is previewed in that design. The fact that the text's already present makes it easier to choose a design that best suits it.

 MOS PowerPoint Exam Objective(s): 2.1.4, 3.3.2

1. Right-click the list, and choose **Convert to SmartArt** from the context menu.

   There's no need to select the list before you convert it.

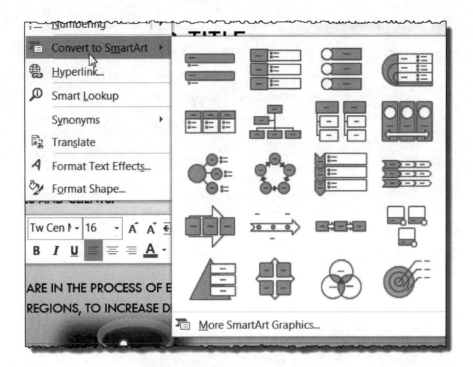

2. Click to select a design.

    For a broader selection of designs, click **More SmartArt Graphics**, then select a design.

    The list appears in the SmartArt graphic.

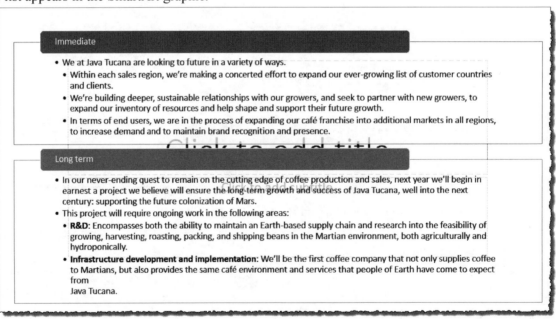

3. To edit SmartArt text, select the graphic, and in the Text pane, edit the text.

    If the SmartArt graphic also contains images, you might need to first select its text component in order for the Text pane to open. As you type, the SmartArt is automatically updated. You can add bulleted (or numbered) items this way as well. For SmartArt that places each item in a box, for example, adding a new item thus adds a new box.

4. To format text in multiple columns, click the **Add or Remove Columns** tool.

    In the Home tab's Paragraph group. There, you can format text as one, two, or three columns, or choose **More Columns** for custom column settings.

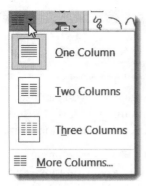

SmartArt Tools tabs

Once you create a SmartArt graphic, and whenever one is selected, two important SmartArt Tools tabs become available: the Design tab and the Format tab.

 MOS PowerPoint Exam Objective(s): 3.1.2, 3.4.1

The *SmartArt Tools Design* tab contains groups of tools to help you work with the structural aspects of your SmartArt.

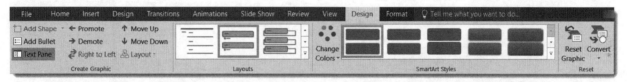

- The *Create Graphic* group contains tools for adding shapes and bullets to your SmartArt; displaying/hiding the text pane; promoting, demoting, and moving individual items (for example, bullet items in lists); reversing the direction of sequentially oriented graphics; and a special layout tool for working with organization charts.

- The *Layouts* group contains a gallery of available layouts, allowing you to change your layout simply by clicking another layout.

- The *SmartArt Styles* group contains a gallery of style variations specific to the selected layout. Once you've selected a layout, then selected a suitable style variant, he Change Colors tool allows you to change the color scheme of the graphic.

- The *Reset* group contains tools for resetting the graphic to its original state. This can be particularly helpful as a kind of "panic button" for those moments when you feel your tweaking and re-tweaking has made a mess of things. The Convert tool allows you to convert the graphic to text or to shapes. Converting a SmartArt graphic to shapes in effect sets it as a collection of graphic shapes, which allows you to work with it using all the standard shape tools. However, it's a good idea to use this feature only after you've finalized all the text and its placement within the graphic.

The *SmartArt Tools Format* tab contains groups of tools for working with shapes, shape styles, WordArt styles, and the arrangement and sizing of the graphic and its components. Many of these tools are similar to those used for working with standard shapes and other PowerPoint objects.

Remember, once created, SmartArt is like any other object on a PowerPoint slide. And you can use many of the same tools to work with it and its contents. Thus, like any other object containing text, if you add text inside a SmartArt shape, you can format that text as you would any other, using the tools on the Home tab.

For example, to apply multi-column formatting to text, whether that text is in a shape or a simple text object, simply select the text; on the Home tab, in the Paragraph group, click Add or Remove Columns, and select the desired column format. As you hover over available options, the selected text previews the results.

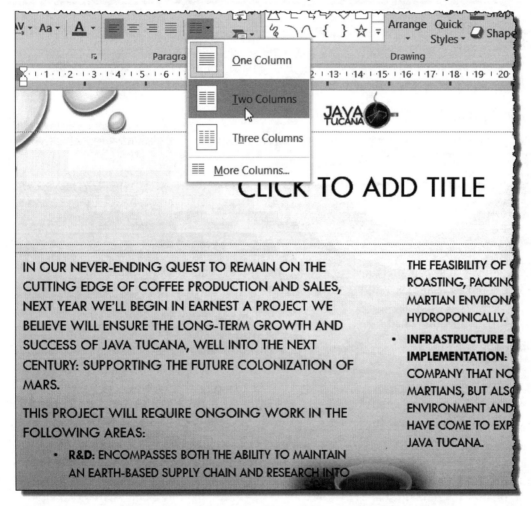

You can also use the Insert tab to add additional shapes to existing SmartArt objects.

Changing layouts

You can change the layout of SmartArt by using the Layouts gallery on the SmartArt Tools Design tab.

1. Select the SmartArt graphic.
2. On the SmartArt Tools Design tab, select a layout.

   From the Layouts gallery. Use the gallery's ▼ (More) button to open the gallery pane. The layouts displayed in the gallery depend on the current layout.

3. For additional options, click **More Layouts**.

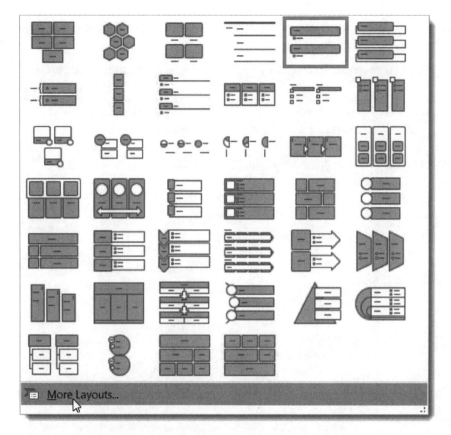

The Choose a SmartArt Graphic window opens.

4. Select a new layout, and click **OK**.

The selected graphic is displayed in the new layout.

Promoting, demoting, and moving list items

Tools for promoting, demoting, and moving SmartArt list items are found on the SmartArt Tools Design tab.

1. Select the SmartArt list item(s) you wish to promote/demote/move.
2. Click the appropriate tool.
   In the Create Graphic group.

   - To promote the item(s), click **Promote**. Each click removes an indentation, moving the item(s) closer to the left margin.

   - To demote the item(s), click **Demote**. Each click indents the item(s) further to the right.

   - To move the item up in the list, click **Move Up**.

   - To move the item down in the list, click **Move Down**.

3. To promote/demote an item using the Text pane, place the insertion point immediately to the right of that item's bullet (or number), then do one of the following.

   - To promote the item, press **Backspace**. Each time you press the key, the item is promoted another level.

   - To demote the item, press **Tab**. Each time you press the key, the item is demoted another level.

   To rotate or reverse the direction of selected SmartArt (or other) text, on the Home tab, in the Paragraph group, click **Text Direction**, then select the desired text orientation. Clicking **More Options** displays detailed text options in the Format Shape pane.

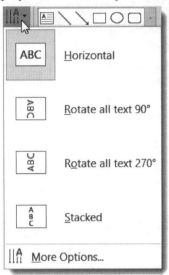

Changing styles and colors

 MOS PowerPoint Exam Objective(s): 3.3.5

On the SmartArt Tools Design tab, you can use the tools in the SmartArt Styles group to change the style and color of your graphic.

1. To change the style, select a new style from the SmartArt Styles gallery.

   Use the ▼ (More) button to display the full gallery.

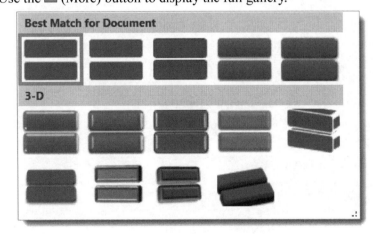

2. To change the colors of the graphic, click **Change Colors**.

The Change Colors options are displayed.

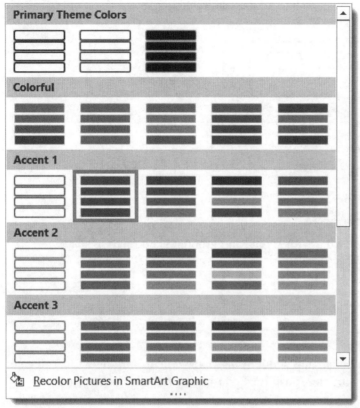

3. Select a color scheme from the displayed options.
4. To change the color of a picture in a SmartArt graphic, choose **Recolor Pictures in SmartArt Graphic**. From the Change Colors options.

    The picture is automatically recolored to match the color variations of the rest of the graphic.

Shapes and shape styles

The SmartArt Tools Format tab contains powerful tools for changing, working with, and embellishing SmartArt shapes, as well as WordArt styles. Working with shapes in SmartArt is just like working with shapes in other kinds of PowerPoint objects. All the same features are available to you, including Shape Styles, Shape Fill, Shape Outline, Shape Effects, grouping, and sizing tools.

 MOS PowerPoint Exam Objective(s): 3.3.3, 3.3.4

In the Shape Styles and WordArt Styles groups, click the **More** button to display more Shape Styles gallery options. Click ▣ (Launcher) to display the corresponding Format pane.

The Shapes group contains tools for changing the selected shape, as well as enlarging or reducing it incrementally.

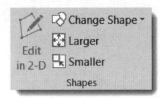

The Shape Styles and WordArt Styles groups contain all the standard tools for working with shapes, which you learned about in *PowerPoint 2016 Level 1*.

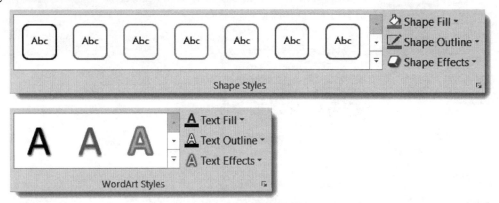

The Arrange tool contains options for working with layers, and grouping and rotating shapes.

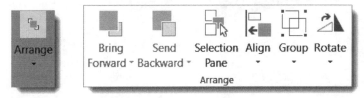

The Size tool lets you specify the exact height and width of the shape you're working with. The launcher in the Size options opens a Format pane to the size, position, and rotation settings for that shape.

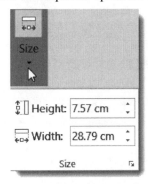

Exercise: Creating and formatting SmartArt

You'll convert bulleted lists to SmartArt, including a process diagram.

Do This	How & Why
1. Open `Creating SmartArt.pptx`, and save it as `My Creating SmartArt.pptx`.	In the `Documents` data folder.
2. Observe the slides in the presentation. After the title slide, the remaining slides are all lists of information.	

Do This	How & Why
3. On slide 2, convert the text to a SmartArt list diagram. a) Right-click the list, and choose **Convert to SmartArt** from the context menu.	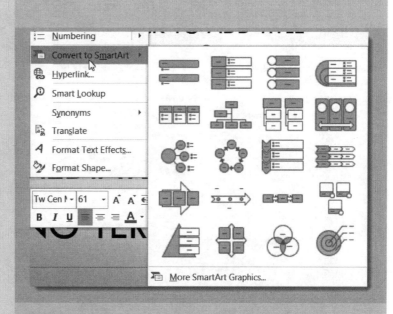
b) Hover over each design preset in the gallery, and preview the results as they are applied to the list, but don't select a design just yet.	Notice that some designs include one or more placeholders for pictures (images).

c) Click **More SmartArt Graphics**.

The Choose a SmartArt Graphic window opens.

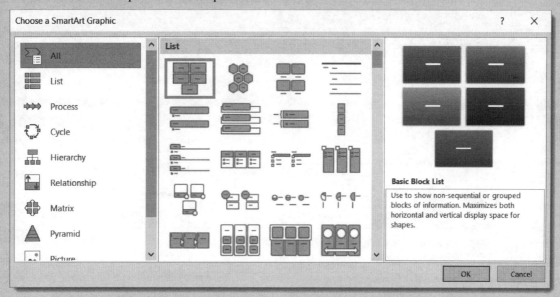

d) In the left pane, click the various SmartArt categories, then click some designs in the central pane.	As you click each one, its description is displayed in the right pane. These descriptions help you select a design that's well suited to content.
e) When you're done exploring, click the **List** category.	In the left pane.

Do This	How & Why
f) Select a diagram option that you think best suits the list.	Choose a diagram that *doesn't* contain a picture placeholder.

g) Click **OK**.

The list is converted to the SmartArt diagram you've chosen.

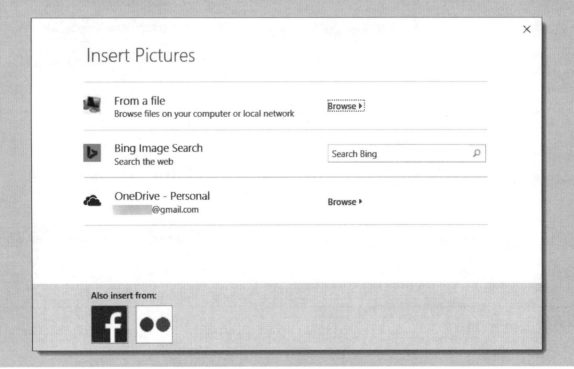

Do This	How & Why
4. On slide 3, convert the list and its heading to SmartArt, choosing a design that contains one image placeholder.	Use the procedure in step 3 as a guide. However, because you're looking for a design that includes a picture placeholder, you can also click the **Picture** category in the left pane of the Choose a SmartArt Graphic window to explore its designs.
5. Insert the `three beans.jpg` image into the picture placeholder.	

a) Click the picture placeholder icon.

The Insert Pictures window opens.

Do This	How & Why
b) Next to "From a file," click **Browse**.	The Insert Picture window opens.

c) Navigate to your data folder, select **three beans.jpg**.

d) Click **Insert**.

The picture is inserted and selected, and the Picture Tools Format tab is displayed. Notice that the image contains a white background that doesn't blend well with the list or the slide background. There is any number of ways we could alter the image to make it look better on the slide.

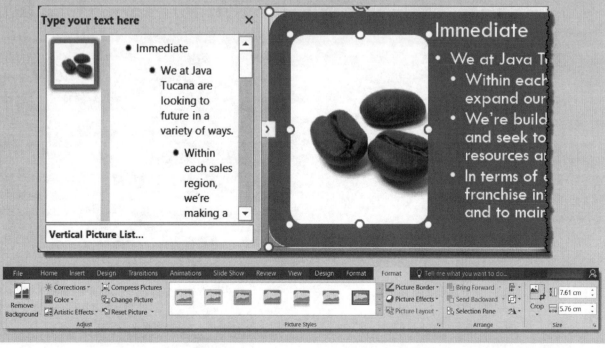

Do This	How & Why
6. Apply color correction to the image by reducing its brightness 20%.	
a) Click **Corrections**.	In the Picture Tools Format tab's Adjust group. The Corrections gallery opens, displaying previews of the image at various settings.
b) Click the **Brightness: -20% Contrast: 0% (Normal)** option.	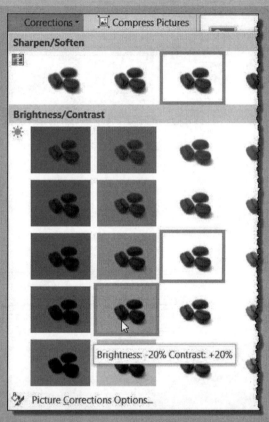
	The image background now blends better with the overall look of the slide.

7. Using the design you selected in step 4, convert the list in slide 4 to SmartArt.	Because the information on slides 3 and 4 have the same status —both elaborate on the "Immediate" and "Long term" bullets shown on slide 2—it makes sense for them to have the same design.

Do This	How & Why
8. Use the same method to insert the `Mars.jpg` image into the SmartArt on slide 4.	From step 5.
9. Use your knowledge of working with pictures to add any effects and so on that you see fit.	Use the tools on the Picture Tools Format tab.
10. Observe slide 5.	It contains the combined text from slides 3 and 4. As it contains two higher-level headings on one slide ("Immediate" and "Long term"), it provides you with an opportunity to apply additional, more intricate types of SmartArt diagrams to it.
11. Convert all the text on slide 5 to SmartArt that includes both the `three beans.jpg` and `Mars.jpg` images.	Use the same technique you just used for the previous two slides. As you explore the different diagramming possibilities, select one that you think will best suit the two headings and relatively long second-level bullet items. Keep in mind that these two bullet items are not sequential steps in a process but represent two parallel, ongoing activities.
12. Use the SmartArt Tools tabs to fine-tune the layout, style, and color scheme of the images and text fill, so that the background images remain somewhat visible.	

13. Resize and, if you wish, reposition the SmartArt to better fit the slide.

With the SmartArt selected, use the sizing handles. Drag the SmartArt to reposition it.

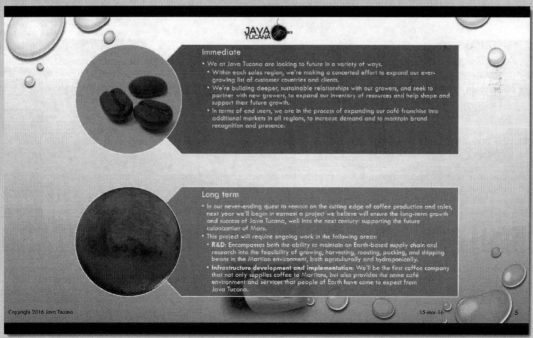

14. Observe slide 6.	It contains a list of numbered steps, meaning that they represent a sequential process. Notice also that some steps contain secondary, bulleted lists, which are non-sequential.

Do This	How & Why
15. Convert the list on slide 6 into a SmartArt graphic that will best suit it.	As you explore and preview designs, you'll notice that some designs that include separate shapes for second-level lists aren't well suited to this list, because not every step contains a secondary bulleted list. These designs often result in empty boxes. Other designs only include boxes for populated lists and are thus better suited to this list. A good place to start might be in the Process category of the Choose a SmartArt Graphic window.
16. Change the layout, as necessary, using the Layouts gallery.	On the SmartArt Tools Design tab. Use the **More** button to open the gallery. Click **More Layouts** to open the Choose a SmartArt Graphic window, if you wish.
17. Fine-tune the style and colors of your graphic.	Use the SmartArt Styles gallery, then use the **Change Colors** tool.

18. Once you're satisfied, save and close the file.

SmartArt charts

You can use PowerPoint's SmartArt feature to create charts. One very common type of chart that's a favorite of PowerPoint presentations is the organization, or "org," chart. Organization charts are typically used to illustrate the structure of a company, institution, and so on. However, they can also be useful in working out structural relationships when writing computer programs, or even tracing family genealogies.

Organization charts tend to be hierarchical, and connecting lines between boxes display those relationships. These charts are most often oriented vertically, clearly displaying a top-down chain of command. However, they can also be displayed horizontally, which can help to de-emphasize the hierarchical nature of working relationships.

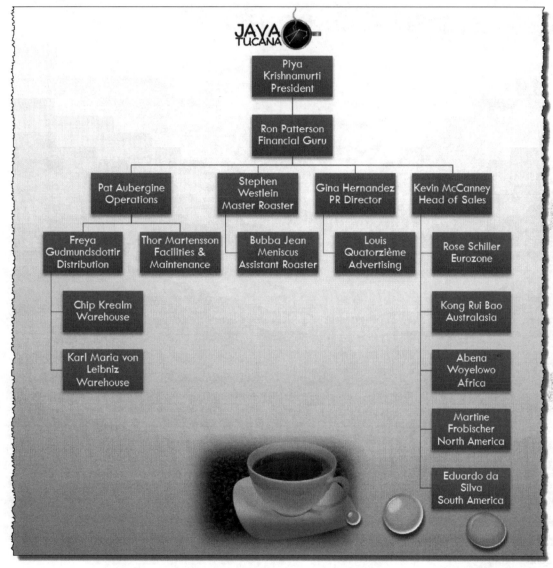

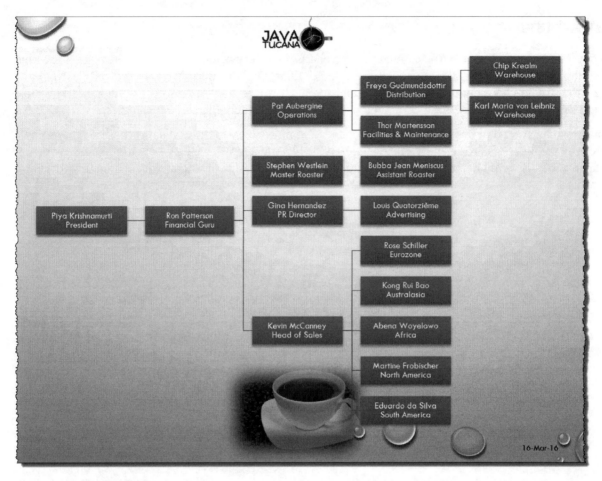

Creating an organization chart

When creating organization charts, as with other SmartArt designs, it's always easiest to start with a list of items. And your list need not be complete. You can still add, delete, promote, demote, or move items later.

PowerPoint provides a variety of organization-chart designs, some of which are intentionally structured to be more hierarchical than others. For example, even a fully hierarchical chart appears less so when displayed horizontally, which is an option that's also provided. As with other SmartArt designs, some of those in the Hierarchy category also contain picture placeholders, allowing you to include images. Likewise, you can change the design at any time, using the SmartArt Tools Design tab. For additional formatting options, use the SmartArt Tools Format tab.

1. Right-click the list you wish to convert to an organization chart, and click **Convert to SmartArt**.
2. In the gallery options, click **More SmartArt Graphics**.
   The Choose a SmartArt Graphic window opens.
3. In the left pane, click **Hierarchy** to display its design options.
   In the center pane.

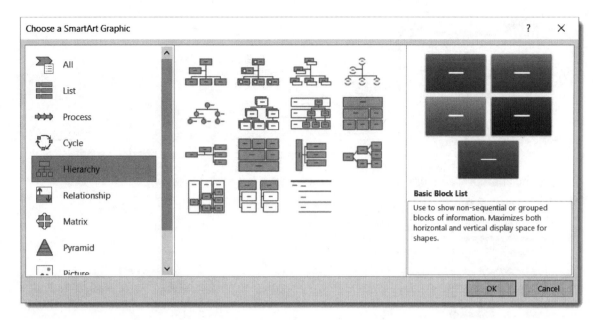

4. Click a design in the gallery, then click **OK**.

   The SmartArt design is applied to the list.

5. Once you've decided on a chart design, if you'd like to change the way the its layers branch, click the **Layout** tool, and select a branching option.

   Each option displays an icon illustrating its function.

- **Standard** results in left and right treelike branches.
- **Both** results in a central "stem," off of which the layers branch on both sides.
- **Left Hanging** results in a stem, off of which the layers branch to the left.
- **Right Hanging** results in a stem, off of which the layers branch to the right.

Adding shapes to the chart

You can add shapes to SmartArt that's already created, using the Add Shape feature options of the SmartArt Tools Design tab. The "shape" that's added is the same as the others in the graphic. For example, if the graphic consists of boxes, the added shape will be a box; if it consists of circles, the added shape will be a circle.

1. Select a shape that's immediately adjacent to where you want to place the new one.
2. Click the drop-down arrow next to the Add Shape tool.

   In the Create Graphic group.

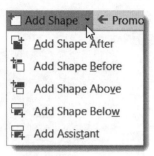

3. Click the appropriate command.

   - **Add Shape After** inserts a shape at the same hierarchic level as the one selected, and it appears farther down the "chain."

   - **Add Shape Before** inserts it at the same hierarchic level, and it appears farther up the chain.
   - **Add Shape Above** replaces the selected shape with the new one, making the selected one subordinate to it.
   - **Add Shape Below** inserts a shape and makes it subordinate to the one selected.
   - **Add Assistant** inserts a shape next to the selected one but places it outside the hierarchy. The difference between Add Shape Below and Add Assistant is subtle: The surest way to ascertain an assistant shape is that in the Text pane, it's always listed below other shapes that are at the same hierarchic level and preceded by a right-angle symbol, rather than a bullet.

Exercise: Creating and modifying an organization chart

You'll create an organization chart, add shapes to it, change its layout, and format it.

Do This	How & Why
1. Open `JT Org Chart.pptx`, and save it as `My JT Org Chart.pptx`.	In the data folder.
2. Observe the slides in this presentation.	There are a few with SmartArt lists, and slide 5 contains a sequential process design. Slide 6 contains a partial list of Java Tucana employees. You'll convert it to an organization chart.
3. On slide 6, right-click in the list, and choose **Convert to SmartArt** from the context menu.	To display the SmartArt options. Don't click on a word in the list that's marked as possibly misspelled. If you do so, the context menu will contain possible spelling option. Instead, click anywhere else in the list.

Do This	How & Why
4. Click **More SmartArt Graphics**.	The Choose a SmartArt Graphic window opens.

5. In the left pane, click **Hierarchy**.

Its design options are displayed in the center pane. Notice that a couple of the designs include picture placeholders. You'll select one that doesn't.

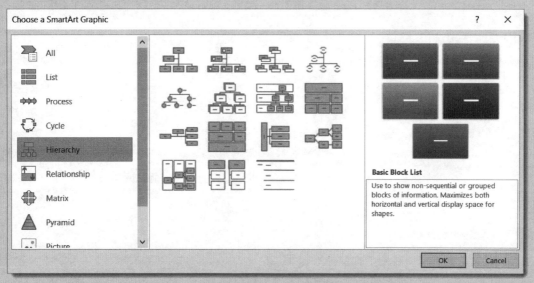

6. Explore the different designs.	Click a design in the center pane, and read its description in the right pane.
7. Click the **Organization Chart** design, then click **OK**.	The one in the top left. The vertically oriented chart appears on the slide. However, there's a problem with the chart hierarchy that you'll need to fix. Thor Martensson should be on the same level as Freya Gudmundsdottir, both of whom report to Pat Aubergine. Rose Schiller should be on the same level as the other sales team, who all report to Kevin McCanney.

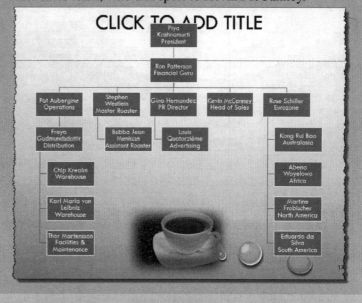

8. Promote Thor Martensson's box.

Do This	How & Why
a) Select Thor Martensson's box.	
b) Click **Promote**.	On the SmartArt Tools Graphic tab, in the Create Graphic group.
c) Click away from the graphic to deselect it, and observe the results.	Thor's box is moved to the same level as Freya's. 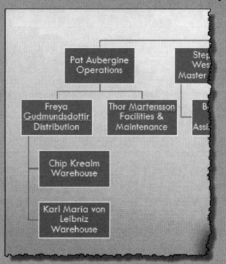
9. Demote Rose Schiller's box.	
a) Select Rose's box, then click **Demote**.	
b) Deselect the graphic, and observe the result.	Rose's box now falls under Kevin's, as do all the boxes that were misplaced under Rose. 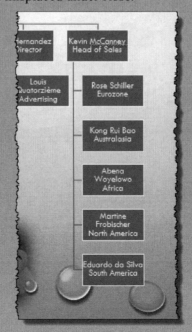

Do This	How & Why
10. Change the chart design to a horizontal orientation. a) If necessary, select the chart. b) Select a horizontal layout.	Java Tucana's management is concerned that the chart resembles a dictatorship.

On the SmartArt Tools Design tab, in the Layouts group. You can click the **More** button to view more designs at once. There, you can even click **More Layouts** to open the Choose a SmartArt Graphic window, where you can click the **Hierarchy** category. The Horizontal Organization Chart design is one possibility. The chart is displayed horizontally. Notice that all the same relationships still hold.

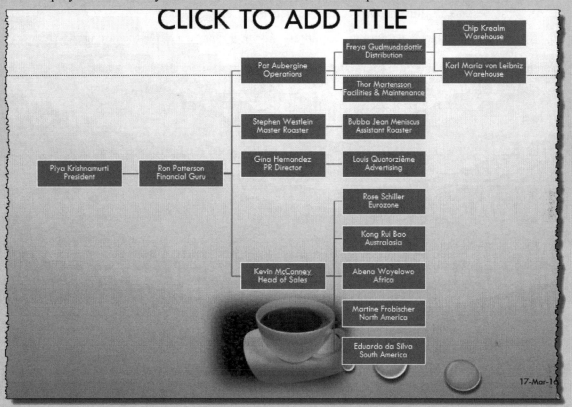

11. Resize and re-position the chart to best fit the slide.	Use the object handles to resize, and drag to re-position.
12. Spruce up the chart's design, first by selecting a style, then by changing the color scheme.	On the SmartArt Tools Design tab, in the SmartArt Styles group. Use the gallery to select a style, then use the **Change Colors** tool to change the color scheme.
13. As a final touch, use the SmartArt Tools Format tab to make additional formatting changes.	Use the tools in the Shape Styles and SmartArt Styles groups.
14. Save and close the file.	

Assessment: Inserting and formatting SmartArt

1. The only way to create SmartArt is from existing text, even if it's incomplete. True or false?
   - True
   - False

2. Which of the following statements is *not* true?
   - You can copy SmartArt and paste it into an Excel 2013 workbook.
   - The List category of SmartArt can be used to illustrate both hierarchies and non-hierarchies.
   - Process designs all illustrate an ordered sequence of steps.
   - A good place to start when looking for an organization-chart design is the Hierarchy category.

3. You must select all text before right-clicking to convert it to SmartArt. True or false?
   - True
   - False

4. Which of the following tools can be useful when adjusting the relationship of shapes in an organization chart?
   - Promote, Demote, and Move
   - Arrange, Size, and Shape Effects
   - Reverse, Add Bullet, and Reset
   - Change Colors, Convert, and Ameliorate

Module B: Additional formatting options

PowerPoint contains other important formatting options, including creating and working with multiple slide masters, and page setup options.

You will learn how to:

- Work with multiple slide masters

Working with multiple slide masters

As you learned prior to this course, all PowerPoint presentations contain at least three masters: a slide master, a notes master, and a handout master. Each presentation can have only one handout master and one notes master. However, it can have any number of slide masters. The reason for having multiple slide masters is that each can govern the layout and appearance of any number of slides, thus allowing you to have and easily apply different layouts to individual slides, have different sections of the presentation, each with its own look.

The Edit Master group

As you know, the Slide Master tab contains tools for working with slide masters. The tools in the Edit Master group are useful for creating, renaming, saving, and deleting slide masters, as well as adding layout elements to them.

Adding a slide master to a presentation

You create new slide masters in Slide Master view. When you create a new slide master from scratch, PowerPoints default settings are applied to it. Thus, it's a "clean slate"—none of the formatting from any other part of the presentation is applied to it.

1. Display the presentation in Slide Master view.
   On the View tab, in the Master Views group, click **Slide Master**.

   The Slide Master tab becomes active.

2. In the Edit Master group, click **Insert Slide Master**.

   A new slide master is added to the Slides pane, and along with it its layout thumbnails, which are displayed under it. The new slide master is selected.

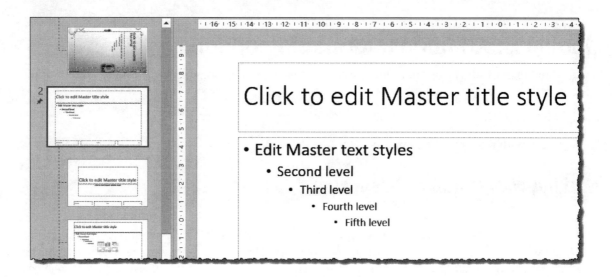

Duplicating a slide master

If you want to add a new slide master but want it to have the appearance and settings of another slide master that's already been created, it's far more efficient merely to copy or duplicate the original slide master. Best of all, you can do so in the same presentation or copy it to a different one.

1. In Slide Master view, right-click the slide you wish to copy/duplicate.

    The slide-master context menu is displayed. Notice that many of the same options available on the Slide Master tab are also present here.

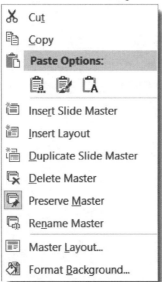

2. Copy/duplicate the master using one of these options, depending on your intended result.

    - To duplicate a master for use in the same presentation, click **Duplicate Slide Master**. The added duplicate preserves all the formatting of the original, merely adding another iteration of it to the presentation. One benefit of doing so is that you can then make subtle (or not-so-subtle) changes to one of the masters that are applied only to the slides that it governs, not to those governed by the other master.

- To duplicate a master for use in another presentation, click **Copy**. Display the destination presentation in Slide Master view; then right-click in a blank are of the Slides pane, and under Paste Options, click **Keep Source Formatting**. This adds the copied master (and its associated layouts) after the current master(s) and layouts in the Slides pane.

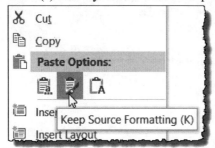

Whenever you copy even a single slide using a different slide-master layout from another presentation, then paste it keeping the source formatting, its governing slide master is copied with it to the destination presentation. This is another quick way to existing content and layouts to your presentations.

3. To save, or "preserve," a slide master, right-click it, and choose **Preserve Master**.

Before you preserve a slide master, a pushpin icon is displayed next to it, indicating that it isn't currently preserved.

It's good to get into the habit of doing this for any presentation that contains multiple masters. If one of the masters isn't applied to any slides in the presentation, PowerPoint will sometimes "clean house" by deleting that master because it's deemed superfluous and therefore unnecessary.

If the master isn't currently applied to any slides, a message window opens, informing you of that fact and asking you to confirm deletion of the master. Click **No** to keep the master and preserve it. Once a master is preserved, PowerPoint won't delete it. Also, the pushpin icon disappears.

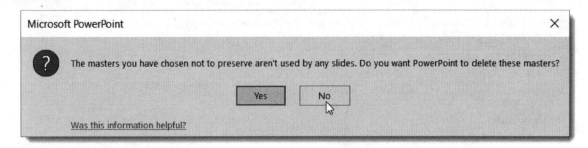

4. To rename a slide master, right-click it, and choose **Rename Master**.
   Or click the **Rename** tool in the Edit Master group.

   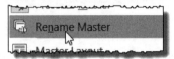

   The unfortunately named Rename Layout window opens.

   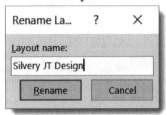

5. In the "Layout name" box, type the new name, and click **Rename**.
6. Hover over the newly renamed slide master.

   The only place the new name is visible is in the tooltip displayed over the slide master.

7. To delete a slide master, right-click it, and choose **Delete Master**.
   From the context menu. Or click **Delete** in the Edit Master group.

   The master and its associated layouts are removed from the presentation.

    Note: Before you delete a slide master, make sure that it's not applied to any slides containing formatting you wish to keep. Unfortunately, PowerPoint doesn't warn you about deleting masters that *are* applied to existing slides; it merely deletes them. Upon deletion, the affected slides revert to their prior format; they don't retain the format of the deleted master.

Applying a master to slides

By default, all PowerPoint presentations have a single slide master. For those with multiple masters, you can easily apply the layouts of any of the masters to any of the slides in the presentation. To do so, the presentation must be displayed in Normal view or Slide Sorter view.

1. Select the slide(s) to which you wish to apply a different slide master layout.
2. Click **Layout**.

In the Home tab's Slides group; or right-click the selection, and choose **Layout**. If you're using the right-click method and applying a slide-master layout to only one slide, you need only right click the slide; selecting it first is unnecessary.

The Layout gallery opens. In the gallery, layouts are categorized by their governing slide masters.

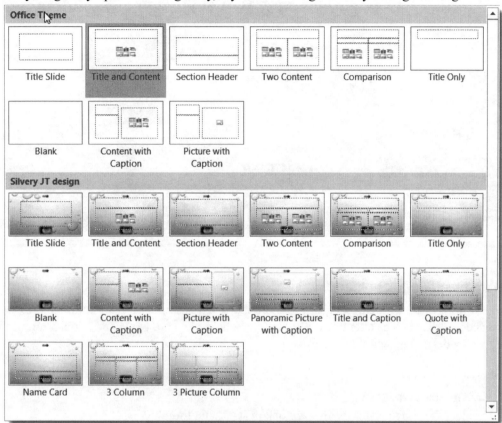

3. Click the desired layout to apply it to the slide(s).

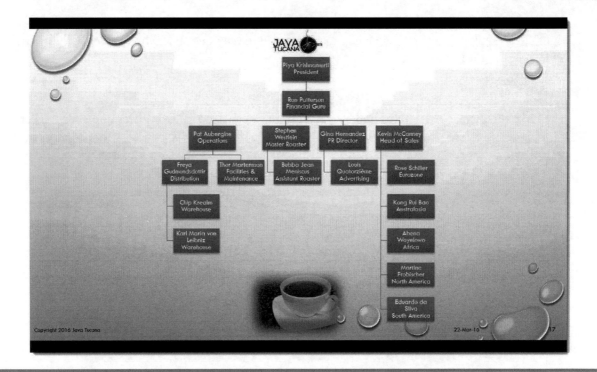

Restoring slide-master placeholders

In the course of working with a slide master, it's possible that you (or someone else) might delete one or more of its original placeholders, such as a text box, a footer element, and so on. However, should you need to, you can easily restore any deleted placeholders.

1. Display Slide Master view.
2. Select the slide master in question.

    Be sure to select the slide master itself—*not* one of its layout thumbnails.

3. Click **Master Layout**.

    On the Slide Master tab, in the Master Layout group.

    The Master Layout window opens. In the list of placeholders, any currently missing are unchecked.

4. Check the placeholder(s) you wish to restore.

5. Click **OK**.

    To restore the selected placeholder(s).

Creating presentation sections

Particularly for very long presentations, dividing them into sections can be useful, primarily as an organizational tool. It can often be much easier to get a good sense of the whole when you're clear about its parts, and vice-versa. To create sections in your presentations, you must be in Normal view or Slide Sorter view. Once you've created sections, there are some useful tools for working with them.

 MOS PowerPoint Exam Objective(s): 1.4.1, 1.4.2, 1.4.3

1. Select a slide to begin the new section.
2. Click **Layout**.
    On the Home tab, in the Slides group.

    Layout options are displayed, but most of these are dimmed, as the new section doesn't yet exist.
3. Click **Add Section**.

    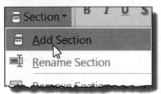

    The new section is added.

4. Observe the new section indicator.
    The section is currently untitled. A collapse/expand triangle icon is displayed next to its current name, "Untitled Section." This icon lets you collapse/expand all slides in the entire new section, which can make a large presentation easier to navigate.
5. With the first slide in the new section still selected, click **Section** again.

    Now the other Section options are available. Notice that from here you can, for example, give the new section a meaningful name by clicking **Rename Section**. You can also easily remove the current section or all sections in the presentation. The Collapse All and Expand All options allow you to collapse or expand all sections at once, respectively. Another handy feature is that you can select all the slides in a section by clicking the section header.

    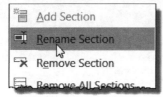

     Note: When you create a section that begins at any slide after slide 1, PowerPoint automatically creates a section that begins at slide one, which it names "Default Section." However, you can also rename this section using Rename Section.

    You can reorder entire sections of presentations, just as you would individual slides, simply by dragging the section name to its new location. You can do this in Normal view, but especially with larger presentations, it's much easier to do in Slide Sorter view.

Page setup options

MOS PowerPoint Exam Objective(s): 1.5.1

In PowerPoint, the default orientation is widescreen (16:9). The Slide Size tool, located on the Slide Master tab (in Slide Master view) and on the Design tab (in Normal view), allows you to change the orientation to standard (4:3). It also allows you to select a custom slide size, which can be particularly useful if you wish to print your slides to a custom size. However, it's important to remember that PowerPoint doesn't allow you to mix slide sizes and orientations in a single presentation. Clicking **Standard (4:3)** or **Widescreen (16:9)** to change the orientation of any slide or master changes them all. However, the widescreen option sets notes, handout, and outline pages to display in Portrait orientation by default.

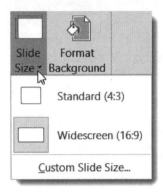

When changing the orientation, you're prompted to set the scaling of slides, either to maximize them or to ensure their fit.

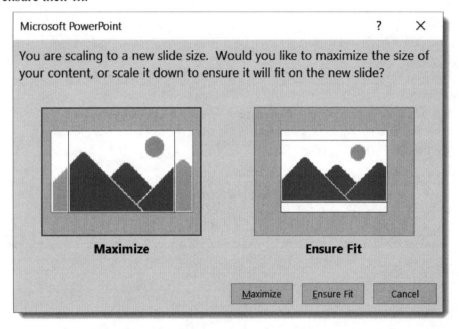

- Clicking **Maximize** ensures that content will remain at its largest; however, elements could be cropped from view in the process.
- Clicking **Ensure Fit** retains full visibility of all slide elements at the expense of reduced size.

To customize the size of your slides, click **Slide Size > Custom Slide Size**. This opens the Slide Size window, which contains options for sizing and orientation. Here, you can set notes, handouts, and outlines in an orientation that's the same as or different than that of the slides. Note that the units of measurement (centimeters or inches) displayed for width and height reflect the general Microsoft Office settings.

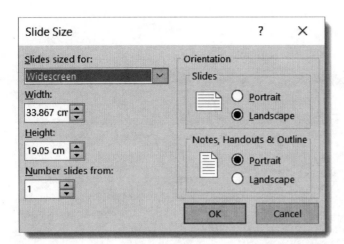

To display further custom sizing options, open the "Slides sized for" drop-down list. Selecting a custom option automatically changes the values in the Width and Height boxes.

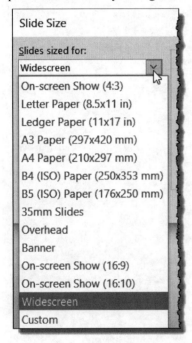

Exercise: Working with multiple slide masters

You'll create new slide masters and apply a slide-master layout to selected slides.

Do This	How & Why
1. Open `JT Slide Masters.pptx`, and save it as `My JT Slide Masters.pptx`.	In the data folder.
2. Observe the slides of the presentation.	It's the draft of a company presentation, currently consisting of only five slides, all of which are governed by a single slide master. You'll create another slide master to prepare for some slides that you'll add from another presentation later.
3. Open Slide Master view.	 Notice the single slide master in this presentation.
4. Right-click in a blank area of the Slides pane, and click **Insert Slide Master**.	In the context menu. 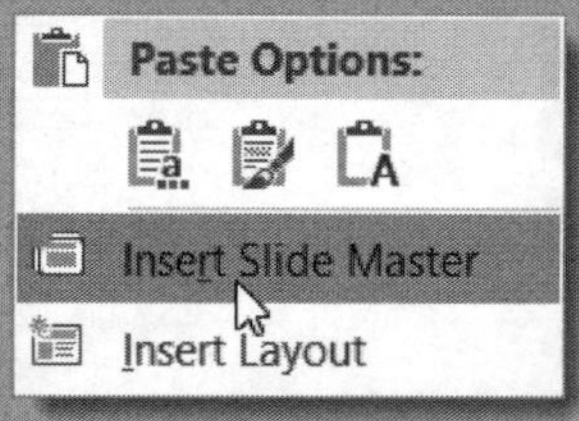 A new slide master and its associated layouts are added in the Slides pane. The new slide master appears below the original one.
5. Return to Normal view.	
6. Open `JT sales info.pptx`.	This presentation contains the slides you'll be adding to the My JT Slide Masters presentation.
7. Copy all three slides, then close the JT sales info presentation.	

Do This	How & Why
8. In My JT Slide Masters, paste them at the end of the presentation, using source formatting.	Right-click below the last slide in the Slides pane, and click the **Keep Source Formatting** option in the context menu. 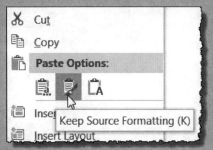 The slides are added at the end of the presentation, with their original formatting intact. 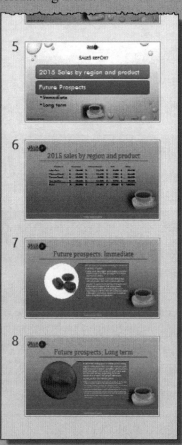
9. Observe the format of slide 5.	It begins the sales portion of the presentation, which is continued with the newly added slides. However, its format doesn't match those slides. You'll fix this shortly, but first some "house cleaning."

Do This	How & Why
10. Open Slide Master view, and scroll through the slide-master and layouts thumbnails.	Following the original slide master is the one you added earlier, labelled "2." Notice also that an additional slide master has been added. As the copied slides were pasted into the presentation together with their original formatting, slide master 3 was also added to govern their formatting. You'll be applying a different layout to slide 5, but the layout you want already appears on the added slides, so you won't need the slide master you added earlier.
11. In the Slides pane, scroll to slide master 2, right-click it, and choose **Delete Master**.	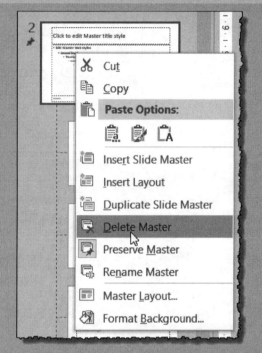 The master and its layouts are deleted, and the "imported" slide master is now slide master 2.
12. In Normal view, right-click slide 5, choose **Layout**.	From the context menu. The Layout gallery is displayed. Notice that the original presentation theme, Droplet, and its layouts are displayed at the top of the gallery. The newly added Retrospect master and its layouts are also displayed.

Do This	How & Why
13. Under Retrospect, click **Title and Content**. This is the layout currently applied to slides 6–8. 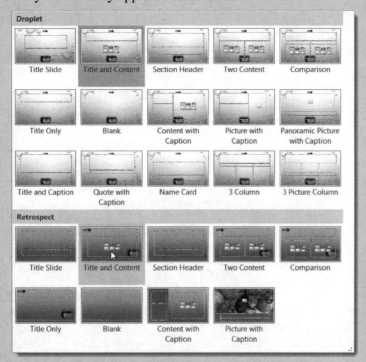 Slide 5 reflects the new layout, which now matches the rest of the sales report slides. 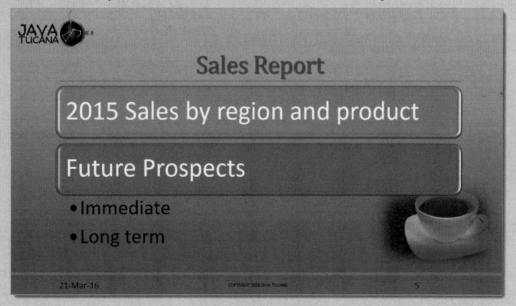	
14. Right-click slide 5, and choose **Add Section**.	From the context menu. 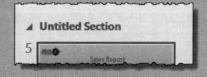

Do This	How & Why
15. Right-click "Untitled Section," and click **Rename Section**.	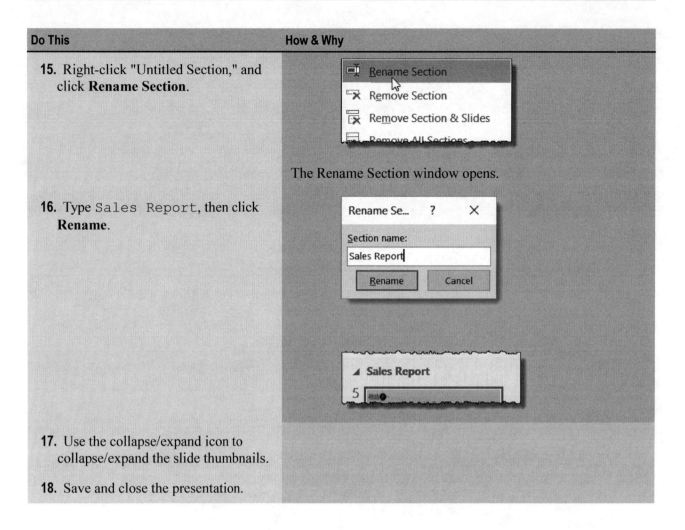 The Rename Section window opens.
16. Type `Sales Report`, then click **Rename**.	
17. Use the collapse/expand icon to collapse/expand the slide thumbnails.	
18. Save and close the presentation.	

Assessment: Additional formatting options

1. Name the tools group that's especially useful for creating, renaming, saving, and deleting slide masters, as well as adding layout elements to them?

    - The Edit Master group
    - The Customize group
    - The Set Up group
    - The Master Layout group

2. Once you've added a new slide master to your presentation, you must add all layout elements separately.

    - True
    - False

3. Which of these methods is the easiest for using slides from another presentation while keeping their content, preserving their appearance, and creating a new slide master to govern them?

    - Copy the source slides, paste only their contents to their destination, create a new slide master, and copy the formatting of the source presentation's slide master to that of the destination presentation.
    - Drag the source slides to the new presentation, create a section for the added slides, create a new slide master, and copy the slides' formatting to the new master.
    - Copy the source slides, and paste them using the Keep Source Formatting option.
    - Create a new slide master, copy the source slides, and paste them to the new slide master, making sure to retain all formatting.

4. If you need to restore a deleted placeholder, you can do so in Slide Master view, using the options in the Layout Placeholder window.

    - True
    - False

Summary: Advanced formatting

In this chapter, you learned how to:

- Create SmartArt; convert lists to SmartArt and change their layout; promote, demote, and move SmartArt list elements; change styles and colors; add and change shapes; and create and modify organization charts
- Add slide masters to presentations, by creating them from scratch and by duplicating them; apply master layouts to slides; restore master layout placeholders; create presentation sections; and work with page setup and orientation options

Synthesis: Advanced formatting

In this exercise, you'll create and format SmartArt, and work with multiple slide masters.

1. Open `Assessment - Advanced formatting.pptx`, and save it as `My Assessment - Advanced formatting.pptx`.
2. Observe the presentation's slides.
   There are two different main layouts that are haphazardly applied to the slides. Many of the slides consist of lists that require different types of formatting for maximum effect.
3. Convert the list on slides 2, 4, 5, and 6 to SmartArt, making sure that the result is a design that is neither hierarchic nor sequential. Select the designs you think are most appropriate to conveying the information. Also, make the designs match on slides 4–6. Don't worry about final layout and color schemes just yet.
4. On slide 2, demote the "Office coffee," "Wholesale," and "Cafés" elements to fall under "Our Services," and promote "Our coffees."
5. Convert the list on slide 3 to a SmartArt organization chart. Select an appropriate format that conveys all the relationships accurately and clearly. Don't worry about final layout and color schemes just yet.
6. Convert the list on slide 7 to a process (sequential) SmartArt design. Again, don't worry about fine-tuning layout and color schemes.
7. Convert the lists on slides 11 and 12 to a SmartArt design that will leave a picture placeholder on each slide. Use the same design for both slides.
8. On slide 11, insert the `three beans.jpg` image in the picture placeholder. On slide 12, insert the `Mars.jpg` image in its picture placeholder.
9. Begin a new section at slide 4, and name it `Our Services`. Begin another section at slide 9, and name it `Sales Report`. Then rename the first, default, section as `About Us`.
10. Apply the Droplet Title and Content master-slide layout to slides 3–7.
11. Apply the Retrospect Title and Content layout to slides 10–12.
12. Now go back to each slide and tweak the lists' sizes, positions, layouts, and colors to your heart's content, so that they convey information appropriately, and so that slides match where necessary.
13. On slide 3, add a text box shape to include the title "Our Team," and place it where it seems to best suit your org chart, and format it appropriately.
14. Make sure that title capitalization, size, and color match those of other slides, where appropriate.
15. Save and close the presentation.

Chapter 8: Animation, time effects, and media

You will learn how to:

- Create and modify animations
- Insert and work with media

Module A: Animating slide content

The ability to create and modify different types of animation is an important feature of PowerPoint. You can also customize the timing of animation effects, a feature that's also applicable to transition effects.

You will learn how to:

- Create and work with animations
- Set timing for animations and transitions

About animation

A great way to add visual impact and underscore salient text on your slides is through animation effects. PowerPoint provides some powerful tools to help draw visual attention to wherever you need it. There are three categories of animation in PowerPoint.

- *Entrance effects* determine how text appears on a slide.
- *Emphasis effects* are methods of visually enhancing text.
- *Exit effects* determine how text is removed from the slide, or "disappears."

The most commonly used effects are entrance and exit effects. Of these two, the more prevalent one is the entrance effect. An often used entrance effect is to have bullet items appear on a slide, one by one. In the world of graphic design, this type of entrance effect is often referred to as a *build effect*, because the text is built up in some order.

The Animations tab

The tools for working with animation effects are located on the Animations tab. The most commonly employed PowerPoint animations are text animations. However, you should know that any slide object can be animated, such as shapes, pictures, and charts. And the animation procedures used for any one apply to all.

- The *Preview* tool lets you preview your animation effect.
- The Animation group consists of the *Animation gallery* and an *Effect Options* tool. As with other PowerPoint galleries, you can use the more button to display the full gallery plus some additional effects options. Besides additional entrance, emphasis, and exit effects, there are options for specifying their motion paths. A *motion path* is the trajectory the animation follows through its duration. The group's launcher button opens an Edit Options window that's tailored to the selected animation.
- The Advanced Animation group contains tools useful for creating custom animation effects. Perhaps the most commonly useful tool in this group is the *Animation Painter*, which allows you to copy an object's animation effect(s) to another object. The group's launcher opens the Animation pane, which contains comprehensive controls for all animation effects.
- As its name denotes, the Timing group contains all the tools you need to specify the timing of animation effects, including the triggering of the effects. In addition, when you're using multiple animation effects on an object, there are tools for reordering the effects.

Animating text

 MOS PowerPoint Exam Objective(s): 4.2.2, 4.2.3

The method for applying animation to text is much the same as applying other kinds of effects in PowerPoint.

1. Select the text box containing the text you wish to animate.
2. Select an animation effect from the Animation gallery.

    On the Animations tab. To display the full gallery, click .

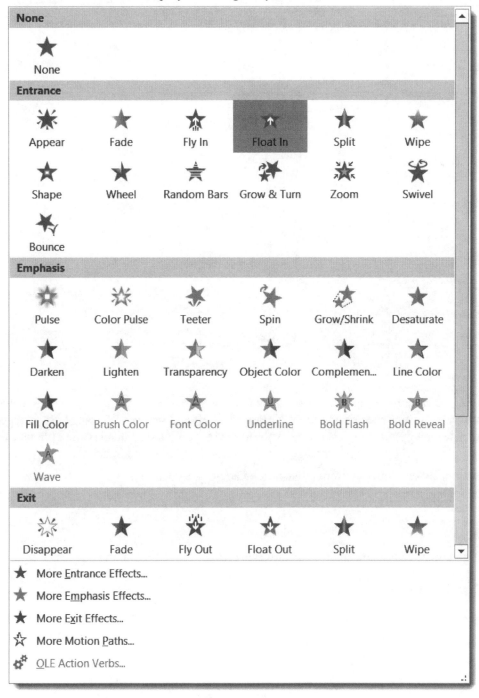

Or, in the Advanced Animation group, click **Add Animation**, and select an effect from the gallery.

The animation effect is applied to the text.

3. To further refine your effect, click **Effect Options**.
   In the Animation group.

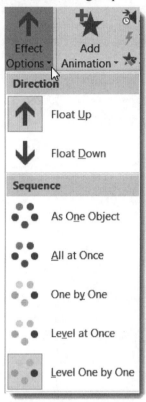

The Effect Options gallery opens. The options displayed are specific to the effect you've selected. The figure above shows options specific to the Spin effect. The effect options are arranged by category; thus, you can select an option from each category. However, you must re-display the options each time to do so. In this example, options are arranged by Direction, Amount, and Sequence.

4. Select effect options by clicking one from any or each category, as desired.

Animating shapes

In the same way you animate text, you can animate any PowerPoint object, including shapes.

 MOS PowerPoint Exam Objective(s): 4.2.1

1. Select the shape (or other object) you wish to animate.
2. Use the Animation gallery to select an effect.
   On the Animations tab.
3. Use the other tools available, such as **Effect Options**, to further refine the animation.

Modifying animations

Changing an animation effect is easy.

1. Select the animated object.
2. Apply a different effect and/or other options.
    Use the tools on the Animations tab.

The Animation pane

 MOS PowerPoint Exam Objective(s): 4.3.3

The Animation pane lists all animations on the current slide in sequential order.

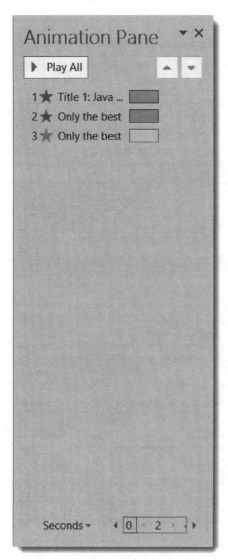

Each animation is listed in sequential order of its occurrence and is given an identifying number, name, and color. A horizontal bar gives a graphic representation of its duration, and you can hover over the bar to see the exact duration of that animation. Before you create any animations, the Animation pane is blank. As you create them, they're are all displayed in the pane, in the order in which you create them.

With no animation selected in the list, the Play All button is displayed above it. You can click **Play All** to cause all animations on that slide to run, in the order in which they're listed.

Selecting an animation in the list changes this button to Play From. Clicking **Play From** runs all animations from the selected one on.

Also, once you select an animation in the list, other tools become available.

- Clicking on the arrow at the right edge of the listing opens a timing drop-down list with additional options.

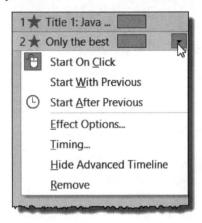

- In the upper-right corner of the Animation pane, you can use the available arrow button(s) to move the selected item up/down in the list. Or, you can simply drag the items in the order in which you'd like them to appear.

To make it easier to see how items in the Animation match up with their slide objects, their item numbers are displayed on the slide as you create each animation. Again, the number tells you in what order animations will run. When you select an animation in the Animation pane, its number is also selected on the slide.

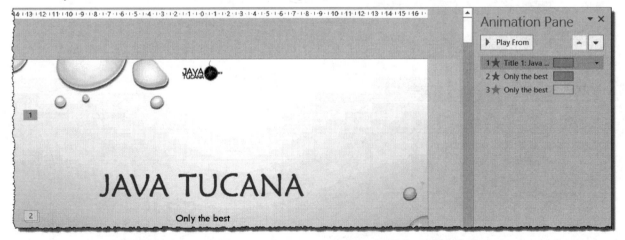

 Note: It's important to remember that the animation effects numbers only appear on slides when the Animations tab is displayed.

To remove an animation effect, open the timing drop-down list for that effect, and click **Remove**.

Customizing animations

Customizing an animation can be as simple or complex as you want it to be. You can customize your animation using the tools on the Animations tab. However, it's a good idea to customize an animation with the Animation pane open, as it lists all animations for that slide at a glance.

 MOS PowerPoint Exam Objective(s): 4.2.4

1. Select the slide with the Animation(s) you wish to customize.
   In Normal view.

2. Open the Animation pane.
   Click **Animation Pane**.

3. Select an animation effect.
   Click **Add Animation**, or click the Animation gallery ⏷ button; then select an effect.

4. With the full gallery displayed, select one of the custom options.
   At the bottom of the gallery. Clicking an option opens its own dedicated window for selecting custom effects.

   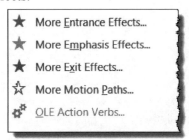

   - **More Entrance Effects**: Select from among 52 different effects provided.

- **More Emphasis Effects**: Select from among 31 different effects provided.

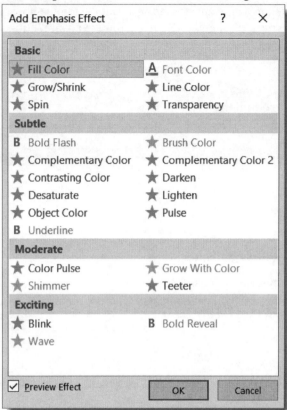

- **More Exit Effects**: Select from among 52 different effects provided.

- **More Motion Paths**: Select from among 64 preset paths provided, or draw your own custom path.

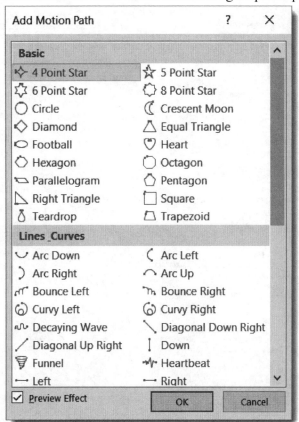

Copying animations

PowerPoint allows you to copy the animation settings of any object and apply them to another object using the Animation Painter. The source and destination objects can reside on the same slide, on different slides, or even in different presentations. The Animation Painter is a very powerful tool, but to get the most out of it, be sure to finalize the animation effects of your source object before copying its animation. Doing so will result in your spending less time—or no time at all—fine-tuning the destination object's animation.

1. Click the object from which you wish to copy the animation.
2. Click the **Animation Painter**.
    In the Advanced Animation group.

    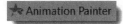

    The mouse pointer is accompanied by a paintbrush icon (like the Format Painter).

3. Click the object you wish to apply the copied animation to.
    The animation is copied to the destination object.

Exercise: Creating and working with animations

You'll create and work with animations in a presentation.

Do This	How & Why
1. Open `JT Animation.pptx`, and save it as `My JT Animation.pptx`.	
2. Observe the slides in the presentation.	The presentation consists of three sections of slides: About Us, Our Services, and Sales Report. Most of the slides consist of lists, including a hierarchy, several non-hierarchic and non-sequential lists, and a process list.
3. On slide 1, select the text box containing the subtitle "Only the Best."	Click in the box. You don't need to select the text.
4. Apply the Fade animation effect. • In the Animation tab's Animation group, click **Fade** in the gallery. • In the Advanced Animation group, click **Add Animation** to open the Animation, and under Entrance, click **Fade**.	The Fade effect is added to the text and the result is previewed once. The AutoPreview option is selected by default.
5. Preview the applied effect again, just to make sure it's working.	Click **Preview**. You'll apply a second effect to the same text.
6. Apply the Color Pulse emphasis effect to the "Only the Best" text. a) Select the text box. b) Open the Animation gallery: Click ▼ in the Animation group, or click **Add Animation** in the Advanced Animations group.	Two animation effects are now applied to the text.

Do This	How & Why
c) Click the **Color Pulse** effect.	
7. Observe the numbered effects boxes on the slide.	

8. On slide 1, apply the Expand animation effect to "Java Tucana."

All three effects are now numbered on the slide.

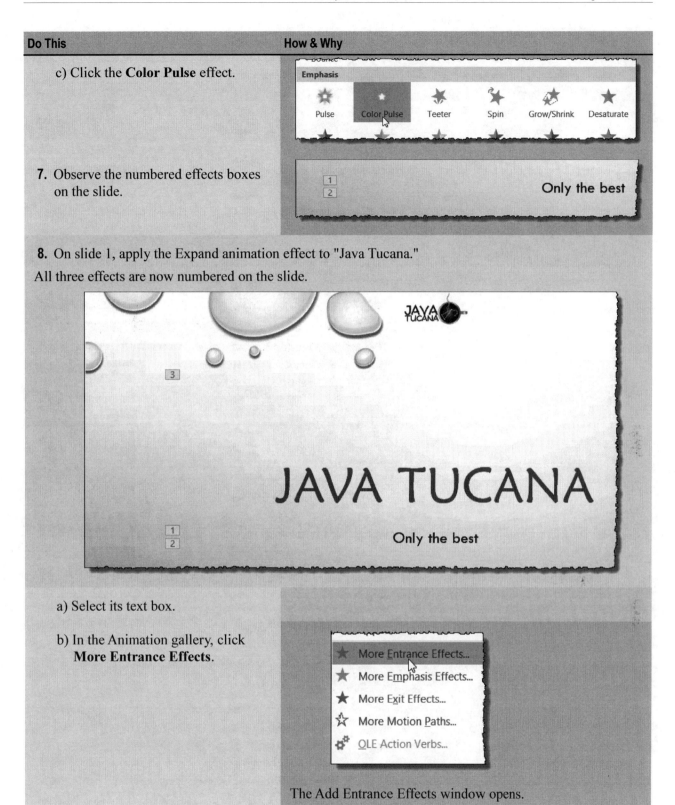

a) Select its text box.

b) In the Animation gallery, click **More Entrance Effects**.

The Add Entrance Effects window opens.

Do This	How & Why
c) In the Subtle category, click **Expand**, and click **OK**.	
9. Select each numbered box in turn, and observe its settings on the Animations tab as you do so.	Its effect is highlighted in the Animation gallery, and its timing information is displayed.
10. Select effect 2, and observe the ordering buttons in the Timing group.	The Reorder Animation buttons become available. This is another convenient way to change effect order without using the Animation pane. You'll change the order of effects on this slide.
11. Change the order of effects to have the Expand effect on the "Java Tucana" heading run first. a) Select effect 3.	

Do This	How & Why

b) Click **Move Earlier** twice.

The effects are reordered on the slide. Although the two effects on "Only the Best" are renumbered as well, they remain in the same order with respect to each other.

12. On slide 2, animate the list items to fly in from the right, one by one.

   The effects are applied and run in preview. The slide numbers five ordered effects. Each number reflects the fly-in of each listed item. The three bullet items under "Our Services" entire as a single group (effect 3).

   a) Select the list.

Do This	How & Why
b) Open the Animation gallery, and click the **Fly In** effect.	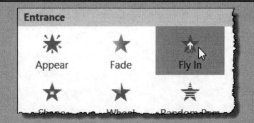
c) Open the Effect Options gallery, and click From Right.	In the Direction category. 
d) Reopen the Effect Options gallery, and under Sequence, select **One by One**.	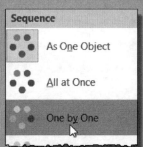
13. Observe slides 1 and 2 in the Slides pane.	Under the slide numbers, animation symbols appear, indicating that the slides contain animation.  You can click a slide's animation symbol to preview the animation.

Do This	How & Why
14. Animate the org chart on slide 3, and at least one other list on any of the remaining slides.	Use any effects you like. Tip: the Float In effect with the Level One by One effect option works really nicely on this one! Feel free to use the Animation pane, especially if you're planning to customize multiple effects on a slide. Should you need to copy an animation (and all its effects), remember that you can use the Animation Painter.
15. When you're finished, save and close the presentation.	

Timing of animation and transition effects

  MOS PowerPoint Exam Objective(s): 4.3.1

The Animation tab and the Transition tab both contain powerful options for working with the timing of effects. You've already seen that the types of effects you use—for example, having each bullet list item fly in, one at a time—are built-in timing devices. But PowerPoint provides tools dedicated specifically to the timing of events, most of which are located in the Timing group on both tabs.

In the case of the Animation tab, there's also an important timing tool that's located in the Advanced Animation group. Clicking the Trigger tool displays context-sensitive options for signaling the activation of an effect. For example, the result of setting the special start condition shown in the figure below would be that the selected effect would run when the presenter clicks Subtitle 2.

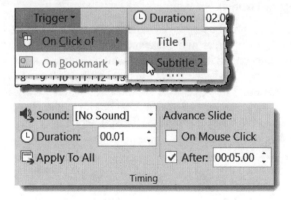

You can make the timing of effects simple or complicated. As with all other tools for the enhancement of your slides, the "trick" is in conveying slide content to maximum effect and not obscuring it. Timing effects can be boiled down to three important factors: how they start, when they start, and how long they last.

Animation timing tools

Tool	Description
Start: On Click	Tells the selected animation when to start. *On Click* starts it on mouse click. *With Previous* starts it at the same time as the previous animation. *After Previous* starts it after the previous animation is completed.
Duration: 02.00	Specifies how long the animation lasts.
Delay: 00.00	Specifies how long the animation should wait before it begins to run.
Reorder Animation / Move Earlier / Move Later	Changes the order of animation effects on a slide. As you've already seen, the sequencing of effects can also be an effective timing tool.
Trigger	Used to set a special start condition, in which, for example, clicking an object causes an effect to run. Think of the Trigger tool as one to use (or not) after all your other timings are set.

Transition timing tools

Tool	Description
Sound: [No Sound]	Specifies a sound to play during the transition from the previous slide to the current one. Options include a variety of sounds that come with PowerPoint, but you can use the *Other Sound* option to load your own sound file. *Loop Until Next Sound* causes the selected sound to replay continuously until the next sound is triggered. As its name implies, *No Sound* results in no sound being played during transition.
Duration: 00.01	Specifies how long the transition lasts. Don't confuse this with how long the slide is visible (see the Advance Slide options below).
Apply To All	Applies all current transition settings to all slides in the presentation. This is a very powerful tool, but it's important to understand its effect before using it. For example, if you've already created award-winning transition effects for some of the slides in your presentation, if you apply transitions you've tweaked on the current slide to all the other slides, you could possibly undo some or all of that great work you did on those slides. Speaking of which, this is when Undo could be the very tool that saves you from having to give up those well-earned awards.
Advance Slide / On Mouse Click / After: 00:05.00	These options don't concern the transition effect per se, but rather how long the slide is visible and what triggers its disappearance. Checking *On Mouse Click* gives the presenter direct control: when the mouse is clicked, the slide disappears. Checking *After* removes the slide after it's displayed for the amount of time (in minutes and seconds) you specify in the box. Checking both options results in a lag between the moment the mouse is clicked and the removal of the slide. In other words, at mouse click the timer starts; when the time has elapsed, the slide disappears.

Additional timing considerations

As you've already seen, certain types of effects can be used to determine a sequence of animations. These effects can be used in combination with specific timing tools to determine the running of the presentation. Regarding types of animation effects, the following points summarize some things to think about when considering text animation.

- *Entrance effects*: These are relatively obvious ways to present text, and the most commonly used entrance effect is to build a list one item at a time. You can set the timing of this "build" automatically, but you might want to allow the presenter time to elaborate on each item as it's presented, in which case you'd instead set each build element to appear on mouse click, and so on.

- *Emphasis effects*: Using the above example, rather than having the items appear individually, you may instead want an emphasis animation to run on each individual item (a bounce, spin, color change, enlargement, or other). Again, each effect can be timed to run automatically at a predetermined interval, or manually at the click of a mouse.

- *Exit effects*: Although these effects obviously don't affect, for instance, the entering of text on a slide, the very fact that you can make it disappear, fade, spin off, fly off, and so on does imply a sequence of events that provide or set the stage for a focal point.

MOS PowerPoint Exam Objective(s): 4.3.2

The best way to set these effects—particularly for complex sequences—is to use the Effect Options window. This window is context-sensitive, and is named and provides specific options for the selected effect.

You already know how to open the Effect Options window by clicking the Animation group's button. But you can also do so in the Animation pane by clicking the arrow at the right of the selected effect; then clicking **Effect Options**, which opens the window with the Effects pane displayed, or **Timing**, which opens the window to the Timing pane.

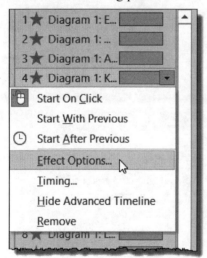

The Effect Options window contains a few tabs. Depending on the selected effect, options appropriate to it are available; others are dimmed, as they don't apply to that effect. The Effect tab contains options for fine-tuning effects. For example, the figure below shows available sound enhancements.

The Timing tab contains additional timing options. Clicking Triggers displays options for triggering the effect as part of a click sequence.

The SmartArt Animation tab allows you to specify how elements—for example, items in a list—are grouped. These are the same options available when you click the Effect Options tool in the Animation group.

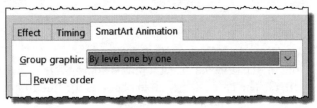

Exercise: Setting timings of animations and transitions

You'll set animation and transition timings by setting effect and timing options.

Do This	How & Why
1. Open `JT Timings.pptx`, and save it as `My JT Timings.pptx`.	
2. Run the slideshow, and observe all the current transitions and animations.	Click the **Slide Show** icon. The slides are currently set to advance automatically every 5 seconds. The presenter will need more time to show and talk about the contents of each slide, so you'll change the current transition settings.
3. In Normal view, set all the slides to advance at the click of a mouse and after 3 seconds.	
a) On the Transitions tab, check On Mouse Click.	In the Timing group. Because your changes will affect all slides, any slide can be selected.
b) In the After box, use the spinner button(s) to set the timing to 3 seconds.	You can instead enter the value directly in the box by typing it.
c) Make sure that **After** is checked.	Advance Slide ☑ On Mouse Click ☑ After: 00:03.00
d) Click **Apply To All**.	To apply these settings to all slides in the presentation. Apply To All The transition effects on all slides are currently very short. You'll increase their duration.
4. Increase the duration of all the slides to 7 seconds.	Slides 1, 4, and 9 each begin their respective sections. The presenter informs you that she'll need more time to introduce each section, and she'd like to be able to determine when to advance to the next slide.
a) Use the Duration spinners, or enter the value in the box.	Duration: 07.00
b) Click **Apply To All**.	
5. Set slides 1, 4, and 9 to advance to the next slide only when the presenter does so manually.	The new settings are applied to the three slides.

PowerPoint 2016 Level 1

Do This	How & Why
a) Select slides 1, 4, and 9.	You could, of course, change the settings of each slide separately, but doing so collectively is much faster.
b) Uncheck **After**.	In the Timing group, under Advance Slide.
c) Ensure that **On Mouse Click** is checked.	
6. Run the slide show, and observe the results of the transition timing changes.	Next, you'll customize the Animation settings.
7. After you've run the presentation, in Normal view, observe slide 3.	The org chart is currently grouped as a single object that floats up. The staff at Java Tucana would like the chart to better highlight each individual and their position.
8. Set the org chart on slide 3 so that each individual's box floats up separately.	The animation now affirms the personhood of each individual on the chart, and revealing the organizational layers in reverse order makes it seem less of a dictatorship. **Note:** Although you could instead use the Effect Options tool to select the Level One By One setting, doing so doesn't allow you to reverse the order of the effect. So in this case, using the Effect Options window is more expedient.
a) Select the chart.	
b) Click ▫ in the Animation group.	The Float Up Effect Options window opens.
c) Display the SmartArt Animation tab.	
d) Open the "Group graphic" drop-down list, and select **By level one by one**.	
e) Check **Reverse order**.	

Do This	How & Why
9. Slide 7 is also grouped as single object. Set the individual steps in the process to fly in one by one.	Use the procedure in step 8 as a guide. However, *do not* check the Reverse order option. 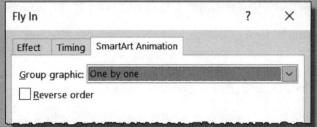
10. Run the slide show again, and observe the results.	The presenter is satisfied with your results, but she'd like you to tweak the settings of some of the animations in the presentation to be significantly longer, but they don't all have to be the same. You can use your discretion. She'd also like you to remove any delay time where it seems appropriate.
11. Increase the duration of each of the animations in the presentation to values that seem to best highlight the content. a) Select each animated object on a slide. b) Change its Duration setting to a higher value. c) Try removing or reducing any Delay time. d) Preview the changes, and tweak as necessary. e) Repeat this process for all the animations. f) Run the slide show again to check your results.	Durations and delay times are shown in seconds (and decimals).
12. When you're done tweaking all the timings, save and close the presentation.	

Assessment: Animating slide content

1. You can use the Animation gallery to combine an entrance effect, an emphasis effect, an exit effect, and a motion path. True or false?

    - True
    - False

2. Which of these statements about animating PowerPoint objects is correct?

    - When selecting text to be animated, you must be sure to select all the text.
    - To animate text, you need only select the slide containing the text.
    - Once you've stacked multiple effects in an animation, their order can't be changed.
    - The most efficient way to fine-tune an effect, including timing and grouping settings, is in the Effect Options window.

3. The Animation Painter is a tool for copying all animation settings from one animation to another. True or false?

    - True
    - False

4. Which of these statements about the timing of effects is true?

    - Setting an animation to start *With Previous* causes it to start at the same time as the previous animation.
    - For both animations and transitions, the Duration setting effects how long the slide remains visible.
    - The Advance Slide settings allow you to advance either at a mouse click or after a set amount of time, but not both.
    - Timing effects can be boiled down to three important factors: how they start, when they start, and who started them.

Module B: Inserting and formatting media

Besides animation and transition effects, another powerful way to further enhance a presentation is by turning it into a multimedia experience by adding audio and/or video.

You will learn how to:

- Insert and work with audio and video in your presentations

About media

A PowerPoint presentation is naturally visual, and by default each slide is static. As you've seen, there are many wonderful ways to visually enhance each slide, even giving it some motion through animation and transition effects. However, another powerful way to further enhance a presentation is by turning it into a multimedia experience. Doing so can be as simple as adding sound effects when a slide or an object appears, or as sophisticated as triggering a full-length video to run at a certain point in the presentation.

As you already know, you can insert a hyperlink on a slide that links to another slide in the same or another presentation. You can also use the Hyperlink tool, in the Insert tab's Links group, to insert a hyperlink to external media, such as a video on a website. However, if you intend to do so, be sure to check whether the link remains active just prior to your presentation; otherwise, you could be in for an unintended surprise. For this reason, we recommend downloading any media and inserting it onto a slide, whenever possible, rather than simply linking to it.

Types of media

The Media group, on the Insert tab, contains the tools necessary for directly inserting media onto a slide. If you want insert a sound effect, the best way to do so is via the Sound tool in the Transition tab's Timing group.

In PowerPoint, you add sound to your presentations in the form of audio files. An *audio file* contains a digitized sound recording. The recording can be as short and simple as a single sound effect, such as a bell ringing, which might signal the appearance of a new slide. At the other duration extreme, the recording could be of Bruckner's *Ninth Symphony*, which plays in the background during your presentation. PowerPoint can accommodate audio files of a variety of types.

It's important to note that when you add audio and/or video to a PowerPoint presentation, it's saved with the presentation itself. Thus, even if the original source file is moved or deleted, the version saved with the presentation remains intact.

Supported audio file types

File extension	Format
.aiff	The Audio Interchange File Format, developed by Apple. This is an uncompressed format, resulting in high-quality sound.
.au	A simple format developed by Sun Microsystems
.mid, .midi	A Musical Instrument Digital Interface file, which is not a recording but instructions for the playing of musical notes via a soundcard
.mp3	A compressed format of generally low, "lossy" audio quality. However, it remains the most common format for compressed audio, because of its relatively small file size. It was developed by the Moving Picture Experts Group (MPEG).
.m4a, .mp4	The .m4a format is a compressed, audio-only file; .mp4 format is an Apple Quicktime format that can include video images.
.wav	The Waveform Audio File Format developed by Microsoft and IBM. It's an uncompressed format that results in high-quality audio.
.wma	The Windows Media Audio format, which is compressed and typically used to stream audio. It was developed by Microsoft.
.flac	The Free Lossless Audio Codec, developed by the Xiph.org Foundation, is a lossless compression format. The result is high-quality—potentially even high-definition—audio, but with file sizes close to half what they would be uncompressed.

Supported video file types

File extension	Format
.asf	The Advanced Systems Format is a multimedia container format, developed by Microsoft and used for streaming audio and video.
.avi	The Audio Video Interleave format, developed by Microsoft.
.mp4, .m4v, .mov, .qt	The .m4v is a compressed audio-video file; the others are Quicktime formats.
.mpg, .mpeg	Compressed video formats developed by the MPEG.
.swf	The Adobe Flash Media format. Adobe Flash Player must be installed to play media in this format.
.wmv	The Windows Media Video format, which is compressed and typically used to stream video. It was developed by Microsoft.

For .mp4 files, Microsoft recommends that you use files encoded with H.264 video, also known as MPEG-4, and AAC audio. For audio, they recommend .m4a files encoded with AAC audio. AAC is a compressed, lossy audio format developed by Apple.

Adding sound effects

Sound effects can be a great way to add some spice to your presentations. As with any features designed to enhance slide content, though, it's important only to add what the content will benefit from. Simply drawing attention is usually not a prudent tactic. Also keep in mind that the sound effects provided in PowerPoint are of very low audio quality.

MOS PowerPoint Exam Objective(s): 3.4.1

The best way to add sound effects to a presentation is through the Transitions tab's Sound tool or the Animations tab's Effect Options window.

1. Select the object to which you wish to add the sound effect.
2. Apply the sound effect.
    Both these methods are useful for having the sound play automatically.

    - In the Transitions tab's Timing group, select the desired sound effect from the Sound drop-down list. To select a sound file from your computer, click **Other Sound** to open the Add Sound window; navigate to and select the file; then click **Open**. Once you've selected a sound, to replay it continuously until the next sound is triggered, in the Sound drop-down list, click **Loop Until Next Sound**.

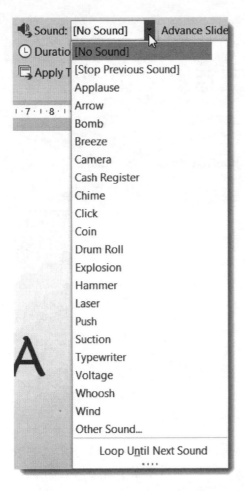

- For an animated object, open the Effect Options window, and on the Effect tab, open the Sound drop-down list. Then select the desired effect, and click **OK**. To select a sound file from your computer, click **Other Sound** to open the Add Sound window; navigate to and select the file; then click **Open**.

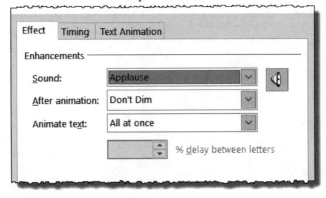

 Note: If you have Internet access, you can also download sounds to your computer, then use the Other Sound option to insert it. You can find sounds using any search engine. Simply search for the type of sound you're looking for, for example, `"elephant trumpeting sounds."`

Inserting an audio object on a slide

Audio in a presentation need not be part of a transition or animation effect. It can be simply audio meant to be played when a slide is visible, and it can be triggered by the presenter or set to play automatically. You can insert audio files directly from your computer. When you insert a sound file onto a slide, it becomes an *audio object*.

 MOS PowerPoint Exam Objective(s): 3.4.1

1. Display the destination slide.
2. On the Insert tab, click **Audio**, and click **Audio on My PC**.
   In the Media group.

   The Insert Audio window opens.
3. Navigate to the audio file, select it, then click **Insert**.
   If you have a network connection, you can also use this window to access another network location.

   The sound is inserted onto the slide, and a loudspeaker icon is displayed to represent it.

4. To play the audio in Normal view, click the **Play** button.
   Hover over or select the audio object to view the transport buttons. Once you click Play, the button toggles to its Pause function.

   To play the audio during the slide show, click (once) the loudspeaker icon.

The Audio Tools tabs

MOS PowerPoint Exam Objective(s): 3.4.2, 3.4.5

The Audio Tools Format tab and Playback tab contain powerful tools for working with audio files. These tools become available when an audio object is selected on a slide.

The Audio Tools Format tab is exactly like the Picture Tools Format tab. The reason for this is that the tools affect the *appearance* of the audio object, not its sound.

As its name implies, the Audio Tools Playback tab enables you to set how the audio object is played. You'll probably never use most of these tools, but there are a few that are worth mentioning here, especially those in the Audio Options, Audio Styles, and Editing groups.

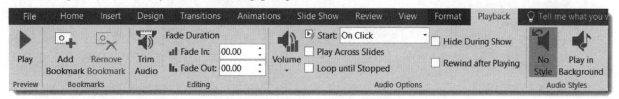

- *Audio Options*: Here, there are tools for setting how the audio file is activated, whether it plays across slides or stops when the current slide is no longer displayed, whether it loops until the presenter stops it, and so on. You can also adjust the audio volume.

- *Audio Styles*: Here, you can set the audio to play continuously in the background during the entire presentation. Use the No Style button to reset the "styled" audio to its original settings.

- *Editing*: Here, you can set fade-in and fade-out times for the audio, as well as trim the length of the audio file. The Trim Audio window contains and audio wave-file timeline. The green slider represents the starting point; the red represents the end point. You can drag the sliders to effectively trim away the portions of the audio file (at either or both ends) that you don't want to play. The Start Time and End Time values tell you exactly at what points along its length it will start and stop playing, respectively. You can use the transport buttons to preview the results of your trimming as you work. Click **OK** when you've finished trimming the audio.

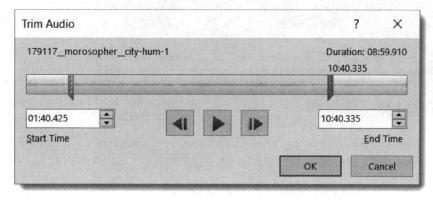

You can always use the Play button to assess how your work's going.

Adding video

Adding video to your slides can be a great way to spice up a presentation. You add video in much the same way that you add audio. However, a video object requires much more room on the slide in order to render it sufficiently visible. Therefore, it's a good idea to add it to a blank or largely blank slide.

 MOS PowerPoint Exam Objective(s): 3.4.1

1. Download the video to or place it on your hard drive.
   Video files can be exceptionally large, so the process of adding a video to a slide can go much more smoothly and quickly if you're working from your hard drive.

2. On the Insert tab, click **Video > Video on My PC**.
   In the Media group.

   The Insert Video window opens.

3. Navigate to the location of the video file, select it, and click **Insert**.
   The new video object appears on the slide.

4. Size and position the object on the slide.

   Generally, you'll want to make the video object as large as possible on the slide for maximum viewability during presentation of the slide show.

5. Play the video.

   In Slide Show view, click the image on the slide. In Normal view, hover over or select the video object, and click **Play**.

Online videos

You can download videos from online sources by selecting the destination slide and then clicking **Video > Online Video**.

In the Insert Video window, you can navigate to or search for videos.

You can download video from your SharePoint or OneDrive account, and you can insert a video from Facebook. However, two common methods of inserting an online video are searching for a YouTube video, and copying and pasting a video embed code.

- To search YouTube for a video, type a search string in the Search YouTube box, and press **Enter**. In the search results window, select the desired video, and click **Insert**.

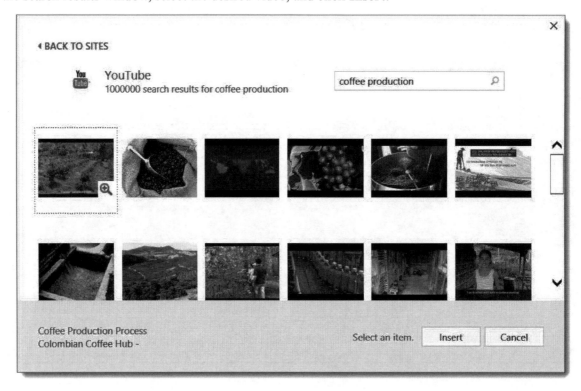

- To paste an embed code from an online video, open the video in your browser, right-click it, and select **Copy embed code**. Then return to (or open) the **Insert Video** window, and paste the embed code into the "Paste embed code here" box.

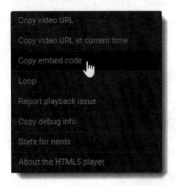

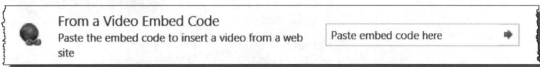

 Note: PowerPoint doesn't allow you to paste an embed code from YouTube videos, among others. To download a YouTube video, use the YouTube search option in the Insert Video window.

The Video Tools tabs

The Video Tools Format tab and Playback tab contain powerful tools for working with video files. These tools become available when a video object is selected on a slide.

 MOS PowerPoint Exam Objective(s): 3.4.2, 3.4.3, 3.4.4, 3.4.5

The Video Tools Format tab is similar to the Audio Tools Format tab. However, the Video Tools Format tab contains tools specific to working with video. Here, you can format the appearance of the video object in much the same way as you would format a picture, including applying styles, making color corrections, adding borders and other effects, and so on. The Reset Design tool allows you to revert the video object back to its original state.

The Video Tools Playback tab contains all the features you need to set how the video is played. Most of the tools you'd normally use are in the Editing and Video Options groups.

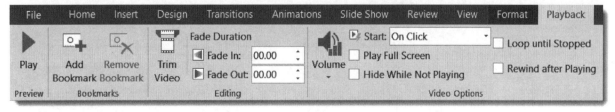

- *Editing*: Here, you can set fade-in and fade-out times, as well as trim the video using the Trim Video window. The green slider represents the starting point; the red represents the end point. You can drag the sliders to effectively trim away the portions of the video file (at either or both ends) that you don't want to play. The Start Time and End Time values tell you exactly at what points along its length it will start and stop playing, respectively. You can use the transport buttons to preview the results of your trimming as you work. Click **OK** when you've finished trimming the video. Because video files tend to be very large, you'll likely need to trim longer clips, particularly if you're using a short clip from a feature-length film.

- *Video Options*: Here, you have access to the same tools used for working with audio. There are tools for setting how the video file is activated, whether it plays across slides or stops when the current slide is no longer displayed, whether it loops until the presenter stops it, and so on. If the video contains audio, you can also adjust volume.

Exercise: Working with media

You'll insert and work with audio and video in a presentation.

Do This	How & Why
1. Open `JT Media.pptx`, and save it as `My JT Media.pptx`.	
2. On slide 1, play the animations.	In the Slides pane, click the slide 1 Play Animations icon. You'll add an audio effect to accompany the first animation on the slide.
3. Display the Animations tab.	The animations are now numbered on the slide.
4. Click [1], then click [icon] in the Animation gallery.	To select the animation and open the Effect Options window.
5. In the Sound drop-down list, select the **Applause** sound effect.	On the Effect tab.
6. Click **OK**.	The animation immediately plays, along with its applause effect.
7. Replay the slide's animation.	Click the slide 1 **Play Animations** icon for slide 1. Now that the animation tab is displayed, you can use the Preview tool. However, doing so only previews the animations, not the transition effects. The transition and animations play. Note that because the applause effect is part of the first animation, there's no applause until the animation runs, not when the slide is fading in from black.
8. On slide 7, add an audio object from your hard drive.	The audio object appears on the slide.
a) Select slide 7.	
b) Click **Audio > Audio on My PC**.	On the Insert tab.
c) Navigate to `Evening Woodland.mp3`, and click **Insert**.	In the data folder.

Do This	How & Why
9. Position the audio object so that it's centered horizontally on the slide and under the title.	Drag the object to position it.
10. Set the audio object to play automatically when the slide is displayed.	
a) Select the audio object, if necessary.	
b) Display the Audio Tools Playback tab.	Remember, you're adjusting the audio settings, not the animation (or transition) settings.
c) In the Start drop-down list, select **Automatically**.	In the Audio Options group.
11. Play the slide show from slide 7.	Notice that the sound doesn't play until the animation is completed. You'll select the same audio effect to play as soon as the slide appears.

Do This	How & Why
12. Display the Transitions tab, open the Sound drop-down list, and click **Other Sound**.	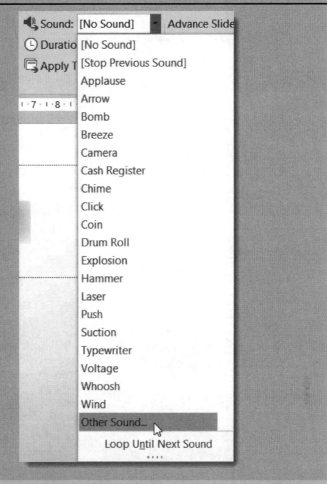
13. Navigate to and open `Evening Woodland.wav`.	In the Add Audio window, select the file, and click **Open**. You can't use the .mp3 version of this file, because PowerPoint recognizes only .wav files as sound effects.
14. Play the slide show from slide 6.	So that you can experience the transition to slide 7. As slide 6 begins to fade, the sound effect plays. On slide 7, as the visual part of the animation ends, the audio object begins to play along with the transition effect. The sounds are currently set to stop playing when they each come to the end. However, the audio file is currently well over two hours long! So, first you'll trim it to a reasonable size.
15. Trim the audio file to 30 seconds duration. a) Select the audio object. b) Click **Trim Audio**.	Now the audio will play for only 30 seconds. In the Editing group of the Playback tab.

Do This	How & Why
c) In the Trim Audio window, change the duration of the audio file to play for only the first 30 seconds of its length.	Drag the end (red) slider, enter the value in the End Time box, or use the spinner (increment and decrement) buttons to change the value. 
d) Click **OK**.	

16. Add a new slide after slide 7.

17. Insert the `Mixing Coffee Beans.mp4` video onto the new slide, size it to fit most of the slide, and center it on the slide.

   a) Click **Video > Video on My PC**.

   b) In the Insert Video window, navigate to and select the file, and click **Insert**.

   c) Use the sizing handles to resize the video object.

   d) Drag it to the center of the slide, using the guides.

Chapter 8: Animation, time effects, and media / Module B: Inserting and formatting media

Do This	How & Why
18. Set the following Video Options.	On the Video Tools Playback tab.
a) Start: **Automatically**.	
b) **Play Full Screen**.	
c) **Loop until Stopped**.	
19. Observe the video as its previewed.	Repeat the preview, if necessary. Roughly the second half of the video is blank, so you'll need to trim it.
20. Use the Trim Video window to trim it so that no blank part of it is visible.	The video now stops before the blank portion of the file.
a) In the Editing group, click **Trim Video**.	On the Audio Tools Playback tab. The Trim Video window opens.

b) Drag the Start Time and End Time sliders so that only the part of the file that actually contains video is selected.

PowerPoint 2016 Level 1   267

Do This	How & Why
c) Click **OK**, and observe the preview.	
21. Use the Video Tools Format tab to make any additional style changes to the video object.	
22. When you're finished making changes, play the slide show and observe the results of your work.	
23. Save and close the presentation.	When you save a file after inserting audio and/or video objects, it takes longer to save because these objects greatly increase the file size.

Assessment: Inserting and formatting media

1. Which of the following statements about using sound effects in a presentation is not true?

    - You can download audio files from an online source for use as sound effects.
    - You can use .mp3 files for sound effects.
    - Audio files can be used as sound effects, transition effects, *and* animation effects.
    - Three allowable file formats for audio objects are .mp3, .wav., and .aif.

2. The tools you use to work with the audio itself are located on the Audio Tools Format tab. True or false?

    - True
    - False

3. Which of the following are important factors to consider when adding audio and video to your presentation? Choose the best response.

    - File format, file size, and quality.
    - File format, file size, and noise suppression.
    - Whether the audio and video add to or detract from the presentation and its purpose, and whether the files are of high definition.
    - File size, file format, and whether the audio and video add to or detract from the presentation and its purpose.

4. Adding audio and video objects to a PowerPoint presentation increases the size of the file only slightly. True or false?

    - True
    - False

Summary: Animation, time effects, and media

In this chapter, you learned how to:

- Create animations from text and shapes; modify, customize, and copy animations; and set timing options for animation and transition effects
- Insert sound as effects, as audio objects, and as transition and animation effects; insert and trim video; and set options for audio and video playback

Synthesis: Animation, time effects, and media

In this synthesis exercise, you'll create and work with animation effects, including timing options, and insert and work with audio and video.

1. Open `JT Animedia Assessment.pptx`, and save it as `My JT Animedia Assessment.pptx`.
2. Use your animation skills to add some animation to every slide.
   - Try some animation styles you haven't yet used.
   - Experiment with timing options.
   - Use settings in the Effect Options window.
   - Use Advanced Animation tools.
   - Experiment with settings in the Timing group, and reorder animations on each slide, as necessary.
   - Add sound effects to some of the animations.
   - Copy one or two animation settings to other objects.
3. Add transition effects to each slide.
   - Experiment with some transition effects you might not have used before, and experiment with transition effect options.
   - Apply settings from the Timing group, and add sound effects to some (or all) of the transitions.
   - Experiment with Advance Slide settings and values.
4. Add one or more audio objects to your presentation, where you think it's appropriate to do so.
   If you have an Internet connection, download one or more audio files in a PowerPoint-approved format. Ask your instructor for guidance, if necessary.
5. Use the Audio Tools Playback tab to customize audio playback.
6. Trim the audio files, if necessary.
7. Experiment with Audio Options group and Editing group tools to fine-tune the audio. If you wish, have the audio fade in and/or fade out.

8. Use the Audio Tools Format tab to change the appearance of the audio objects.
9. Pick an appropriate location, and on a new slide, add a video. You can use Mixing Coffee Beans.mp4 or download a YouTube video, if you have an Internet connection.

    If you download a YouTube (or other) video and it also has audio, adjust the audio settings, such as Volume, where necessary.
10. Use the Video Tools Playback tab to adjust Video Options and Editing settings.
11. Trim the video, if necessary.
12. Resize and position the video.
13. View the slide show.
14. Save and close the presentation.

Chapter 9: Reviewing content, tracking changes, and saving in other formats

You will learn how to:

- Review presentation content and track changes
- Save your presentations in other formats

Module A: Reviewing content and tracking changes

PowerPoint provides useful tools for reviewing the contents of your presentations, both as you enter information and after the fact. In addition, PowerPoint helps you keep track of changes made by multiple reviewers and merge the results as you see fit.

You will learn how to:

- Review the content of your presentations and track changes made by multiple reviewers

Proofing your presentation

 MOS PowerPoint Exam Objective(s): 5.2.3

The Review tab provides you with tools for checking your spelling, punctuation, and capitalization, as well as a thesaurus for finding just the right word.

The Proofing group contains often-used tools for working with presentation content. Clicking any of these tools opens its respective pane, which contains information specific to the term currently highlighted.

- *Spelling*: The Spelling pane highlights any potentially misspelled words, often provides alternatives, and provides the tools for implementing them. In the lower part of the pane, clicking the speaker icon plays a recording of the spoken word. Below this are synonyms for the highlighted word. If you know that the highlighted word is in another language, you can use the drop-down list at the bottom of the pane to select that language.

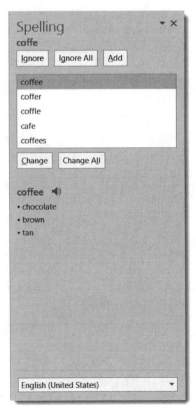

- *Smart Lookup*: The Smart Lookup tool opens the Insights pane, which contains tools for exploring selected text and topics in depth online. Clicking **Explore** at the top of the pane allows you to explore selected words or topics through various online sources, including Bing and Wikipedia. Clicking **Define** displays the definition of selected words.

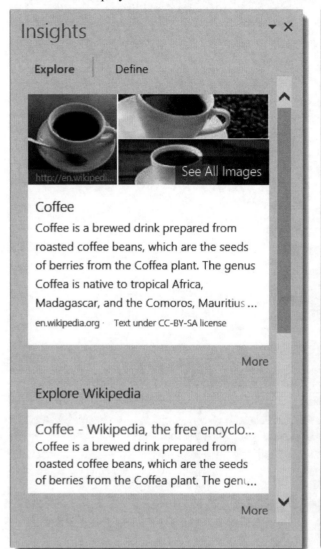
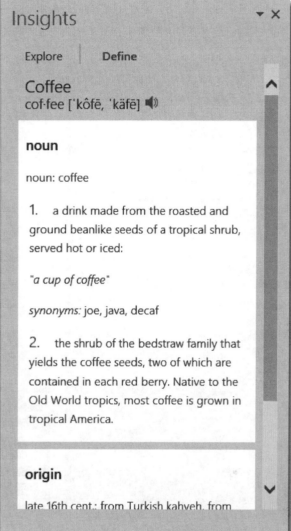

 Note: The first time you use Smart Lookup, in the Insights pane a message is displayed, asking you to read a privacy statement and accept its terms and conditions. To continue, click **Got It**.

- *Thesaurus*: The Thesaurus pane contains a list of synonyms found for the highlighted word. This pane is a kind of verbal "rabbit hole," in that clicking any of the synonyms listed makes it the focus of its own list of synonyms, and so on. Hovering over a word in the list displays an arrow to the right of it. Clicking that arrow displays the Insert command, for replacing the highlighted word on the slide, and Copy, for copying the word, which then allows you to paste it anywhere you'd like.

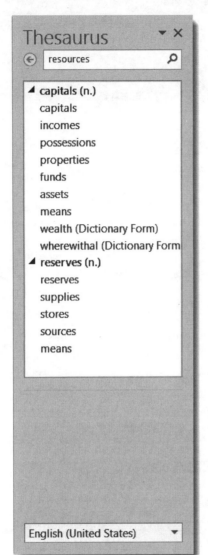

Automatic spell checking

MOS PowerPoint Exam Objective(s): 5.2.3

PowerPoint checks spelling continually and automatically by default. When it finds a possible error, it underlines the word or phrase with a red, wavy line, which indicates that it's either misspelled or not in the current dictionary.

At this point, you have a few options.

- Retype the word to correct it.
- Right-click the underlined text, and click the appropriate option. PowerPoint may suggest one or more terms, though it doesn't always have a suggested correction. To tell PowerPoint to ignore all instances of that particular spelling of the word in the entire presentation, click **Ignore All**. To make it a recognized word (or spelling), click **Add to Dictionary**.

- Sometimes a proper name or an uncommon word is flagged as a misspelling. In this case, you can choose to ignore all instances of the word in the document, or you can add the word to the dictionary so that it won't be flagged in the future.

If you're used to some of the more powerful proofing tools in Microsoft Word, for example, it's important to keep in mind that they're far more limited in PowerPoint.

To enable grammar checking in PowerPoint, make sure the **Check grammar with spelling** proofing option is checked in the PowerPoint Options window. PowerPoint does have limited ability for checking errors in grammar, and also underscores those with a red, wavy line, but you shouldn't rely on it to catch all errors. However, this is where the Research tool might come in handy.

Using the Spelling pane

Although PowerPoint continually checks spelling and grammar on the fly, you might want to check an entire presentation at once, for instance, if you're editing or reviewing someone else's presentation. It's easiest to do so by using the Spelling pane.

MOS PowerPoint Exam Objective(s): 5.2.3

1. On the Review tab, click **Spelling**.

    In the Proofing group. It's a good idea to check spelling from the beginning of a presentation, but you can instead do so from any point within it. In the latter case, when the spell check reaches the end of the presentation, it will ask you whether you wish to continue checking spelling from the beginning of the presentation.

    The Spelling pane opens.

2. Take one of several actions:

    - Click **Ignore** to remove the underlining and move to the next issue.
    - Click **Ignore All** to remove the underlining from and ignore all instances of the term.
    - Click **Add** so that PowerPoint will consider the term correct and add it to the dictionary, making it available to other presentations.
    - Select a suggestion, or edit in the window, and click **Change** or **Change All**.

- Retype the selected word correctly, and then click **Resume** to continue checking the rest of the presentation.

Once the end of the presentation (or the point at which you started) is reached, a message indicates that the spell check is complete.

Proofing options

To open proofing options, click **Options** on the File tab, then click the **Proofing** category in the left pane.

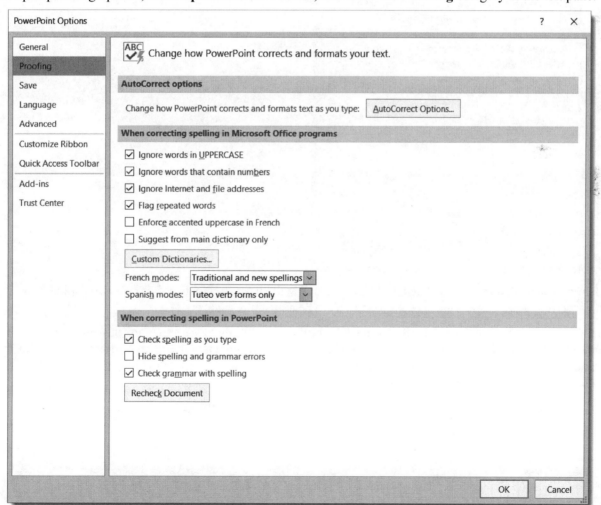

There are check boxes for many spelling and grammar options, as well as buttons to open AutoCorrect options, custom dictionaries, and grammar settings. To have PowerPoint check grammar along with spelling, click **Check grammar with spelling**. When you're finished making changing to proofing options, click **OK**.

To change the language PowerPoint uses to proof a document, click **Language** on the Review tab.

AutoCorrect options

The term AutoCorrect is a bit of a misnomer: In many cases, Autocorrect replaces a combination of common characters with characters or symbols that aren't on a typical keyboard. For instance, the characters (c) are replaced by the copyright symbol.

To open the AutoCorrect window from Proofing options, click the **AutoCorrect Options** button.

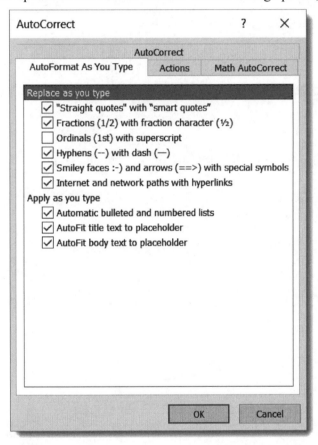

AutoCorrect will capitalize the first letter of a sentence. It will also correct when there are two capital letters starting the first word of the sentence, assuming this to be a mistake, such as "THe."

Although AutoFormat and AutoCorrect features are normally useful, there are situations in which the automatic replacements are an unwelcome nuisance, in which case you can turn off the corrections you don't want. For instance, to tell PowerPoint not to automatically apply bullets or numbers to lists, uncheck **Automatic bulleted and numbered lists** on the AutoFormat As You Type tab.

The Actions tab allows you to create custom settings for automating additional actions that you routinely and repeatedly perform.

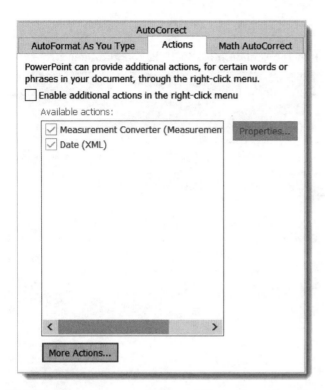

The Math AutoCorrect tab is used for options geared specifically toward mathematical symbols and equations.

Exercise: Proofing your presentation

You'll explore PowerPoint's proofing options, then check the presentation for spelling and grammar errors.

Do This	How & Why
1. Open `JT Proofing.pptx`, and save it as `My JT Proofing.pptx`.	
2. Click **File > Options**, then click **Proofing**. In the left pane. The Proofing options are displayed in the PowerPoint Options window.	

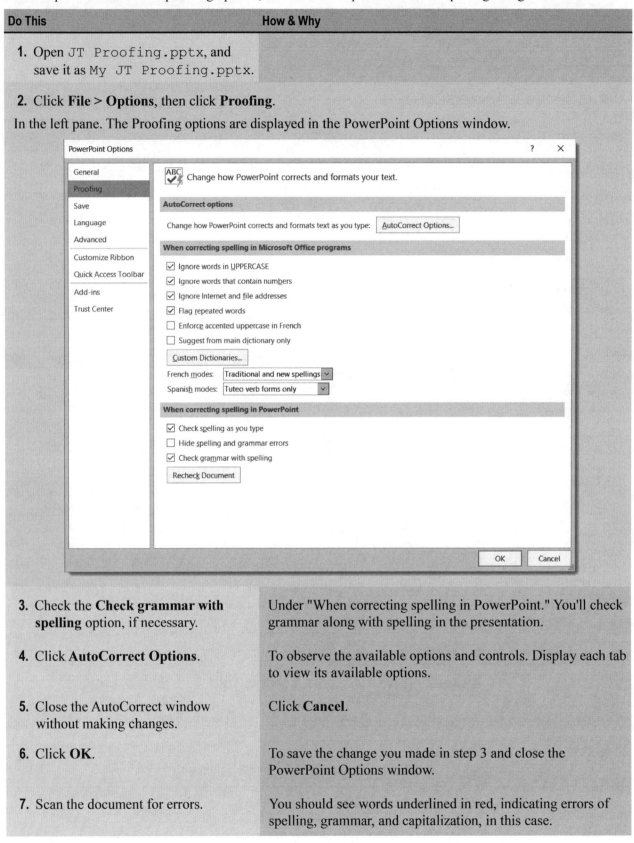

3. Check the **Check grammar with spelling** option, if necessary.	Under "When correcting spelling in PowerPoint." You'll check grammar along with spelling in the presentation.
4. Click **AutoCorrect Options**.	To observe the available options and controls. Display each tab to view its available options.
5. Close the AutoCorrect window without making changes.	Click **Cancel**.
6. Click **OK**.	To save the change you made in step 3 and close the PowerPoint Options window.
7. Scan the document for errors.	You should see words underlined in red, indicating errors of spelling, grammar, and capitalization, in this case.

Do This	How & Why
8. On slide 2, right-click the first error underlined ("coffe"), then click **coffee**.	This is a handy method to use when you're sure of the correct spelling of a word.  The misspelled word is replaced with the correct spelling. You'll continue proofing the presentation using the Spelling pane.

9. On the Review tab, click **Spelling**.

The Spelling pane opens, and the next potential error is highlighted on the slide. The correct spelling highlighted in the Spelling pane.

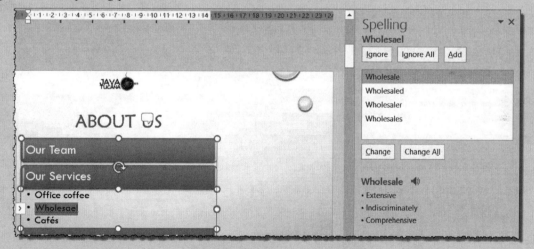

10. Click **Change**.	To replace the incorrect spelling with the correct one.
11. Edit the remainder of the presentation. a) Review each flagged item. b) If there is an error, select the right suggestion, and click **Change**.	

PowerPoint 2016 Level 1   281

Do This	How & Why
c) If the word is correct but unrecognized, click **Ignore**.	On slide 3, ignore the proper names. On slide 9, ignore the coffee-variety names Supremo, Tarrazu, and Coban. You could instead click **Ignore All** in all these cases. On slide 6, one grammar error is found ("your" instead of "you're"). On slide 13, the wrong correction is suggested ("Marians"). You'll need to click **Martians** in the list, then click **Change**.
12. When the spelling and grammar check is complete, and PowerPoint informs you that you're "good to go," click **OK**.	
13. Save and close the presentation.	

About comments

When you're working on a presentation with other people, you might want to make comments on the content or add reminders for later. Likewise, you could write a comment as a reminder for your own use. You could just add a note in the slide text and remove it later, but it might be hard to spot or left in by mistake—making it visible to an audience during a slide show! Instead, PowerPoint lets you add comments as markup, rather than as presentation content. Thus, comments are not visible in Slide Show view.

Comments are displayed as balloons on slides.

You can view comments in the Comments pane.

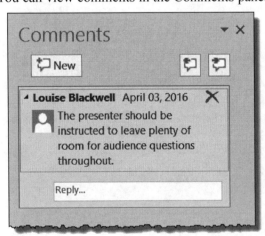

Commands for managing comments are located on the Review tab, in the Comments group.

Adding comments

When you add a comment, it's always attached to a part of the presentation's content. When you're commenting on something like a sentence or graphic, this helps point it out. However, if you're used to using comments in Microsoft Word, for example, it's important to know that unlike those in Word, comments in PowerPoint don't point to selected objects or text; they're merely placeholders.

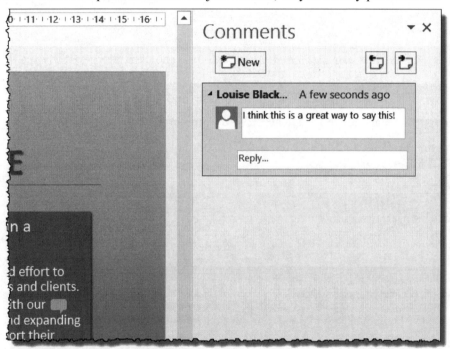

 MOS PowerPoint Exam Objective(s): 5.1.3

1. Place the insertion point or make a selection.
   Select the object, a portion of text, or simply place the insertion point at the desired location.
2. In the Comments group, click **New Comment**.
3. Type the comment.
   Usually, you only need to create comments as plain text, but you can apply limited formatting, such as changing font type or applying bold or italic formatting. However, you can't change paragraph formatting.
4. Click away from the comment when you're done writing it.

Managing comments

 MOS PowerPoint Exam Objective(s): 5.1.4

You can edit or delete existing comments. You can also navigate easily through all comments in a long presentation.

- To edit a comment, click anywhere in its text, and make any changes you like.
- To delete a comment using the Comments group, select the comment, and click **Delete**.
  The upper part of the Delete button.

- To delete a comment from the Comments pane, hover over the comment, and click the (Delete) icon.
- To delete multiple comments, click the lower part of the Delete button, and select an option.
  - To delete all comments on the current slide, click **Delete All Comments and Ink on This Slide**.
  - To delete all comments in the presentation, click **Delete All Comments and Ink in This Presentation**.

> **Note:** In PowerPoint, "ink notes" are manual markup that can be added to a presentation via touch-enabled computers.

- To navigate between comments, click **Previous** or **Next**.
  In the Comments group or Comments pane.

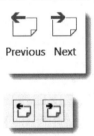

- To move a comment, simply drag it to a location on the slide.
  Remember, even if you first select a slide object or specific text, adding a comment merely inserts a generic comment balloon that points to nothing in particular. However, by moving the balloon manually to point it to its referent, you can at least make the balloon appear more content-specific.
- To reply to a comment, in the Comments pane, click in the comment's Reply box, then type your reply.

- To hide comments and markup in a presentation, click the lower half of the Show Comments button, and uncheck **Show Markup**.

    Doing so hides the comment balloons and closes the Comments pane.

     Note: Even though comments aren't visible during a slide show, you might not want others to view comments and markup in the file itself.

    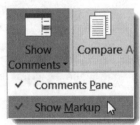

- To hide only the Comments pane, uncheck **Comments Pane**.

    Or click ☒ in the Comments pane. The comment balloons (and any additional markup) remain visible on the slides.

- To show comments and markup, click **Show Comments**.

    The upper half of the button.

Exercise: Adding and working with comments

In this exercise, you'll use comments to review a document.

Do This	How & Why
1. Open `JT Comments.pptx`, and save it as `My JT Comments.pptx`.	This presentation already contains several comments.
2. In the Comments group, click **Next**. On the Review tab. 	

The first comment in the presentation is displayed, both as a balloon on slide 2, and in the Comments pane, which is now open. In the Comments pane, you can see the commenter's name and when the comment was made.

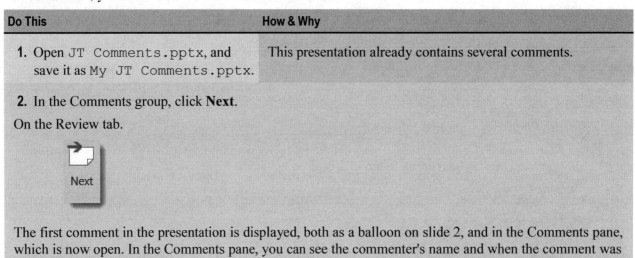

3. In the comment text, edit "The presenter should be instructed" to read `Instruct the presenter`.	You can edit a comment just as you would any other text. 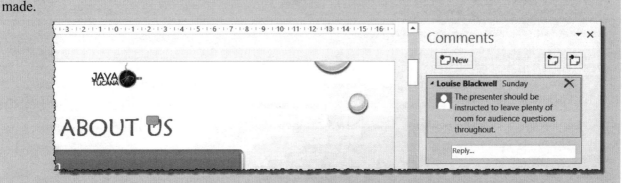
4. Click away from the comment to view it completed.	
5. Click **Next** to move to the next comment.	In the Comments group or the Comments pane. The comment on slide 3 is displayed. 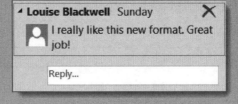

Do This	How & Why
6. Delete the comment.	Click ✕ in the comment itself, or click **Delete**. The Comments pane informs you that there are comments on other slides, the subtext being that there are none on this one.
7. On slide 5, you'll add a comment that refers to the last bullet item. • In the Comments group, click **New Comment**. • In the Comments pane, click **New**. **Note:** The tooltip for this button reads "Insert Comment."	The new comment appears in the Comments pane and includes your name. On the slide, a balloon appears in the upper-left corner.
8. Type the comment text `Is the last bullet item true for both coffees and teas?`	
9. Drag the balloon for your new comment to the left of the last bullet item on the slide.	This will make the balloon easily visible while scanning the slide.

Do This	How & Why

10. While you're at it, drag Louise Blackwell's comment balloon to the left of the second bullet item. Then click away from the comments.

Now both bullets are easily seen. This can be particularly helpful when scanning slides with the Comments pane hidden.

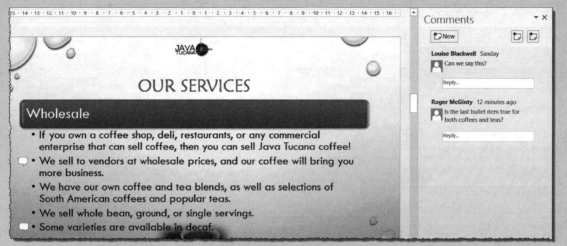

Do This	How & Why
11. Display the remaining comments in the presentation, then use the **Previous** button to move to a preceding comment.	
12. Add any additional comment you'd like.	
13. Move to a slide that contains at least one comment.	
14. Click **Show Comments**.	The upper part of the button. The Comments pane closes, but the balloons remain visible.
15. Click **Show Comments** again.	The Comments pane reappears, and the balloons are still visible.
16. Click **Show Comments** > **Show Markup**.	The balloons and Comments pane are both hidden from view.
17. Click **Show Comments**.	The upper part of the button. In this instance, because no markup was visible, this action is the equivalent of clicking **Show Comments** > **Show Markup**.
18. Save and close the presentation.	

Presentation comparison

 MOS PowerPoint Exam Objective(s): 5.1.1, 5.1.2

Tracking changes over multiple presentation versions can be difficult, especially when multiple editors are involved. To make the process easier, PowerPoint provides the Compare tool, which merge different versions of a presentation into a single one. This allows you to review any changes all at once.

When you use the Compare tool, Word looks at the content differences between the two presentations, merges them into a single onscreen presentation, and marks them as changes for you to accept or reject.

It's important to remember that once you've compared and merged slides from two presentations, once you've completed this process, you also have the option of reusing slides from other presentations.

1. With the destination presentation open, on the Home tab, click **New Slide > Reuse Slides**.
2. In the Reuse Slides task pane, click Open a PowerPoint File.
3. Select the source presentation, and click **Open**.
4. To retain the original formatting, check **Keep Source Formatting**.
5. Select the slide(s) you want to reuse.
6. Close the Reuse Slides pane.

Comparing presentations

 MOS PowerPoint Exam Objective(s): 5.1.2

Use the Compare tool to compare two versions of the same presentation.

1. Open the original version of the presentation.
2. On the Review tab, click **Compare**.
   In the Compare group.

   The Choose File to Merge with Current Presentation window opens. This is very much like the Open window.
3. Select the file name of the revised version you wish to compare the original presentation to.
   The Open button becomes the Merge button.

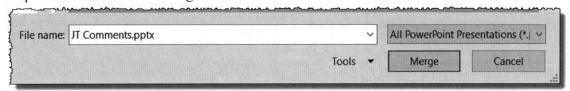

4. Click **Merge**.

   The Revisions pane opens (alongside the Comments pane, if comments have been added and displayed), listing all changes (and comments) made by reviewers.

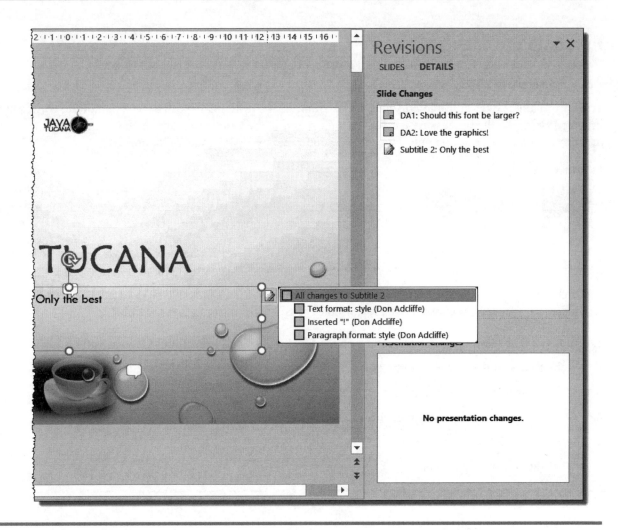

Reviewing changes

 MOS PowerPoint Exam Objective(s): 5.1.2, 5.1.4

When comparing versions of a presentation, accepting or rejecting changes is straightforward.

1. In the merged presentation, with the Revisions and Comments panes displayed, review each change.
   In the Revisions pane list, click the change.

   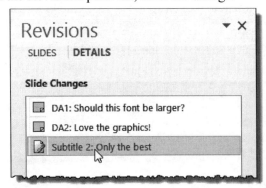

   The change or changes are listed on the slides and are preceded by check boxes.

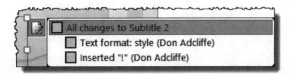

 Note: It's not necessary to display the Comments pane when reviewing changes. However, viewing comments alongside changes can sometimes clarify reviewers' intentions, which can make it easier to judge the efficacy of a given change.

2. Accept or reject the change.

   - To accept a change using the Revisions pane, click to check it. (Click again to uncheck it.) To accept multiple changes applied to a slide object, check the "parent" box. Once you accept a change, you can see the change applied to the slide object.

   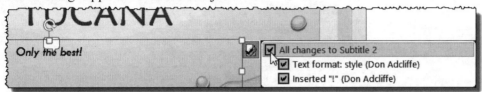

   - To accept a change using the Ribbon, click the lower part of the Accept button. To accept all changes to an object, click **Accept Change**. Otherwise, click **Accept All Changes to This Slide** or **Accept All Changes to the Presentation**.

   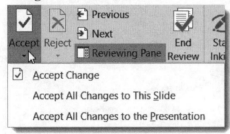

   - To reject a change, simply ignore it. (If it's already checked, uncheck it.) Doing so prevents the change from being applied to the merged version.

   - The Reject tool also provides options for rejecting one or more changes. To reject all changes to an object, click **Reject Change**. Otherwise, click **Reject All Changes to This Slide** or **Reject All Changes to the Presentation**.

   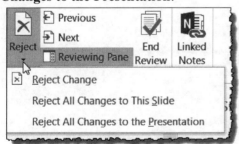

    Note: The Reject options only become available if a change is previously accepted.

3. Save the compared document with accepted/rejected changes.

   For impeccable "version control," it's a good idea to give the document a new name that reflects this completed step in the process of developing a presentation. For example, you could use descriptors such as "compared," "changes reviewed," "final review," and so on. That way, should you need to re-examine any step in the review process further down the road, you always have the individual files created at each step for comparison.

Exercise: Comparing presentations and reviewing changes

You'll compare two versions of a presentation, review the changes, then save the resulting merged version.

Do This	How & Why
1. Open `JT Original.pptx`.	This is a proofed version of a presentation saved prior to being reviewed or commented upon. You'll compare it to a fully reviewed version.
2. Compare JT Original.pptx with JT Revised.pptx.	
a) On the Review tab, click **Compare**.	In the Compare group. The Choose File to Merge with Current Presentation window opens.
b) Navigate to `JT Revised.pptx`, then click **Merge**.	
The presentations are merged, the Revisions pane opens, and changes are displayed with their check boxes.	

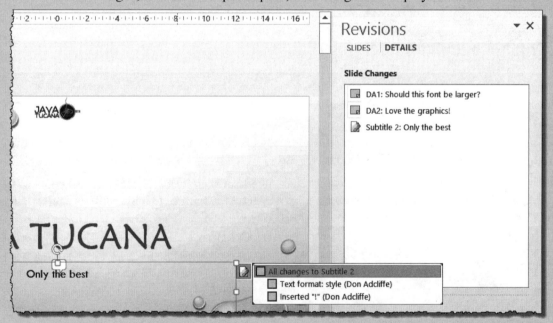

3. If you'd prefer to review the changes with the Comments pane visible, open the pane.	Click **Show Comments**. If the way the comments are displayed in the Revisions pane is sufficient, then there's no need to do so.
4. Observe the Revisions pane.	You can display revisions according to Slides or Details. The Details view is handy because it lists the details, which you can click one by one to view in greater detail.
5. Review the changes in the presentation.	You'll leave the comments intact for now, just in case there might be further revisions down the line.

Do This	How & Why
a) In the Revisions pane, click the Subtitle 2 change.	The changes to Subtitle 2 are listed in detail next to the object on the slide. Next to each change is the reviewer's name. 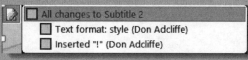
b) Check the **Inserted "!" (Don Adcliffe)** change.	To accept the change.
c) Reject the other change to Subtitle 2.	Simply ignore it, thus leaving it unchecked. Any unchecked changes won't be incorporated into the latest version of the presentation. Note that there is now a problem with Subtitle 2. Because Don made two changes—the insertion of an exclamation point and a formatting change to italics—selecting only the exclamation-point change results in its appearing in italics. The rest of the subtitle is in roman (normal) type.
d) On the slide, remove italic formatting from the exclamation point.	
e) In the Compare group, click **Next**.	To move to the next change. On slide 3, a message is displayed, informing you that the animation change that a reviewer made can't be merged. PowerPoint can't merge features such as animation effects. However, in this case, Don Addcliffe has only fixed some spelling errors; he didn't actually change any animation effects. 
f) In the rightmost row of blue boxes, observe the name Abena Woyelowo.	Her last name was misspelled. One of the misspelled names Don corrected was Abena's.
g) Accept the change to made to slide 3, and observe the result.	Click to check the box. The names in the boxes are now spelled correctly, including Abena's.
a) Advance to the next change.	In the Compare group, click **Next**. The next change, also involving an animation, is displayed. Fortunately, none of the reviewers has change any animation effects. All remaining changes are textual, so you can accept them without worrying about their having any effect on the animations.
b) Click **Accept > Accept All Changes to This Slide**.	Be sure to click the lower part of the Accept tool first to display additional options. All changes are accepted on slide 4.

Do This	How & Why
c) Jump to the next tracked change.	You may have to click **Next** twice—first to re-display the checked option on slide 4, then to advance to the next change. The next change is on slide 5. If you wish to view any of the comments, which aren't completely visible in the Revisions pane, and you haven't yet opened the Comments pane, you can use any of the techniques you know for doing so.
d) Click the change listed.	Slide properties.
e) This time, accept all the remaining changes made to the presentation.	Click **Accept > Accept All Changes to the Presentation**.
f) Click through each slide, and observe the results of your comparison and review.	Notice that each slide with one or more accepted changes is displayed with an icon showing a check mark, just like those shown in the Revisions pane.
6. Close the Revisions pane, as well as the Comments pane, if necessary.	On each pane, click ⊠.
7. Save the presentation as `My JT Comparison.pptx`. Then close it.	

Assessment: Reviewing content and tracking changes

1. The category of PowerPoint options that govern spelling, grammar, capitalization, and so on is called AutoCorrect. True or false?

   - True
   - False

2. What's the spell-checking option that tells PowerPoint to remember terms for future use in other presentations? Choose the best response.

   - Ignore All
   - Remember Term
   - Add to Dictionary
   - New Word

3. When adding a new comment, you need to select a destination slide, then select the object or word(s) you're commenting on, then click New Comment. True or false?

   - True
   - False

4. When you use the Compare tool to merge two presentations, and then finish reviewing all reviewers' changes, which response best describes the state of the presentation(s)?

   - All changes are merged, except for those rejected, and the merged presentation is automatically saved.
   - All changes are merged, except for those rejected, and the original presentation is saved with the new changes.
   - All changes are merged, except for those rejected and any style effects that can't be merged, and the reviewed presentation is automatically updated to reflect the new changes.
   - All changes are merged, except for those rejected and any style effects that can't be merged. The two compared presentations remain intact and unchanged, and the new, reviewed version awaits saving.

Module B: Saving a presentation in other formats

When you make presentations, you might plan to share them with others. If you're going to print them or save them to a shared folder for other PowerPoint users, that's simple enough, but you have many other options for saving them.

You will learn:

- How to save a presentation as a template, and about other saving options

Available formats

 MOS PowerPoint Exam Objective(s): 5.2.4, 5.2.5

PowerPoint's default file format is all you need most of the time, but you can save in a number of other formats, or *file types*, used by other versions of PowerPoint, or by other programs. Not all file types are interchangeable: some might not support all of PowerPoint's features and formatting options. Some don't even support graphics or text formatting. When you save a document as another file type, it's important to make sure that it's compatible with other users' software, and that it preserves any important information, including formatting, in the document. Whether you simply use **File > Save As** or one of these other routes, you end up at the Save As window.

The most common file types you might need are listed in Backstage view, by clicking **Export > Change File Type**. If you've configured Windows to show file extensions, you can tell file types apart not only by their icons but by their extensions.

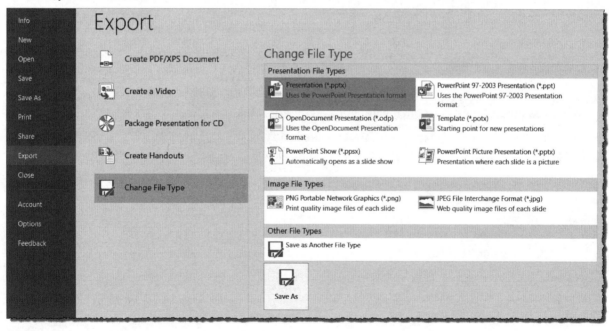

Several different presentation file types are available.

Presentation (*.pptx) — The default file format in PowerPoint 2007 and later. It supports all of PowerPoint's normal functions and is what you should use, unless you have reason not to.

PowerPoint 97-2003 Document (*.ppt) — The file format used by older versions of PowerPoint; .ppt files are usually larger than .pptx files and don't support all of PowerPoint's newer features. However, they're more compatible with older software, such as older Office versions.

OpenDocument Presentation (*.odp) — A file format designed by the Organization for the Advancement of Structured Information Standards (OASIS) and used by many non-Microsoft office suites. It supports most PowerPoint features, but some formatting options might be lost or appear differently.

Template (*.potx) — The default format for templates in PowerPoint 2007 and newer. You shouldn't use this for presentations, but instead to make starting points you'll later use to create presentations.

PowerPoint Show (*.ppsx) — A special PowerPoint format that saves the file as a slide show. Thus, it opens only as a slide show and does not present the slides in editing mode.

PowerPoint Picture Presentation (*.pptx) — A special PowerPoint format in which each slide is saved as a picture. In this format, individual slides cannot be edited.

There are also two image file types available.

Portable Network Graphics (*.png) — This format creates high-quality images of each slide for use in printed materials.

JPEG File Interchange Format (*.jpg) — This format creates lower-quality images of each slide for Web use.

The other option available in the Export pane is **Create PDF/XPS document**.

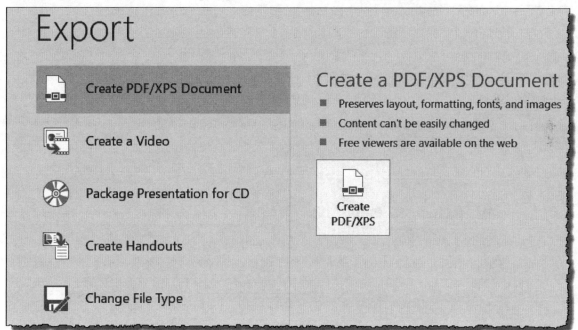

Click **Create PDF/XPS** to open the Publish as PDF or XPS window.

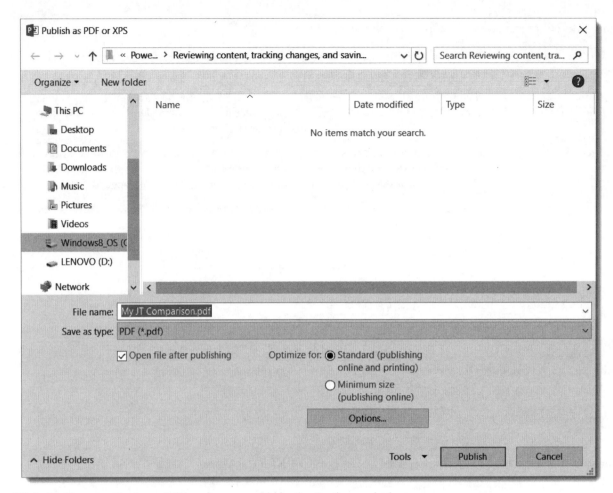

Click **Options** to display additional commands in the Options window.

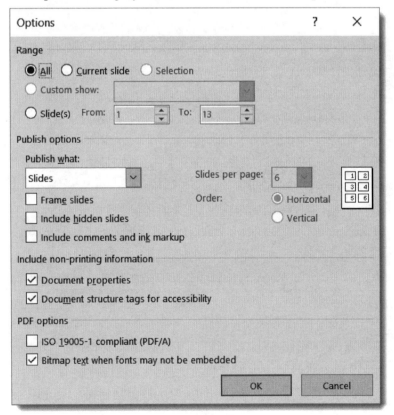

Portable Document Format (.pdf) — Developed by Adobe and broadly supported by many software vendors, PDF was designed to preserve a file's exact formatting and appearance, regardless of viewer or operating system. It is intended for distributing finalized presentations, so PDF files really aren't meant to be edited after they're saved. It supports other publication features as well, such as digital signatures and DRM.

XML Paper Specification (.xps) — Microsoft's own equivalent to PDF, XPS has similar features and limitations. It's natively supported by Windows Vista and later as well as other Microsoft products, but is less widely supported by third-party manufacturers.

By clicking **Change File Type > Save as Another File Type**, or from the Save As window, you can choose some additional formats, such as macro-enabled presentations and templates (.pptm and .potm, respectively), Office themes (.thmx), PowerPoint XML presentations (.xml), outlines in Rich Text Format (.rtf), MPEG-4 videos (.mp4), and Windows media videos (.wmv). You can also choose to save the presentation in an earlier PowerPoint format, in order to retain backward compatibility.

```
PowerPoint Presentation (*.pptx)
PowerPoint Macro-Enabled Presentation (*.pptm)
PowerPoint 97-2003 Presentation (*.ppt)
PDF (*.pdf)
XPS Document (*.xps)
PowerPoint Template (*.potx)
PowerPoint Macro-Enabled Template (*.potm)
PowerPoint 97-2003 Template (*.pot)
Office Theme (*.thmx)
PowerPoint Show (*.ppsx)
PowerPoint Macro-Enabled Show (*.ppsm)
PowerPoint 97-2003 Show (*.pps)
PowerPoint Add-In (*.ppam)
PowerPoint 97-2003 Add-In (*.ppa)
PowerPoint XML Presentation (*.xml)
MPEG-4 Video (*.mp4)
Windows Media Video (*.wmv)
GIF Graphics Interchange Format (*.gif)
JPEG File Interchange Format (*.jpg)
PNG Portable Network Graphics Format (*.png)
TIFF Tag Image File Format (*.tif)
Device Independent Bitmap (*.bmp)
Windows Metafile (*.wmf)
Enhanced Windows Metafile (*.emf)
Outline/RTF (*.rtf)
PowerPoint Picture Presentation (*.pptx)
Strict Open XML Presentation (*.pptx)
OpenDocument Presentation (*.odp)
PowerPoint Presentation (*.pptx)
```

The **Package Presentation for CD** options allows you to save your presentation and burn it onto a CD. It can then be played on most CD drives/players.

Using Save As options

Whether you're changing a presentation's file type, saving a newly created file, or just saving a new copy to a different location, you need to use the Save As window. It contains options for file name and location, as well as additional properties, depending on the file type.

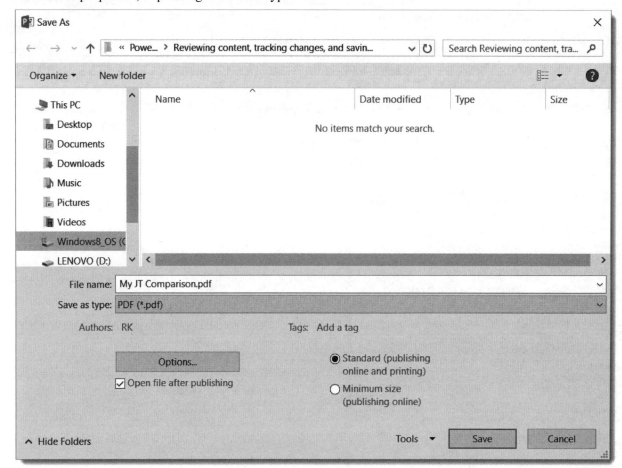

Remember that saving a document with a new name, location, or format doesn't delete the original file. It doesn't update it either. If you want to keep an updated version of the original file, be sure to save it normally before creating the new one. If you don't want to keep it at all, make sure to delete it from Windows Explorer after saving the new file.

 MOS PowerPoint Exam Objective(s): 5.2.5

1. Open the Save As window.
   - Press **F12**.
   - In Backstage view, click **Save As**, click the main destination location, and click **Browse**. If you select a OneDrive location, you first need to sign in to your account.
   - In Backstage view: click **Export > Change File Type**, select a file type, and click **Save As**; or click **Create PDF/XPS Document > Create PDF/XPS** to open the Publish as PDF or XPS window, another form of the Save As window.
2. Choose the file format from the "Save as type" list. If you used the Export pane, this is already chosen for you.
3. Choose the file's name and location.
   - Navigate through folders using the left pane, or type a file path into the address bar.

- Type the file's name, if necessary, in the File Name box.

   Your file type might influence where you want to save it. For example, templates are saved by default in the Templates folder, and you might want to make sure a web page doesn't have any spaces in its file name.

4. Set additional file properties.

   - Many of these vary by file type. For example, PDF documents can be optimized for various publishing methods.
   - Click **Tools** to access additional options, such as file settings or graphics compression.

5. Click **Save**.

   For some file types, you'll be asked to specify additional conversion details in a separate window, or you'll receive warnings about compatibility settings.

Creating PDF and XPS documents

MOS PowerPoint Exam Objective(s): 5.2.5

PDF and XPS documents are both *fixed formats*, which is to say they're meant to be read but not edited, generally speaking. Both can be read by an assortment of free readers, and all fonts, formatting, and images appear the same on nearly any device. The drawback is that once saved, the content can't be easily changed. Think of these formats as a type of printing, even though you can create them as you would any other file type.

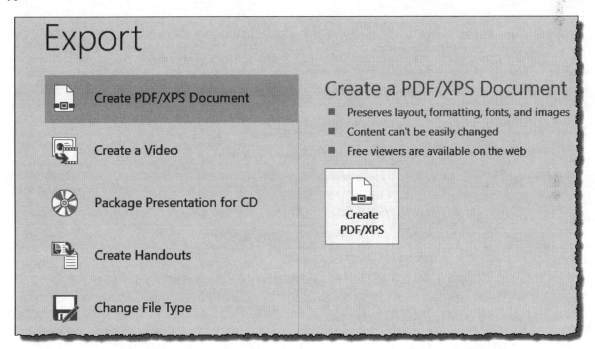

1. Open the Save As window.

   You can also open the nearly identical Publish as PDF or XPS window in Backstage view by clicking **Export > Create PDF/XPS Document > Create PDF/XPS**. The process is otherwise the same.

2. Choose saving options.

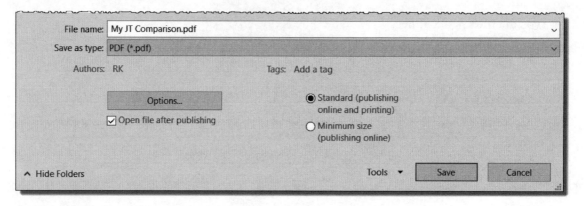

- Choose either **PDF** or **XPS** from the "Save as type" list.
- In the Optimize For section, click **Minimum size** to create a smaller file, and **Standard** to preserve graphical quality.
- Check **Open file after publishing** to automatically open the document in your default PDF or XPS reader.

3. To set additional file options, click **Options**.

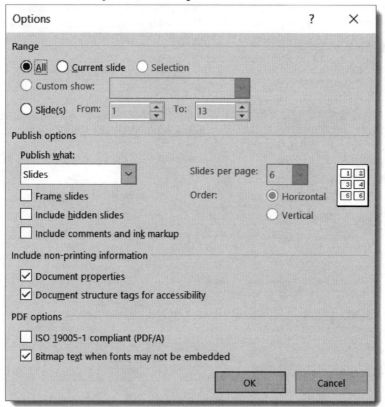

- You can publish the entire presentation, a slide, a range of slide numbers, or a selection.
- You can optionally include markup, bookmarks, document structure, and document properties.
- PDF and XPS each have additional available options.
- Click **OK** when you're done.

4. Click **Save** or **Publish**.

Creating Word handouts

You can create handouts from your presentations that you can print and share with your audience.

1. In Backstage view, click **Export** > **Create Handouts** > **Create Handouts**.

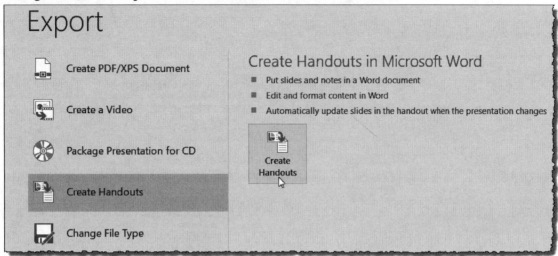

The Send to Microsoft window opens.

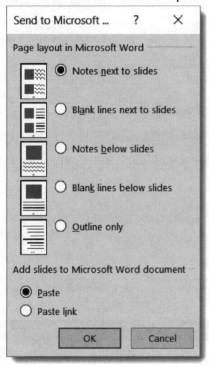

2. Select a page-layout option.

    The illustration preceding each selection gives a rough idea of the resulting layout.

    For printing, you'll want to use the default Paste option under "Add slides to Microsoft Word document," as this pastes the slides' contents, rather than mere links to them.

3. Click **OK**.

    After some processing, the handouts document is created and opened in Word. The resulting document can now be edited normally in Word.

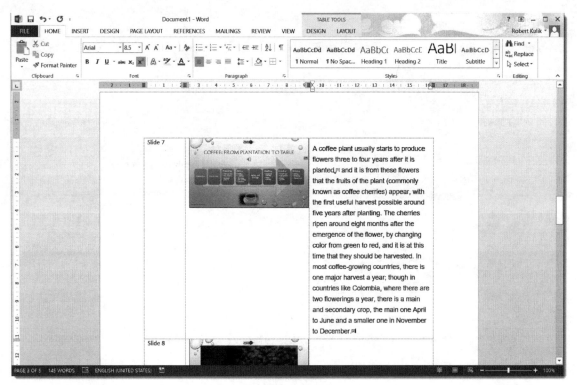

 Note: Remember to save your handouts document! A Word handouts document can only be saved in Word, not in PowerPoint.

Handout Master view

 MOS PowerPoint Exam Objective(s): 1.3.5

You can change the appearance of your presentation handouts in Handout Master view, which you access by clicking **Handout Master**, in the View tab's Master Views group.

In Handout Master view, the Handout Master tab is displayed, as well as a preview of a handout page and its layout.

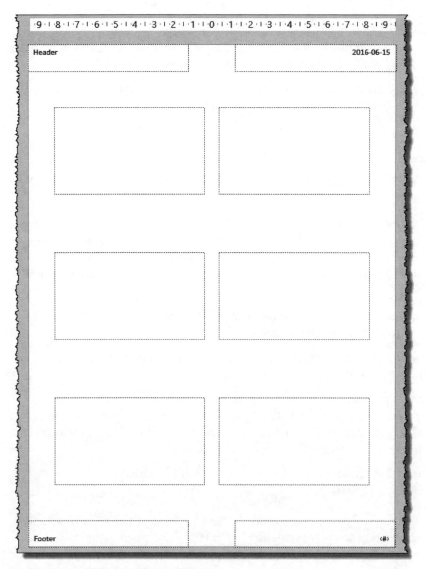

There are several tool groups on the Handout Master tab that you can use to change the appearance and formatting of handout pages and their elements.

- *Page Setup*: Contains tools for changing page orientation, the size of slides as they appear on the handout page, and the number of slides per handout page.

- *Placeholders*: By default, header, footer, date, and page-number elements are displayed on handouts. However, you can specify which of these elements you'd like displayed on your handouts by checking or unchecking them.

- *Edit Theme*: The Themes tool allows you to apply the theme of your choice to your handouts to give them their own distinctive look.

- *Background*: Use these tools to fine-tune the appearance of elements on your handouts.

Note: If you intend to apply a theme to your handouts, it's a good idea to apply the desired theme first, then alter/fine-tune your design using the tools in the Background group.

When you're finished formatting your handouts, as always, you can use the tools on the View tab or icons in the status bar to change views. Alternatively, if you wish to return to the previous view, you can instead click **Close Master View**.

About videos

What if you need to give a presentation at a location halfway around the world, and it happens to be at a time when you can't be there in person? What if you'd like to give the presentation in multiple locations at once and want to make sure that it runs smoothly and perfectly every time, exactly as you've planned it?

Well, one feature that could be just what you're looking for is PowerPoint's new ability to record a full-length presentation, complete with narration, custom timings, and so on. The result is a video file, saved in the format of your choice.

MOS PowerPoint Exam Objective(s): 5.2.4, 5.2.5

If you're thinking about turning your presentation into a video, there some features you might consider using, depending on your specific needs.

- Record and time your own narration to run with the video. To do so, you'll need a decent microphone. You can use your computer's internal microphone; however, a better choice would be a headset mic. Particularly if the distance from your computer varies as you give the presentation, the sound will not record at a consistent level. A headset mic will ensure that the level and clarity of the sound remains relatively the same.

- Use your mouse as a laser pointer. Like its physical counterpart, a laser pointer can be a great tool for quickly focusing the audience's attention on specific content.

- All the usual animation and transition effects can still be used and recorded. Likewise, any embedded audio and/or video objects remain part of the video.

- You don't have to record the entire presentation in real time. You can pause at any time during recording, and then continue recording when you're ready. Even after you've completed recording, you can always go back and re-record individual slides, including narration, use of the laser pointer, and so on.

- A very important consideration is that viewers need not have PowerPoint installed to view the completed video.

It can take considerable time to record a video of your presentation. At the very least, if you're recording the entire presentation in real time, it will be as long as the presentation itself. However, when planning to record your video, allow plenty of time for any pausing that might be necessary during recording, as well as time for any re-recording that might be necessary later on.

Once you've completed recording your video, and have saved it in the format of your choice, you can distribute it in any number of ways, including emailing it, sharing it via a Cloud service such as OneDrive, or burning it to a CD or DVD. However, remember to check whether the recipient has the capability to play the video in the format in which you've saved it. Also, once you've created a video, you can upload it to a website.

Creating a video

Before you begin to record a video of your presentation, make sure that the presentation itself is completed. Doing so will make the whole process of recording go much more smoothly.

 MOS PowerPoint Exam Objective(s): 5.2.5

1. With your finished presentation open, record your narration and add timings.

    a) On the Slide Show tab, display the Record Slide Show options.

    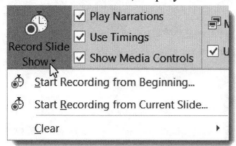

    b) To record from the beginning of the slide show, click **Start Recording from Beginning**; to record from the current slide, click **Start Recording from Current Slide**.

    The Clear option is used to delete narrations and timings.

    The Record Slide Show window opens.

    c) Check/uncheck the appropriate options.

    Slide and animation timings records the time each slide appears, including any animation steps.
    Narrations, ink, and laser pointer records your voice as you narrate each slide, including your use of the pen, highlighter, laser pointer, and eraser tools.

    d) Click **Start Recording**.

    For additional recording options during Record mode, hover the mouse pointer the upper-left corner of the slide to display the Recording toolbar, if necessary.

    Click ➔ to advance to the next slide. Click ▌▌ to pause recording. Click ↶ to re-record the current slide.

    To re-record the current slide from the Slide Show tab, click **Record Slide Show > Start Recording from Current Slide**.

2. Right-click the slide, and select **Pointer Options**, and select a tool, if desired.

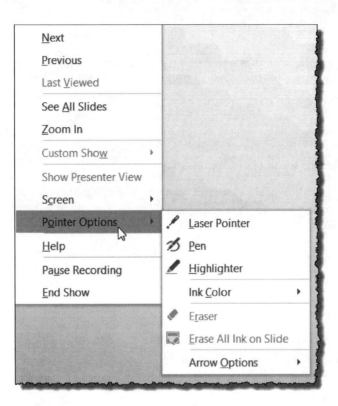

- Laser Pointer
- Pen
- Highlighter
- Eraser (available once there's something recorded to be erased)
  You can further refine the appearance of some of these tools using the Ink Color and Arrow Options choices.

3. To stop recording, right-click the last recorded slide, and click **End Show**.

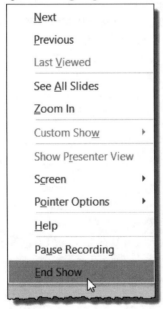

The slide show is automatically saved and opened in Slide Sorter view. When you've finished recording your narration, a speaker icon is displayed in the lower-right corner of your slides. Click the icon to preview the narration. The timing of each slide is displayed below that slide.

Exercise: Saving a presentation in other formats

You'll save a presentation as a PDF file, and use it to create Word handouts.

Do This	How & Why
1. Open JT PDF.pptx.	
2. Click **File > Export > Create PDF/XPS Document > Create PDF/XPS**.	

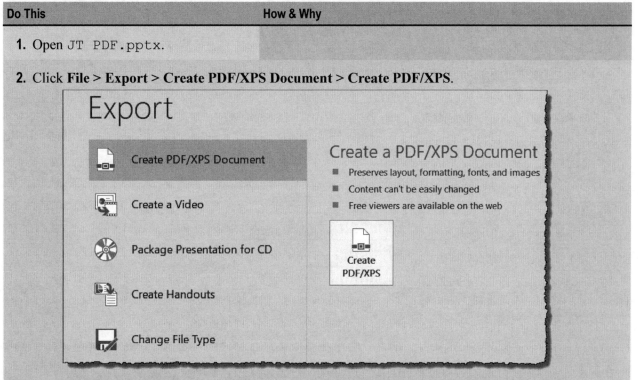

The Publish as PDF or XPS window opens, and the file is given a .pdf extension. Note that the default options will open the file after publishing and optimize it for online and print use, which retains high image resolution and results in larger file size.

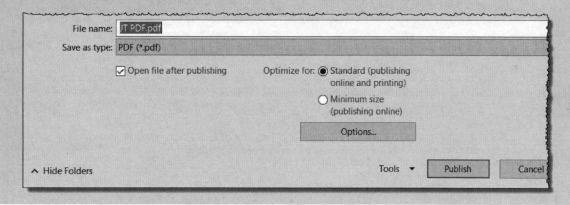

Do This	How & Why

3. Click **Publish**.

JT PDF.pdf is created and opens in a PDF viewer.

4. Close the PDF viewer. | JT PDF.pptx is still open.

5. Click **File** > **Export** > **Create Handouts** > **Create Handouts**.

Do This	How & Why
	The Send to Microsoft window opens. 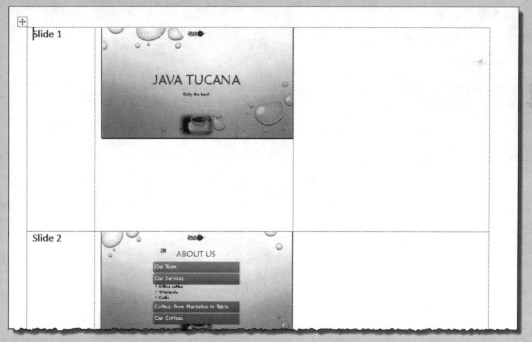

6. Keep the default options, and click **OK**.

After some processing, the handouts document is created and opened in Word. Blank space is provided to the right of each slide for the addition of notes.

Note: When creating handouts pages, many PowerPoint users prefer adding and editing their presentation notes in Word, rather than in PowerPoint. This is because PowerPoint's text-editing and -formatting features are severely limited. In Word, you have all the necessary editing and formatting tools at your disposal.

Do This	How & Why
7. Save the Word handouts document as `My JT Handouts.docx`, then exit Word.	
8. Close the PowerPoint presentation without saving it.	

Assessment: Saving a presentation in other formats

1. If you want to save a PowerPoint presentation in another format that preserves slide contents without allowing other users to edit it, which format could you use? Choose the best response.

   - OpenDocument Presentation
   - PowerPoint 97-2003 Presentation
   - Template
   - PowerPoint Picture Presentation

2. When saving a presentation in other formats, many of the same options are available in both the Save As window and Backstage view. True or false?

   - True
   - False

3. What's an excellent format to use for printing and distributing all presentation materials? Choose the best response.

   - PDF/XPS document
   - Portable network graphics
   - Word handouts
   - PowerPoint Show format

Summary: Reviewing content, tracking changes, and saving in other formats

In this chapter, you learned how to:

- Review content using the automatic spell checker, and check spelling manually; use proofing and AutoCorrect options; add and manage comments; track and review changes; and compare presentations
- Save and/or export presentations in various formats, including PDF/XPS documents and Word handouts; and create a video of a completed presentation, using narration and other presentation tools

Synthesis: Reviewing content, tracking changes, and saving in other formats

In this synthesis exercise, you'll proof a presentation; add, delete, and reply to comments; compare presentation versions; and save a presentation to run automatically as a slide show.

1. Open `JT Assessment Review.pptx`, and save it as `My JT Assessment Review.pptx`.
2. Use the Spelling tool to scan the document for spelling errors.
3. Display all markup in the presentation.
4. Review all the comments currently in the presentation, and reply to a few of them. Use the Revisions pane and/or the Comments pane, where applicable.
5. Delete any comments that you think are no longer necessary; keep any that should probably remain.
    For example, any comments directed to the presenter.
6. Add at least two or three comments to the presentation.
7. Hide the comments and markup.
8. Save your changes, then compare this presentation to `JT Assessment Original.pptx`.
9. Review the changes shown in the merged presentation. Accept necessary changes; reject any that seem unnecessary.
    For example, accept spelling corrections.
10. Advance through all the changes. Use the Accept tool where it might be more efficient to do so.
11. When you're finished reviewing changes, save the edited version as `Final Assessment Review.pptx`.
12. Close the Revisions and/or Comments panes, as necessary.
13. Use the current presentation to create a file that will automatically run as a slide show when opened.
    Remember to use the **Change File Type** command.
14. Test the new file to make sure it runs as a slide show.
15. Close the file, and close the presentation.

Chapter 10: Custom slide shows

You will learn how to:

- Work with notes pages and explore options for viewing them
- Configure and present custom slide shows

Module A: Working with notes pages

Notes are a powerful way to enhance your presentation and connect with your audience. In PowerPoint, there are a number of options for adding and working with notes.

You will learn how to:

- Work with notes pages and explore options for viewing them

About notes

Probably the worst kind of slide show is one in which a presenter merely reads the contents of each slide to the audience. Don't be that presenter! As you've learned, each slide in a presentation should contains salient points, along with any graphics, transitions, animations, and so on that serve to underscore those points. Any additional background information shouldn't appear on the slides. Instead, it should be provided to the presenter in the form of *notes*.

Whether you intend to present your slide show yourself or have created it for another presenter, the best way to ensure that additional relevant information is covered—and any potential audience questions are answered—is by creating notes pages. Of course, you should add notes only for those slides that require them. The notes can be as sketchy or detailed as you like, as only the presenter will be able to view them during the slide show.

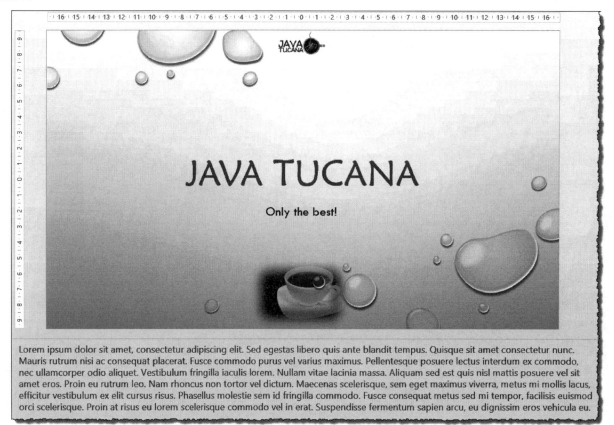

Adding notes to a slide

There are a number of ways to add notes to a slide. The most common method is to use the Notes pane in Normal view.

1. In Normal view, select the slide to which you wish to add notes.
2. Click **Notes**.

On the taskbar.

The Notes pane opens under the slide.

3. Click in the Notes pane, and type your notes.
   To place the insertion point.

4. To enlarge the Notes pane, drag the Notes pane border upward.
   This is particular helpful for viewing longer notes.

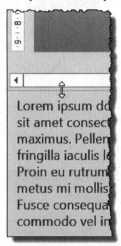

Notes Page view

Notes Page view is a handy way to display a slide and its corresponding notes together as a single page of information. To display Note Page view, in the View tab's Presentation Views group, click **Notes Page**.

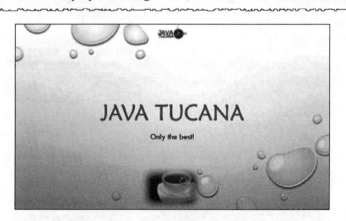

It's important to note that although you can enter, edit, and format text in Notes Page view, it's much easier to do so in Outline view. However, for quick edits in Notes Page view, you can always zoom in to enlarge the notes' display. Also, once you've made formatting changes, they're all displayed in Notes Page view.

 Note: Because PowerPoint's text- and paragraph-formatting options are rather paltry, we suggest creating Word handouts from your presentation. You can then use Word's far more powerful tools to format your notes as you see fit. This is especially useful for creating handouts for printing, when you want notes to look their best.

Notes Master view

 MOS PowerPoint Exam Objective(s): 1.3.6

You can change the appearance of your presentation notes in Notes Master view, which you access by clicking **Notes Master**, in the View tab's Master Views group.

In Notes Master view, the Notes Master tab is displayed, as well as a preview of a notes page and its layout.

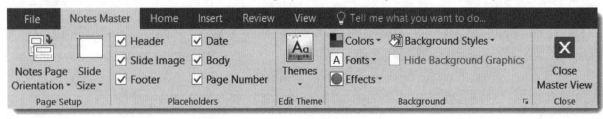

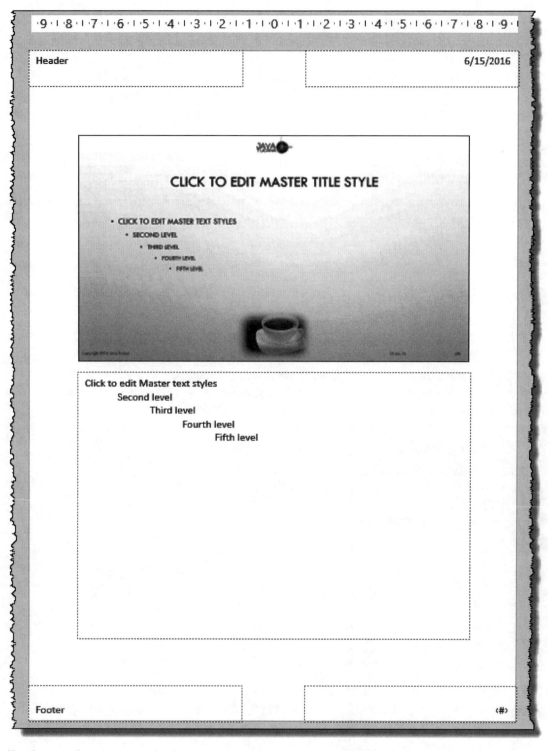

Like the Handout Master tab, there are several tool groups on the Notes Master tab that you can use to change the appearance and formatting of notes pages and their elements.

- *Page Setup*: Contains tools for changing page orientation, and the size of slides as they appear on the notes page.

- *Placeholders*: By default, header, slide image, footer, date, body, and page-number elements are displayed on notes pages. However, you can specify which of these elements you'd like displayed by checking or unchecking them.

- *Edit Theme*: The Themes tool allows you to apply the theme of your choice to your notes pages to give them their own distinctive look.
- *Background*: Use these tools to fine-tune the appearance of elements on your notes pages.

 Note: If you intend to apply a theme to your notes pages, it's a good idea to apply the desired theme first, then alter/fine-tune your design using the tools in the Background group.

When you're finished formatting your notes pages, as always, you can use the tools on the View tab or icons in the status bar to change views. Alternatively, if you wish to return to the previous view, you can instead click **Close Master View**.

Working with note text in Outline view

Although you can edit and format note text in the Notes pane or in Notes Page view, it's much easier to do so in Outline view. Changes in text format likewise display in Normal view.

1. Display Outline view.

In Outline view, the slide's Notes pane is larger and thus easier to work with.

2. In the thumbnails, right-click the slide you wish to edit and/or format, and click.

To display text formatting of notes (and slide titles). This selection is a toggle; clicking it a second time turns off the display of formatting.

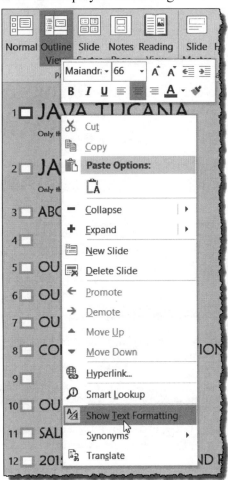

3. Edit and/or format the text, as necessary.
    Use the standard formatting tools on the Home tab.

   Lorem ipsum dolor sit amet, consectetur adipiscing elit.
   Sed egestas libero quis ante blandit tempus. Quisque sit amet consectetur nunc. Mauris rutrum nisi ac consequat placerat. Fusce commodo purus vel varius maximus. Pellentesque posuere lectus interdum ex commodo, nec ullamcorper odio aliquet. Vestibulum fringilla iaculis lorem. *Nullam vitae lacinia massa.* Aliquam sed est quis nisl mattis posuere vel sit amet eros. Proin eu rutrum leo. Nam rhoncus non tortor

    Note: Certain types of formatting, such as bold and italic text, are displayed without turning on Show Text Formatting. However, formatting such as changes in font size or text color displays only with Show Text Formatting enabled.

4. Return to Normal view.
    Enlarge the Notes pane, if necessary. The same types of formatting changes that display in Outline view (with Show Text Formatting enabled) are also displayed in Normal view.

Adding an extra notes page

There might be times when the notes you wish to add to a slide are lengthier than the notes area provided for the slide. Fortunately, you can add an additional page for notes. Unfortunately, PowerPoint doesn't provide an easy method for doing so. However, there is an adequate—albeit lengthy—workaround for adding a notes page.

1. Duplicate the slide you want to create an additional notes page for.
    In Normal view, right-click the slide you wish to duplicate, and click **Duplicate Slide**; or press **Ctrl+D**.

   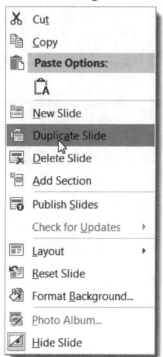

   The duplicate slide is inserted below the original.
2. Display Notes Page view.
    Click **Notes Page** on the View tab.

3. At the top of the duplicate slide, delete the slide object.

   a) Click the slide object to select it.

   b) Press **Delete**.

4. Enlarge the notes object.

   a) Click the notes object to select it.

   b) Drag the top-center handle upward to fill the page with the notes object.

5. Replace the text with the additional notes text.

   To continue the text that's already on the original slide. As a reminder to the presenter, it can be helpful to add a short heading such as "Slide 1 notes continued," for example.

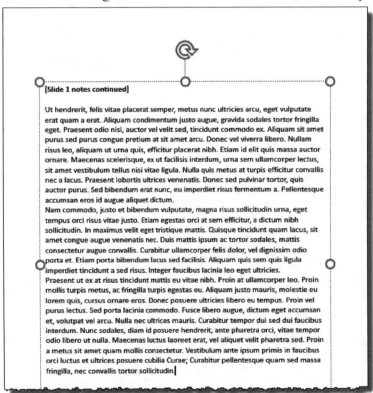

6. Display Normal view.

7. Right-click the duplicate slide, and click **Hide Slide**.

   In the Slides pane thumbnails.

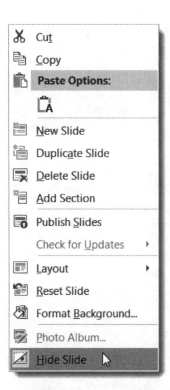

The duplicate slide won't be visible in the slide show; however, its notes will remain visible to the presenter. The slide's number is struck through in the thumbnails.

Printing notes pages

 MOS PowerPoint Exam Objective(s): 1.6.2

Print notes pages from PowerPoint's Print Options.

1. Display Print Options.
   Click **File > Print**.

2. Under Settings, check to make sure that the **Print Hidden Slides** option is checked.

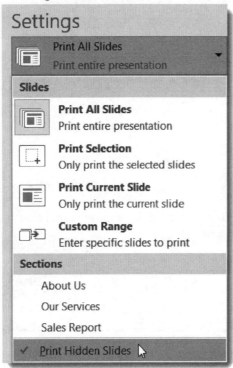

3. Below Slides, display the first set of options, and click **Notes Pages**.
   Among the options displayed are those for displaying slide thumbnails along with their notes.

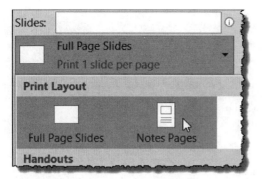

4. Click **Print**.

Exercise: Working with notes pages

You'll add and work with slide notes pages.

Do This	How & Why
1. Open `JT Notes.pptx`, and save it as `My JT Notes.pptx`.	
2. Display the Notes pane, and observe the notes for slides 1 and 2.	Click ≜ Notes in the taskbar. The notes contain some formatted text. Slide 2's notes continue from slide 1, and slide 2 is hidden from the slide show.
3. View the slides in Notes Page view.	
4. Open `JT Notes Text.docx`.	This is a Word file that contains text that you'll add to a slide.
5. Select and copy all the text in the Word document.	Press **Ctrl+A** to select the text, then press **Ctrl+C** to copy.
6. Switch to the PowerPoint window, and scroll to view the notes page for slide 3 ("About Us").	
7. Paste the text into the slide's notes object. a) Click in the notes object to place the insertion point.	The text is pasted into the notes object, but it doesn't all fit and thus spills below it.

Do This	How & Why
b) Press **Ctrl+V** to paste the text.	
8. In the notes object, select all the text below the first paragraph, and then press **Ctrl+X**.	To "cut" the text and save it to the Clipboard.
9. In Normal view, duplicate slide 3.	Right-click slide 3, and click **Duplicate Slide** in the context menu.
10. Select slide 4.	The new duplicate.
11. Delete the slide object.	Click to select it, and press **Delete**.
12. Enlarge the notes object to fill the page.	Drag the top-center handle upward. Leave a top margin that roughly matches those of the sides and bottom.
13. Replace the existing text in the notes object with the text you cut in step 8. a) Select or delete the existing text. b) Press **Ctrl+V**.	The additional text easily fits in the notes object box.
14. In Outline view, set the display to **Show Text Formatting**. a) Display Outline view.	Outline View

Do This	How & Why
b) Right-click a slide in the thumbnail, and click **Show Text Formatting**.	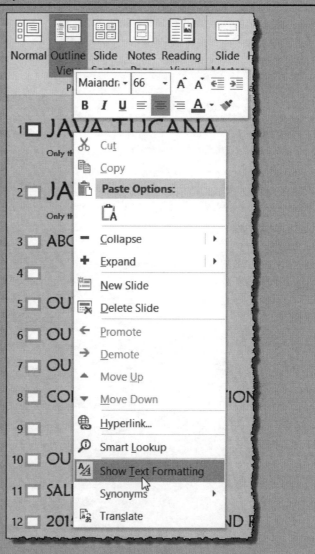
15. Format some of the notes text on slides 3 and 4 as you see fit.	
16. Return to Normal view, and observe the results of your formatting of notes text.	The formatting is displayed in the notes pane. You still need to hide slide 4; otherwise, it will be repeated during the slide show.

Do This	How & Why
17. Hide slide 4 from the slide show.	Right-click slide 4, and click **Hide Slide** in the context menu.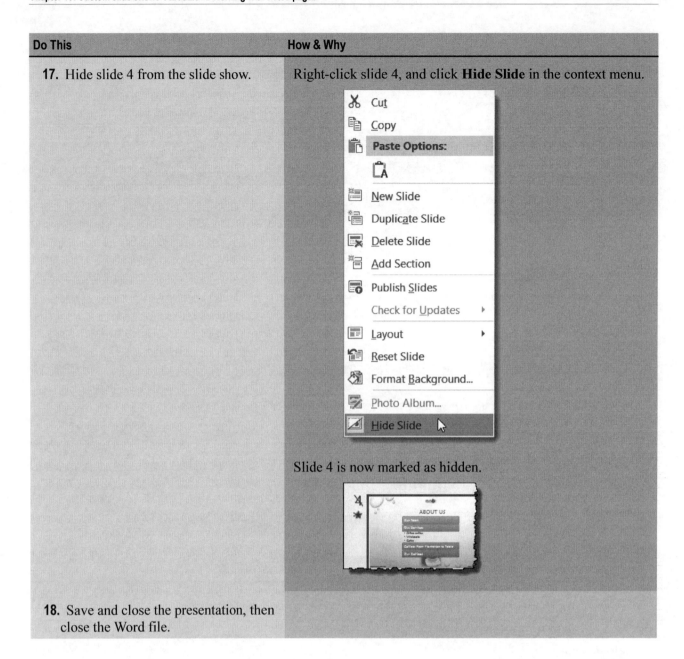Slide 4 is now marked as hidden.
18. Save and close the presentation, then close the Word file.	

Assessment: Working with notes pages

1. You can add slide notes in Normal view, Notes Page view, and Outline view. True or false?

    - True
    - False

2. Which of these statements about working in Normal view is *not* true? Choose the best response.

    - The Notes area can be viewed or hidden.
    - You can enlarge the Notes area to view longer notes.
    - Double-clicking the Notes area border displays the complete notes for that slide.
    - You can place your insertion point in the Notes area and type, or you can paste text there from other sources.

3. Unfortunately, Note Page view doesn't display any formatting of notes text. True or false?

    - True
    - False

4. Which command do you use to create the actual placeholder for an extra notes page? Choose the best response.

    - Duplicate Slide
    - Hide Slide
    - Show Text Formatting
    - Add Notes Page

Module B: Configuring, rehearsing, and presenting slide shows

You will learn how to:

- Configure, rehearse, and present custom slide shows

Presenter view

As your presentation nears completion, you'll want to try running it to make sure that the final product is as you envisioned it. PowerPoint's Presenter view is a powerful tool for testing your slide show, as well as ultimately presenting it to an audience.

MOS PowerPoint Exam Objective(s): 1.7.1, 1.7.2, 1.7.4

Presenter view is intended to run on two monitors, which is how PowerPoint slide shows are typically presented. The presenter's computer, typically a laptop, runs in Presenter view, which shows a dashboard containing panes showing the current and next slide, and all the controls necessary for running the slide show. The audience sees only the finished slide show—without all the notes and controls—on a main monitor, which is connected to the presenter's computer, typically via an HDMI, DVI, or serial cable. The presenter can thus view all notes privately.

Keep in mind that if your slide show contains sound, you'll need to make sure it can be heard. Sound is automatically carried via HDMI connections to the presentation monitor, by which it can be controlled. Other types of connections might require you to run the sound separately through amplified speakers of a public address system.

By default, once you've connected the second monitor, and click (**Slide Show**), Presenter view automatically runs on your computer's monitor. The main slide show runs on the second monitor, which the audience sees. You can also test-run your slide show in Presenter view without having a second monitor connected by pressing **Alt+F5**.

Presenter view contains two main panes: the left pane shows the current slide; the right pane displays the notes for the current slide, as well as a thumbnail of the next slide. A timer is displayed above the current slide, which runs continuously once you've started the presentation. To the right of the timer are ▮▮ and ↻ icons, which pause and restart the timer, respectively. At the bottom of the Presenter view dashboard, the navigation section shows the current slide number, as well as the total number of slides in the presentation. Here, you can also use the Back and Forward buttons to navigate during the slide show.

Presenter view also contains other useful controls for working with and closing the presentation.

Presenter view controls

Control	Description
	Displays the Windows taskbar, allowing you to switch applications during the presentation.
	Use the Display Settings options to swap monitors for Presenter view and the slide show. This isn't something you'd normally do when presenting to an audience. It's provided as a tool for test-running your slide shows.
	One way of ending the slide show.
	Closes Presenter view and ends the slide show.
	Use the pen or laser pointer to draw your audience's attention to information on a slide. The pen lets you draw on slides.
	Use this tool to view all the slides in your presentation, in a kind of slide-sorter view. This allows you to easily select another one for viewing at any time during the presentation.
	Click the zoom tool to select a portion of the current slide to magnify it for the audience.

Control	Description
Black or unblack slide show	Renders the slide show temporarily black. Clicking it again re-displays it. This tool can be helpful when you want to focus the audience's attention on the presenter, or for dramatic effect before presenting the next slide.
More slide show options	Brings together many of the same functions offered by other Presenter-view controls, as well as one that lets you temporarily hide Presenter view.

Mouse and keyboard slide-show controls

 MOS PowerPoint Exam Objective(s): 1.7.4

While playing a slide show in PowerPoint, there are some helpful mouse and keyboard shortcuts you can use for navigation, presentation control, and emphasis. Some of these might already be familiar to you, while others are specific to Presenter view. These lists are by no means exhaustive; they merely provide some more commonly used actions.

Presenter view mouse techniques

Desired result	Action
Advance to the next slide.	Click.
Display a context menu.	Right-click.
Advance through the slides.	Roll the mouse wheel, if available.
Display the first slide.	Press and hold both mouse buttons for two seconds.
Use the laser pointer.	Press and hold **Ctrl+click** while moving the mouse around the slide. Letting go of either key returns the mouse pointer to its normal function.
Draw on a slide.	Press **Ctrl+P** to change the mouse pointer to a pen. Then draw on the slide. When finished drawing, press **Ctrl+A** (or **Esc**) to return the mouse pointer to its normal function.

Presenter view keyboard shortcuts

Desired Result	Action
Advance to the next slide.	**Enter / Spacebar / PgDn / P**
Return to the preceding slide.	**Backspace / PgUp / P**
Display a specific slide.	**[slide number], Enter** (for example, **1** then **Enter** displays slide 1)
Show/hide the pointer.	**A / =**
Change the mouse pointer to a pen.	**Ctrl+P**
Return the pen to a mouse pointer.	**Ctrl+A / Esc**
Erase slide drawing(s).	**E**
End the slide show.	**Esc**

Rehearsing slide timings

 MOS PowerPoint Exam Objective(s): 1.7.3

PowerPoint's has a special tool for rehearsing the timing of the slides in your presentation.

1. On the Slide Show tab, click **Rehearse Timings**.
   In the Set Up group.

   The slide show runs in full-screen mode, and the Recording window opens. It records the elapsed time of each slide and the overall presentation as you run through it. The current-slide timer appears in the white box. The presentation timer is in the gray box. Use the buttons on either side of the current-slide timer to pause or restart the timer.

   Note: When you restart the timer, it restarts the entire presentation, not the current slide.

2. Run through your presentation, advancing slides as you would for an audience.
   After a few seconds of display, the Recording window disappears. Whenever you wish to re-display it, click near the upper-left corner of the screen.

   When you're finished with the presentation, you're prompted whether to save the rehearsal timings.

3. Click **Yes** to save the rehearsal timings, or **No** to discard them.
   Saving your timings can be valuable for comparison, particularly in cases where the live presentation will have a strict time limit imposed on it.

Chapter 10: Custom slide shows / Module B: Configuring, rehearsing, and presenting slide shows

Exercise: Exploring Presenter view and Rehearsal mode

In this exercise, you'll explore Presenter view and PowerPoint's Rehearsal mode.

Do This	How & Why
1. Open `JT Rehearse Timings.pptx`.	
2. Run the slide show in Presenter view. • If you have access and your computer is connected to a second monitor, click ▭ (**Slide Show**) to run the slide show on the second monitor and Presenter view on your computer. • If you don't have an external monitor connected to your computer, press **Alt+F5** to run Presenter view on your computer.	
3. Use the various controls available in Presenter view for navigating slides, viewing notes, and so on.	Use the various dashboard controls, as well as any mouse techniques and keyboard shortcuts you'd like. Be sure to try the pen and laser-pointer tools on slides.
4. Advance through all the slides in the presentation.	
5. When you're finished, end the slide show and close Presentation view.	Use the **End Slide Show** button or the **Close** button.
6. From the Slide Show tab, rehearse the slide show's timings.	In the Set Up group, click **Rehearse Timings**. The slide show runs in full-screen Rehearsal mode, and the Recording window opens. Because you're not actually giving this presentation—least of all in Latin!—just pretend to go through the slide show, clicking to advance through all the transitions, animations, and effects.
7. Try using the **Pause** and **Restart** buttons, and observe the effects of doing so.	They pause the timer and restart the timer (and slide show), respectively.
8. At the end of the slide show, when prompted to save the recorded timings, click **No** to discard them.	
9. Close the presentation without saving any changes.	

The Custom Shows feature

PowerPoint Custom Shows feature allows you to create any number of slide shows from a single presentation. For example, a presentation might contain all the information there is to know about a company, what it does, how it functions, its employees, and so on. But presenting all that information in a single slide show might not be appropriate for every audience.

Custom Shows lets you create a unique slide show geared toward one particular audience that's a subset of the slides in the entire presentation. Thus, you needn't create new presentation files for each slide show that uses slides that are already part of the original presentation. Particularly for large presentation files, this can save valuable disk space, file-transfer time, and so on.

Creating a custom slide show

MOS PowerPoint Exam Objective(s): 1.7.1, 1.7.2

You create custom slide shows in the Define Custom Show window.

1. Open the presentation you wish to use to create your custom slide show.
2. On the Slide Show tab, click **Custom Slide Show > Custom Shows**.
   In the Start Slide Show group.

   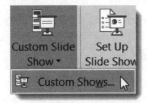

   The Custom Shows window opens. Until you create a custom show, the window is blank.
3. Click **New**.
   The Define Custom Show window opens. Here, you name and select slides for your custom slide show.

   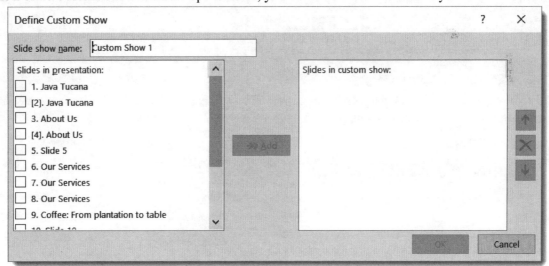

4. Type a name in the "Slide show name" box.
5. Select the slides you want to include in the custom show.
   Under "Slides in presentation."
   Any hidden slides are listed with their numbers shown in brackets. Hidden slides that are selected remain hidden, but their contented is copied to the custom slide show. If these slides serve as extra notes pages, remember to include these, as necessary.

6. Click **Add** to include the selected slides in your custom show.

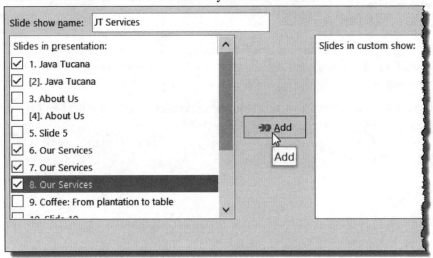

The slides are added to the "Slides in custom show" list. You can use the buttons at right to reorder or delete a selected slide. Doing so only affects the custom slide show, not the "parent" presentation.

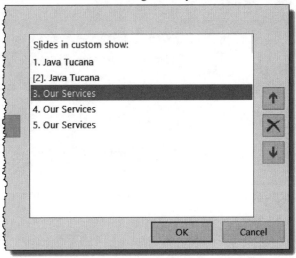

7. When you're finished, click **OK**.

The new slide show is added to the list of custom shows. Once you've created a custom slide show, you can use the buttons at right to edit, remove, or copy it.

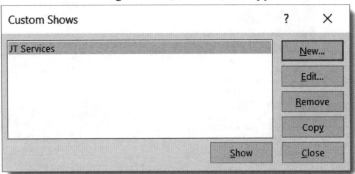

Presenting a custom slide show

 MOS PowerPoint Exam Objective(s): 1.7.4

You can present custom slide shows from Custom Slide Show options or the Custom Shows window.

1. Open the presentation on which your custom slide show is based.
2. Click **Custom Slide Show**, and click the name of the custom show you wish to run.
3. To run your custom show from the Custom Shows window, click **Custom Slide Show** > **Custom Shows**. On the Slide Show tab.

    The Custom Shows window opens.
4. Select the custom slide show you wish to run, then click **Show**.

    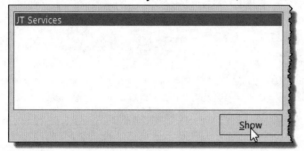

5. When you're finished running your slide show, click to exit and return to the presentation.

Exercise: Exploring the Custom Shows feature

You'll create and run a custom slide show.

Do This	How & Why
1. Open `JT Custom Slide Show.pptx`, and save it as `My JT Custom Slide Show.pptx`.	
2. On the Slide Show tab, click **Custom Slide Show > Custom Shows**.	In the Start Slide Show group. 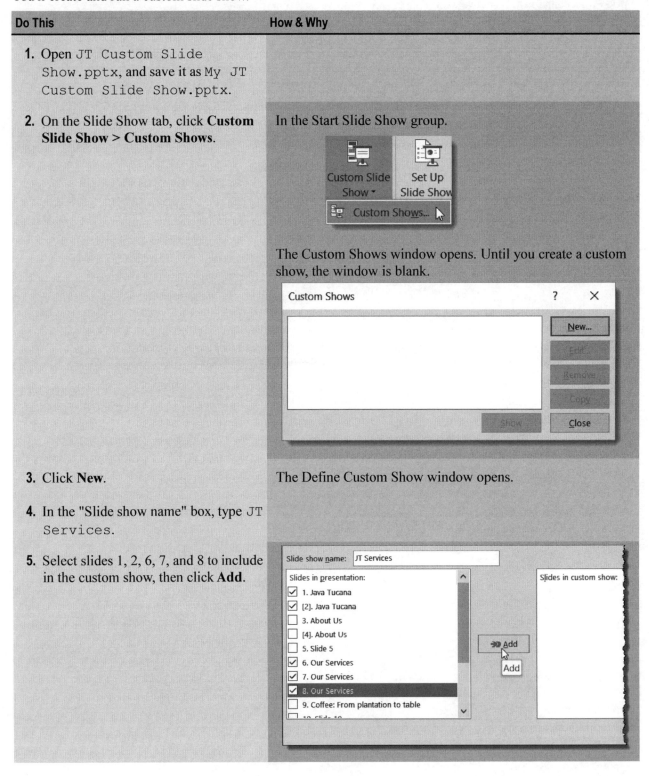 The Custom Shows window opens. Until you create a custom show, the window is blank.
3. Click **New**.	The Define Custom Show window opens.
4. In the "Slide show name" box, type `JT Services`.	
5. Select slides 1, 2, 6, 7, and 8 to include in the custom show, then click **Add**.	

Do This	How & Why
6. Click **OK** to finish creating the custom show.	The new show appears in the list of custom shows. 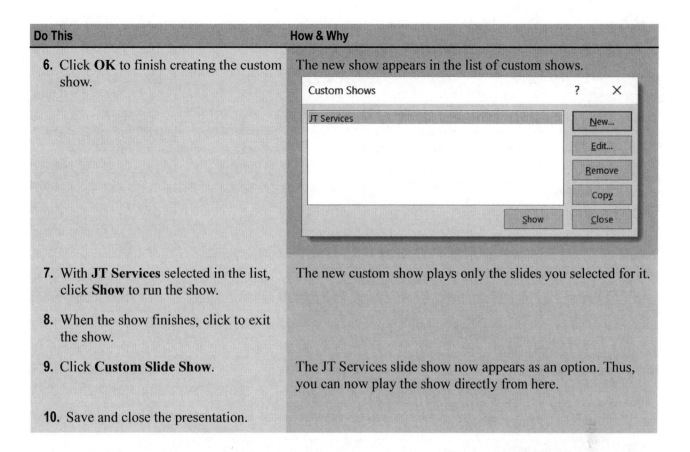
7. With **JT Services** selected in the list, click **Show** to run the show.	The new custom show plays only the slides you selected for it.
8. When the show finishes, click to exit the show.	
9. Click **Custom Slide Show**.	The JT Services slide show now appears as an option. Thus, you can now play the show directly from here.
10. Save and close the presentation.	

Assessment: Configuring, rehearsing, and presenting slide shows

1. In Presenter view, you must use keyboard shortcuts to navigate your presentation, as the mouse pointer is rendered unavailable. True or false?

    - True
    - False

2. Which of the following statements is true? Choose the best response.

    - The Rehearse Timings feature is useful for getting a sense of how long it takes to show individual slides, but not the duration of the entire presentation.
    - The Rehearse Timings feature displays slides, notes, and graphics, but it doesn't show transitions or animation.
    - Presenter view can be displayed on one monitor or multiple monitors.
    - The primary purpose of Presenter view is to display all presentation components to the audience.

3. Once you've created a custom slide show, it must be shown from the Custom Shows window. True or false?

    - True
    - False

Summary: Custom slide shows

In this chapter, you learned how to:

- Create, work with, and print notes pages, and explore options for viewing them
- Work with Presenter view on single and multiple monitors, and explore additional mouse and keyboard control options; use Rehearsal mode to rehearse slide and presentation timings; and create and present custom slide shows

Synthesis: Custom slide shows

In this synthesis exercise, you'll work in Presenter view, work with notes pages, and create a present a custom slide show.

1. Open `Synthesis - JT Custom.pptx`, and save it as `My Synthesis - JT Custom.pptx`.
2. View the slides in Notes Page view.
3. Observe the slides in the presentation.
   This presentation already contains many notes. However, you'll be adding notes to slide 12.
4. Open `Synthesis - JT Slide 12 Notes.docx`.
   You'll copy the notes from this file to slide 12.
5. Copy all the text in this Word document.
6. In Normal view, paste the notes onto slide 12.
   There's more text here than can fit in the notes object.
7. Duplicate slide 12.
8. On the new slide 13, delete the slide object, and enlarge the notes object to fill the page.
9. Leave the first paragraph of notes on slide 12, but move the remaining three paragraphs from slide 12 onto slide 13.
10. In Outline view, display all text formatting, then format the notes text on slides 12 and 13.
    a) Place the first sentence of each notes paragraph on its own line to form a heading.
    b) Make each heading bold, and increase its font size to **14**.
11. Make sure that slide 13 won't be visible in the slide show.
12. In Normal view, observe slides 12 and 13, including their notes.
13. Run the slide show in Presenter view.
    - If you have access and your computer is connected to a second monitor, run the slide show on the second monitor and Presenter view on your computer.
    - If you don't have an external monitor connected to your computer, run Presenter view solely on your computer.
14. Use the various controls available in Presenter view for navigating slides, viewing notes, and so on, including the pen and laser-pointer tools.
15. When you're finished, end the slide show and close the presentation.
16. Rehearse the presentation's timings, also using the pause and restart functions.
17. At the end of the slide show, don't save the recorded timings.
18. Use this presentation to create a custom slide show.
    a) Name it `JT Sales`.   (Continued...)

b) Include slides 1, 2, 5 through 8, and 12 through 16.
19. Run the slide show directly from the Custom Slide Show options.
20. Save and close the presentation.
21. Exit Word without saving the document.

Chapter 11: Sharing, collaborating, and security

You will learn how to:

- Protect your presentations
- Share your presentations

Module A: Protecting your presentations

Being able to share your presentations with others is wonderful. But before you do so, it's a good idea to think about whether you want to give the recipient(s) full editorial access or restrict how the file is used and what's visible.

You will learn how to:

- Protect and limit access to your presentations

The Info window

Clicking **File** opens the Info window, which provides important tools for protecting your presentations.

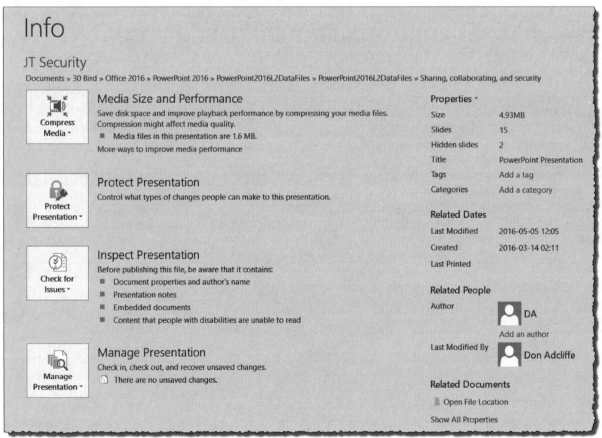

MOS PowerPoint Exam Objective(s): 5.2.1

These tools are located as Protect Presentation options.

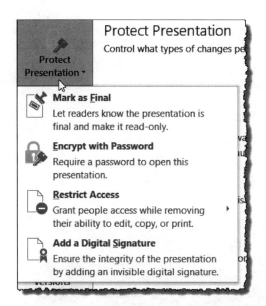

- *Mark as Final*: Renders the presentation "read-only," which means that recipients can't alter its contents. This effectively marks it as "final," although this setting is reversible.
- *Encrypt with Password*: Sets a password that's then required to open the file.
- *Restrict Access*: If your computer is set up for Information Rights Management (IRM), you can use this option to allow viewing of the file. However, viewers can't edit, copy, or print its contents.
- *Add a Digital Signature*: If you have a registered digital signature, you can use this option to add it to the file.

Making a presentation "read-only"

You can make a presentation file "read-only," which means that others can view the file but not alter its contents.

 MOS PowerPoint Exam Objective(s): 5.2.1

1. With the presentation open, click **File**.
   To open the Info window in Backstage view.
2. Click **Protect Presentation**, and click **Mark as Final**.

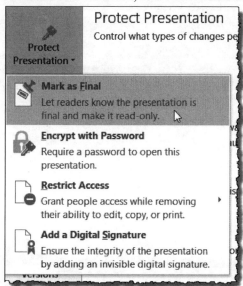

A message window opens.

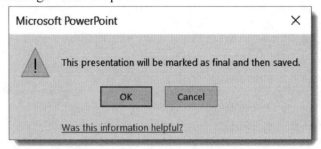

3. Click **OK**.

   A banner appears near the top of the window, indicating that the presentation has been marked as final. On the taskbar, the Marked as Final icon appears. In this state, the file can't be edited.

   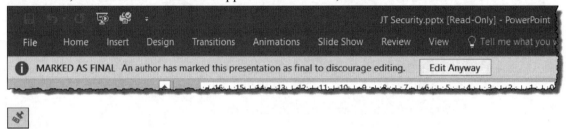

   Note: To remove the file's read-only status, click **Edit Anyway** in the banner. If the banner isn't visible, click **File**, and click **Protect Presentation > Mark as Final** again to toggle off read-only mode.

Protecting a presentation with a password

You can password-protect your presentations, so that only those who know the correct password have access to them.

MOS PowerPoint Exam Objective(s): 5.2.1

1. With the presentation open, open Backstage view.
   Click **File**.

2. In the Info window, click **Protect Presentation > Encrypt with Password**.

   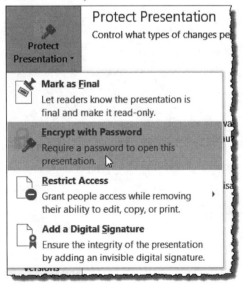

The Encrypt Document window opens.

3. Type a password.

As the information below the Password box states, passwords are case-sensitive. If you forget or lose your password, it can't be recovered. So store it in a separate, safe place.

As you type, the actual characters aren't shown, so choose and type it carefully!

4. Click **OK**.

The Confirm Password window opens, prompting you to re-enter your password.

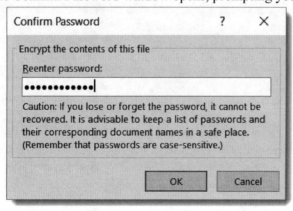

5. Re-type the password, and click **OK**.

In the Info window, you're informed that a password is now required to open the presentation.

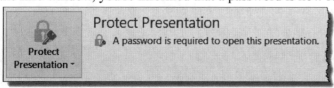

6. Save the file.

    Password protection isn't fully applied until you save the file. If you try to close the file before you've saved it, you're prompted to save it. Click **OK** to do so.

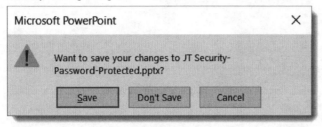

File properties

 MOS PowerPoint Exam Objective(s): 1.5.3, 5.2.2

If you wish to hide (or provide) information about a presentation file, you can do so in the Info window, under Properties. A partial list of properties is displayed by default. To display all properties, click **Show All Properties**.

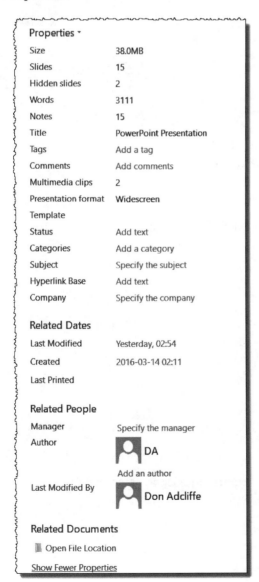

Beginning at the Title field, many of the properties fields can be altered, in case you wish to hide (or specify) certain information from other users of the file. To do so, click in the field, and type the information as desired.

To reduce the number of fields to the default settings, click **Show Fewer Properties**.

Exercise: Protecting your presentation

You'll make a presentation read-only, then you'll password-protect it.

Do This	How & Why
1. Open `JT Security.pptx`, and save it as `JT Security - Read-Only.pptx`.	
2. Open Backstage view.	The Info window is open.
3. Click **Protect Presentation**, and click **Mark as Final**.	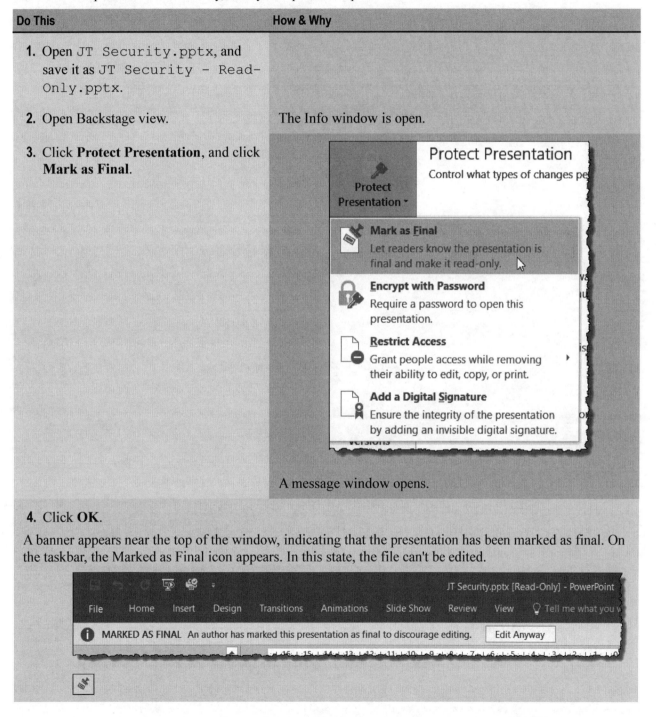
	A message window opens.

4. Click **OK**.

A banner appears near the top of the window, indicating that the presentation has been marked as final. On the taskbar, the Marked as Final icon appears. In this state, the file can't be edited.

Do This	How & Why
5. Open Backstage view.	In the Info window, the Protect Presentation feature states that the presentation is now marked as final.
6. Save and close the presentation.	
7. Open `JT Security.pptx` again, but this time save it as `JT Security - Password-Protected.pptx`.	
8. Click **Protect Presentation** > **Encrypt with Password**.	The Encrypt Document window opens.
9. Type a password, then click **OK**.	You're prompted to retype the password to confirm it.

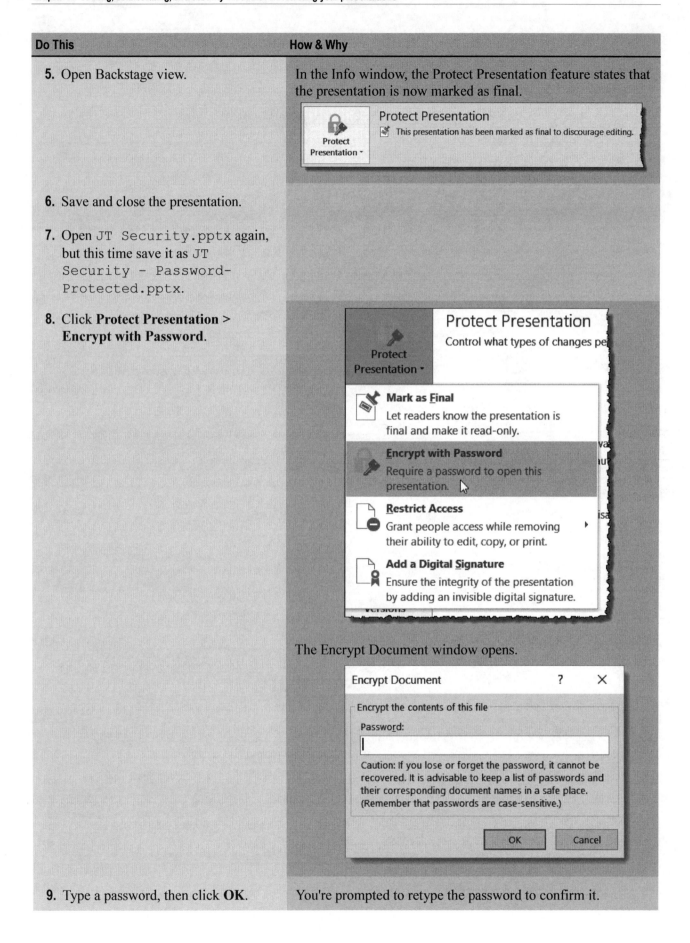

Do This	How & Why
10. Retype the password, then click **OK**.	In the Info window, you're informed that a password is now required to open the presentation. 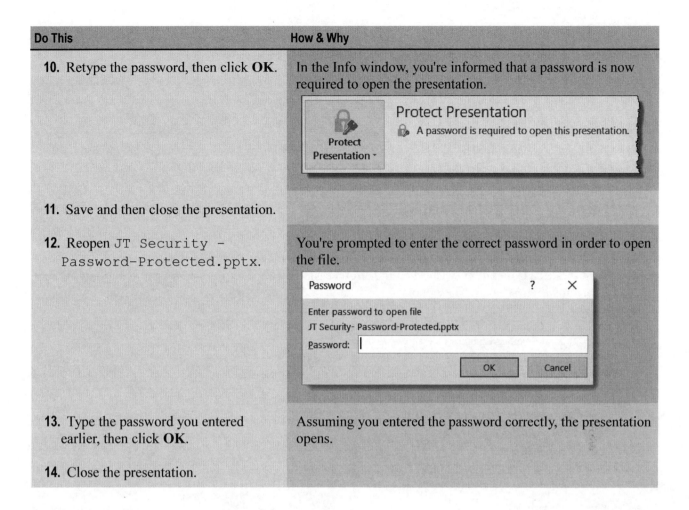
11. Save and then close the presentation.	
12. Reopen `JT Security - Password-Protected.pptx`.	You're prompted to enter the correct password in order to open the file.
13. Type the password you entered earlier, then click **OK**.	Assuming you entered the password correctly, the presentation opens.
14. Close the presentation.	

Assessment: Protecting your presentation

1. Which of the following statements about marking a presentation as final is correct? Choose the best response.

   - Clicking Mark as Final opens the Info window.
   - Mark as Final restricts editorial access to the file.
   - Once you're marked a presentation as final, it can never be edited.
   - Once marked as final, a presentation can only be edited after the correct password is entered.

2. Clicking Edit Anyway turns off read-only mode, allowing full editorial access to the presentation.

   - True
   - False

3. Which of the following statements about password-protecting a presentation is true? Choose the best response.

   - The Encrypt Document window is your one chance to create a password, so you'd better get it right!
   - If you forget a password you've created, you can have Microsoft send you a Reset Password email.
   - Fortunately, passwords are not case-sensitive.
   - When a user attempts to open a password-protected presentation, she must enter the correct password in the Password window.

Module B: Sharing your presentations

There are many powerful ways to share your PowerPoint presentations with others, whether for collaboration or simply for viewing.

You will learn how to:

- Check the compatibility and accessibility of your presentation, and use various tools to share it with others

Compatibility and accessibility

Before you share your presentations with others—and decide how you want to share it—it's important to ensure that it's both compatible with the intended medium/system and accessible to intended users. PowerPoint provides a Compatibility Checker and an Accessibility Checker for finding and repairing potential problems in these areas. These tools are available in the Info window as Check for Issues options.

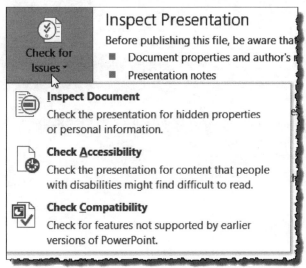

Checking compatibility

 MOS PowerPoint Exam Objective(s): 5.2.2

The Compatibility Checker helps you to troubleshoot and repair potential compatibility problems in your presentations. Found issues pertain primarily to compatibility with earlier versions of PowerPoint.

Important issues to consider when deciding to share your presentation for use with these earlier versions include the playability of transition, animation, and other effects, many of which can only run in PowerPoint 2013 (and later). If you want to that these effects will function in different user environments, we recommend you save your presentation in a more universal format, such as a video.

 MOS PowerPoint Exam Objective(s): 5.3.9

1. With the presentation open, display Backstage view.
2. In the Info window, click **Check for Issues > Check Compatibility**.

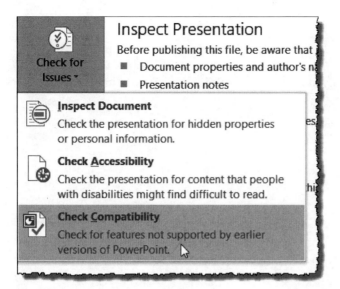

After several seconds, the results of the check are displayed in the Microsoft PowerPoint Compatibility Checker window.

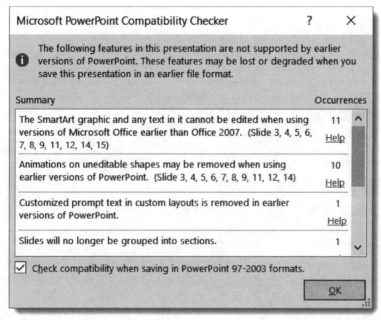

3. If necessary, scroll to view all compatibility issues, and click the **Help** link for detailed information about the problem.

   Each item summarizes the problem and gives its number of occurrences. Whether or not you should address any given problem depends on how intended users will access your presentation. For example, with the **Check compatibility when saving in PowerPoint 97-2003 formats** option checked, any potential issues related to those earlier formats are listed. If your intended users will use those earlier versions of PowerPoint to view your presentation, you'll need to address these issues. If they'll use the latest version of PowerPoint, then you can ignore these issues.

4. When you're finished reviewing the issues found, click **OK**.

   To close the Compatibility Checker.

5. Save any changes.

The Accessibility Checker

PowerPoint's Accessibility Checker helps you find and repair potential accessibility problems in your presentations. When you run this checker, the results are display in the Accessibility Checker pane. Checking accessibility is particularly important for intended users with disabilities such as sight or hearing issues.

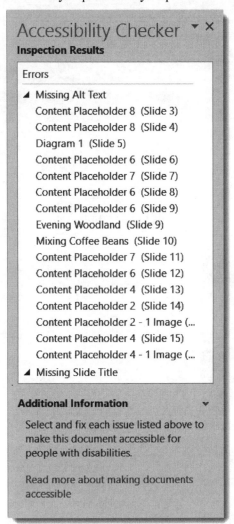

Each potential issue found is labeled as an Error, and Warning, or a Tip.

- *Error*: Contents that might be unviewable, unreadable, or unintelligible to people with disabilities.
- *Warning*: Contents that might be difficult for people with disabilities to understand.
- *Tip*: A suggestion for improving the accessibility of an item to people with disabilities.

Checking accessibility

The Accessibility Checker helps you to troubleshoot and repair potential accessibility problems in your presentations.

 MOS PowerPoint Exam Objective(s): 5.2.2

1. With the presentation open, display Backstage view.
2. In the Info window, click **Check for Issues > Check Accessibility**.

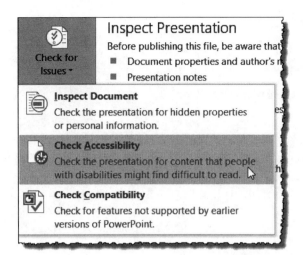

After a few seconds, the Accessibility Checker pane opens, listing potential accessibility errors and/or warnings, and tips for addressing them.

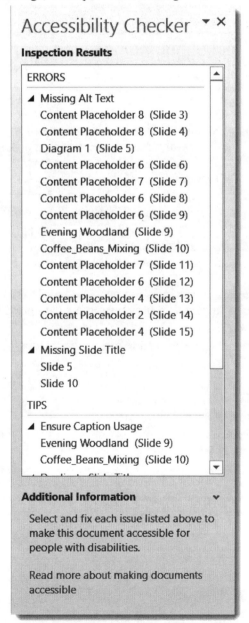

3. For help in fixing a specific issue, click it in the list.

   To select the item and display information about why and how to fix it.

4. Scroll in the pane to read the Why Fix and How To Fix information.

5. Address and fix each item, as necessary.

6. When you're done, close the Accessibility Checker pane.

   Note: Some solutions to accessibility issues might require some creativity in how you apply your PowerPoint skills. For example, to add Alt Text (alternative text) to an object, the tip might instruct you to right-click a slide object, then click Layout & Properties, then fix the issue from that pane. But for some objects, you might instead have to choose **Size & Position** from the context menu (to open the Format Shape pane), and then continue from there as described.

   Note: For additional information about presentation accessibility, click the **Read more about making documents accessible** link in the Accessibility Checker pane.

7. Save the file.

Compressing media

MOS PowerPoint Exam Objective(s): 5.2.4

Another factor to consider before you share your presentation with others is whether any media files it contains should be compressed. Doing so can often improve media playability and save valuable disk space.

Note: Before compressing the media in your presentation, it's important to consider which type—if any—is appropriate for its contents and its intended audience. If you've added media purely for emphasis or to grab attention, you might choose to apply a greater amount of compression. However, if the media are central to your topic and your audience, you might want to preserve media quality and thus apply little or no compression. For example, if you're a graphic designer and the point of your presentation is to highlight key aspects of your design, you might choose not to compress the media, so as to preserve their resolution for maximum impact.

1. With the presentation open, in Backstage view, observe the media summary next to the Compress Media tool.

   PowerPoint display information specific to the current presentation as it relates to any media it contains.

   ### Media Size and Performance
   Save disk space and improve playback performance by compressing your media files. Compression might affect media quality.
   - Media files in this presentation are 34 MB.
   - 2 media file(s) contain trimmed regions.

   More ways to improve media performance

2. Click **Compress Media**.

   In the Info window.

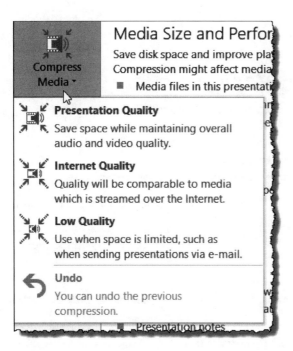

3. Select the desired media compression option.

   - To apply minimal compression but preserve overall media quality, click **Presentation Quality**.
   - To apply a degree of compression compatible with most video streaming scenarios, click **Internet Quality**.
   - To apply as much compression as possible, click **Low Quality**. Depending on the size of the original media file, this could be the best choice for sending the presentations as an email attachment.

   The Compress Media window opens, and the media files are compressed. After compression, the results are displayed. The initial and post-compression sizes of each item are displayed. Near the bottom of the window, the total reduction of file size is displayed.

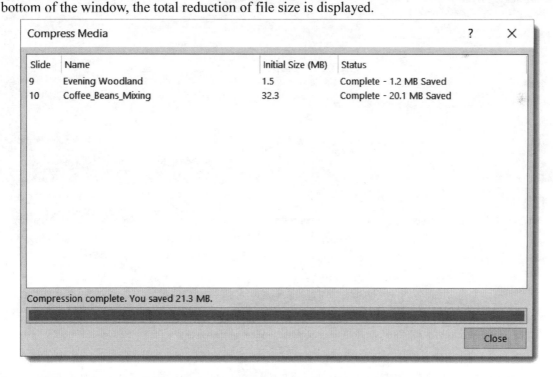

4. Click **Close**, then observe the updated Media Size and Performance summary.

Media Size and Performance
Save disk space and improve playback performance by compressing your media files. Compression might affect media quality.
- Media files in this presentation are 13 MB.
- You compressed this presentation's media to Internet Quality. Run slide show to preview results.
- Undo the compression if the results are unsatisfactory.

More ways to improve media performance

For additional compression information, click the **More ways to improve media performance** link.

5. Run the slide show to view the results of compression.
    Keep in mind that if the results of compression are unsatisfactory, you can always undo the compression.

6. To save the results of compression, save the file.

Exercise: Exploring compatibility and accessibility options

You'll run compatibility and accessibility check on a presentation, then apply media compression to it.

Do This	How & Why
1. Open `JT Prepare to Share.pptx`, and save it as `My JT Prepare to Share.pptx`.	
2. In the Info window, click **Check for Issues > Check Compatibility**.	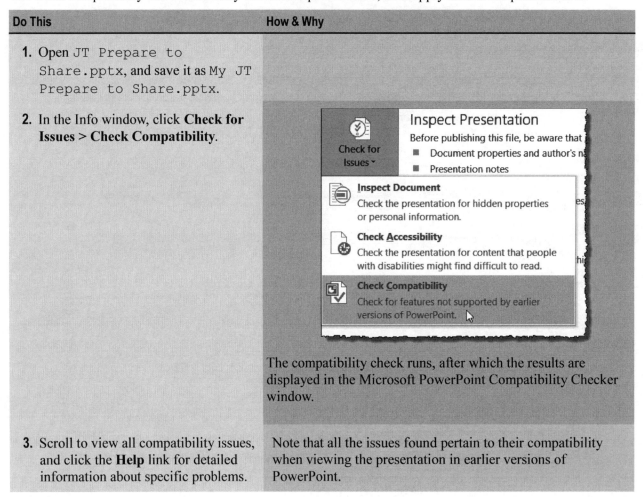 The compatibility check runs, after which the results are displayed in the Microsoft PowerPoint Compatibility Checker window.
3. Scroll to view all compatibility issues, and click the **Help** link for detailed information about specific problems.	Note that all the issues found pertain to their compatibility when viewing the presentation in earlier versions of PowerPoint.

Do This	How & Why
4. In the Help window, click the message that matches the one in the Compatibility Checker window. It contains information about why the message appears, as well as a solution to try. 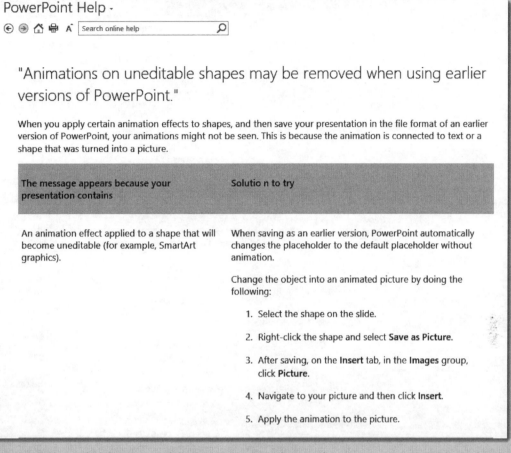 Your presentation is intended for users of the latest PowerPoint version, so you won't need to address any of these issues.	
5. Close the Help and Compatibility Checker windows.	

Do This	How & Why
6. In the Info window, click **Check for Issues > Check Accessibility**.	After a few seconds, the Accessibility Checker pane opens, listing potential accessibility errors and/or warnings, and tips for addressing them.

Do This	How & Why
7. Under Errors, select **Coffee_Beans_Mixing (Slide 10)**, and observe the summary of the problem and solution.	Under Additional Information. You'll need to scroll to see all the information. You're informed that the video object on slide 10 should have alternate text (Alt Text) to be used as a placeholder. Alt Text is helpful when media objects either don't load properly or load slowly. It lets the viewer know what's intended.
8. On slide 10, right-click the video object, and click **Format Video**.	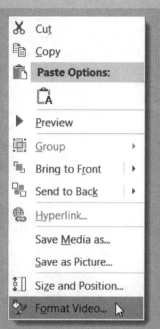 The Format Video pane opens.
9. Click **Size & Properties**.	To display the settings.  Note that the instruction in the Accessibility Checker pane is to click "Layout & Properties," which in this case wouldn't work. Size, Position, and Alt Text categories are displayed.

PowerPoint 2016 Level 1

Do This	How & Why
10. Expand the Alt Text category, then enter to the Title and Description information shown in the figure below.	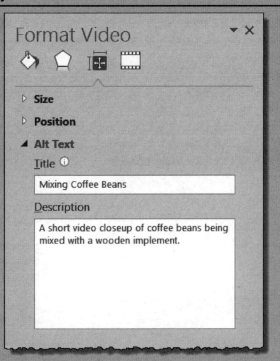 The error message for this slide is no longer displayed in the Accessibility Checker window.
11. Pick one other accessibility error, and address the problem.	
12. Close the Accessibility Checker pane, and any other pane that's open.	
13. Save your changes.	

14. Display the Info window, and observe the media summary next to the Compress Media tool.

 Media Size and Performance
Save disk space and improve playback performance by compressing your media files. Compression might affect media quality.
- Media files in this presentation are 34 MB.
- 2 media file(s) contain trimmed regions.

More ways to improve media performance

Do This	How & Why
15. Click **Compress Media**, and observe the available options.	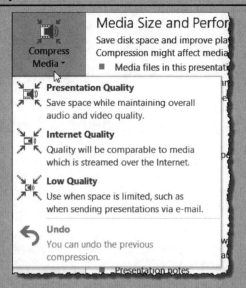

You'll compress this presentation as little as possible, to preserve the quality of the media for slide-show use.

16. Click **Presentation Quality**.

The Compress Media window opens, and the media files are compressed. Observe the initial and final media-file sizes, and the total amount of compression.

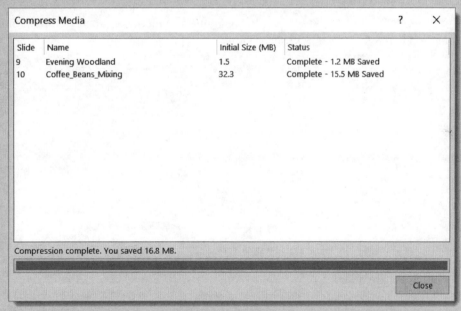

17. Click **Close**, then observe the updated Media Size and Performance summary.

Media Size and Performance

Save disk space and improve playback performance by compressing your media files. Compression might affect media quality.

- Media files in this presentation are 17 MB.
- You compressed this presentation's media to Presentation Quality. Run slide show to preview results.
- Undo the compression if the results are unsatisfactory.

More ways to improve media performance

Do This	How & Why
18. Run the slide show to view the results of compression.	
19. Save and close the presentation.	To save the compressed version of the presentation.

Saving a presentation to a shared location

As you've already seen, PowerPoint provides many different formats in which you can save a presentation for viewing, reviewing, and editing by others. In addition, you can save your presentation to a shared location, to make it easy for others to access it. This could be as straightforward as using a shared location on a corporate network. Recently, it's become more common for people to share files via cloud computing.

Cloud computing refers to the use of storage services that don't have a single physical location but instead take advantage of the seemingly unlimited resources of the Internet (the "cloud"). There are countless services now available for cloud storage. Most offer a certain amount of storage (often at least 1 GB) for free, then more for a subscription fee.

Microsoft Office 2013 (and later) comes with a cloud service called *OneDrive* that offers 5 GB of free storage. You need only sign up for a personal account. Some organizations subscribe to a business account using OneDrive. However, many corporate environments that use Microsoft products subscribe to *SharePoint*, another common cloud service.

With subscription to a cloud service, you can upload (save) your presentations there, then grant others access to them, if necessary. Or, the cloud location may already be shared, and all you need to do is upload the files.

Once you've saved your presentation to a cloud service, PowerPoint provides several ways for sharing it. You can find these options in the Share window in Backstage view.

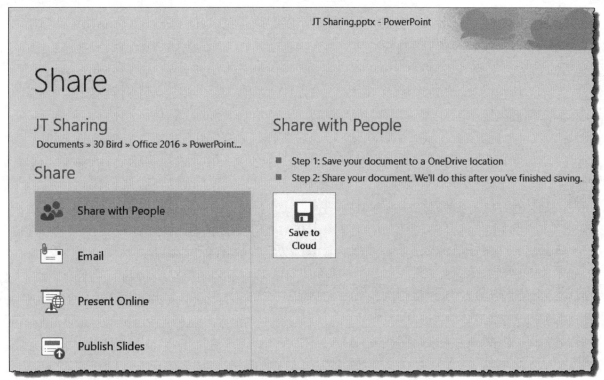

Here, you can select a sharing option.

- *Share with People*: You're prompted to save the presentation to a OneDrive location in the Cloud. You can also choose to require the user to log into OneDrive before they can access the presentation. Once you've done so, the Share with People button appears, which you can then use to select specific recipients.

- *Email*: This is probably the most versatile option, as it allows you to send the presentation as an attachment, a link, a PDF/XPS file, or an Internet fax. For the fax option, you need to have a fax service provider.

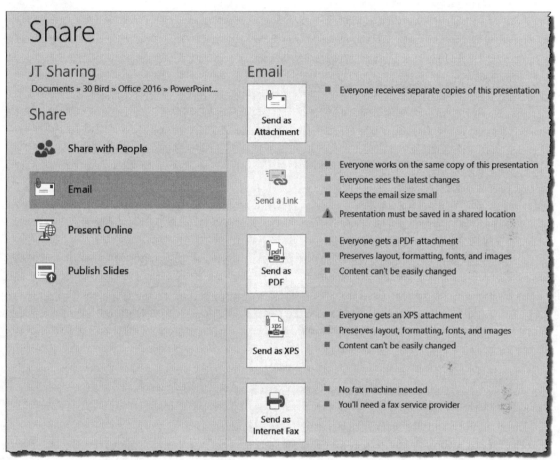

 Note: The *Send a Link* option only becomes available once you've used *Share with People* to save the presentation to a shared location.

- *Present Online*: Allows you to give a presentation online. A link sent to recipients allows them to view the presentation. You can also choose to allow link recipients to download the presentation for later viewing. This option requires a Microsoft account.
- *Publish Slides*: Allows you to publish the presentation's slides to a library or SharePoint site. Others can track and review changes, make comments, and so on.

Saving a presentation to OneDrive

Saving a presentation to a OneDrive location is much the same as saving it to any other physical location. As with other cloud services, when you save a file to OneDrive, it resides both on your computer and in the cloud.

 Note: You can also use **File > Share > Share with People** to share a presentation via OneDrive.

1. With your presentation open, click **File > Save As**.
2. Click **OneDrive**.
    Under Save As. It could be OneDrive - Personal or OneDrive - Business.

 Note: You could just as well use another subscription cloud service, such as Dropbox. To do so, click **Browse** instead, then navigate to your Dropbox (or other cloud service) folder, and save the presentation to that location.

3. Navigate to the desired folder.
    - Click **Browse** to open the Save As window. Create a subfolder, if necessary.
    - Click an available OneDrive folder.
4. If desired, rename the file and change the file type, as necessary.
    For example, you may have chosen to share it as a PowerPoint Show (.ppsx) file.
5. Click **Save**.
    Once you save a file to your designation OneDrive location on your hard drive, if your computer is connected to the Internet, the file will begin to upload to the cloud.

Inviting others to share a presentation

Once you've uploaded your presentation to a OneDrive location, there are a number of ways you can share it with others. One way is if the folder you've uploaded the file to is already shared. Likewise, you can invite others to share a OneDrive folder. However, it's generally a good idea (and often much safer) to simply email others a link to the file.

When the email recipients click the link, they can download the file directly, and they have access only to that file, not to the folder in which it resides. This approach prevents others from having access to other files contained in that (or any other) folder.

1. With the presentation open, click **File > Share**, then click **Email**.
   In the Share options.

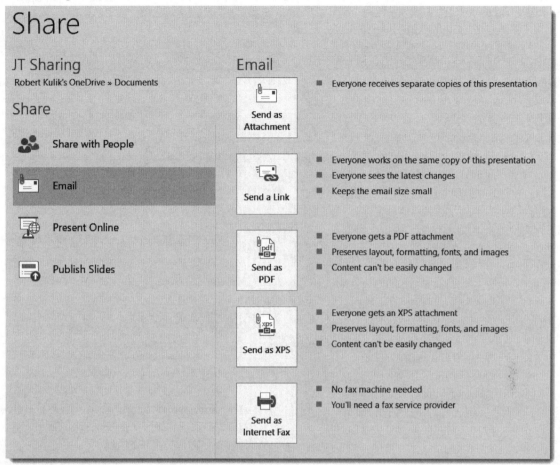

2. Select an Email option.
   - **Send as Attachment**: Opens an Outlook Message window, with the presentation file attached. Specify recipients, type your message, then click **Send**. So far, this has been the most commonly used option for sharing presentations. However, with this option you don't need to use a cloud service, unless the file recipient will also upload the file to a shared cloud location. The biggest drawback to this option is that email services have an upper limit regarding the size of files you can send. Thus, multimedia presentations can easily be too large to send via email.
   - **Send a Link**: Opens an Outlook Message window with the link to the file displayed in the message field, and the file name in the Subject field. Specify recipients, type the remainder of your message, then click **Send**. Because you're not sending an attachment, there's no concern regarding the file size of the presentation.
   - **Send as PDF**: Similar to Send as Attachment, except the presentation is "published" and attached as a PDF file.
   - **Send as XPS**: Similar to Send as Attachment, except the presentation is "published" and attached as an XPS file.
   - **Send as Internet Fax**: Sends the presentation as an electronic fax. This option requires that you have an Internet fax provider.

Exercise: Saving a presentation to a shared location

You need to have access to a OneDrive (or other) cloud account, as well as email accounts set up for at least two other classmates. If not, your instructor will demonstrate a sharing option. You'll save a presentation to a shared location, then invite others to share it.

Do This	How & Why
1. Open `JT Sharing.pptx`.	
2. Click **File > Save As**.	
3. Click **OneDrive**.	Or click **SharePoint**, as the case may be. To save to another cloud service not listed under Save As, click **This PC** instead, then navigate to the available cloud-service folder, and save the presentation to that location.
4. Click **Browse**.	To open the Save As window.
5. Navigate to the desired OneDrive (or other cloud-service) folder.	
6. Click **Save**.	To save the presentation by its current name and in its current format.

Do This	How & Why

7. Click **File** > **Share**, then click **Email**.

In the Share options.

8. Click **Send a Link**.

A Message window opens in Outlook. The link appears in the message field.

 Note: For the Send a Link option to be available, you must have open the version of the presentation that's saved to OneDrive (or another Cloud service).

Do This	How & Why
9. Enter two recipients' email addresses in the To field.	
10. Click in the message field, above the link, and type a brief message letting the recipients know that this is the link to your latest presentation.	

The recipients will be able to click the link to open and view the file in PowerPoint Online, which will open in their default browser. They have full editorial access to the file.

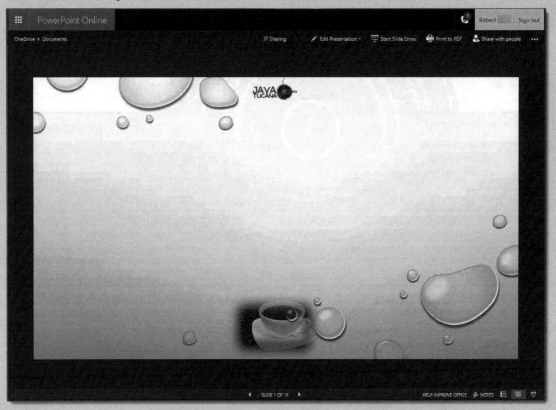

The PowerPoint Online window contains many options for further editing, saving, viewing, and/or sharing of the presentation. If recipients have PowerPoint installed on their computers, they can open the presentation directly in PowerPoint. Otherwise, they can work with it using PowerPoint Online in their browser.

11. Close the presentation.

Assessment: Sharing your presentation

1. The Compatibility Checker is used to assess the compatibility of your presentation with presentation applications other than PowerPoint. True or false?

   - True
   - False

2. Which of the following statements about checking your presentations for accessibility is true? Choose the best response.

   - Besides consideration for people with disabilities, accessibility can help ensure that a presentation is more friendly to international users.
   - In PowerPoint, "accessibility" refers to whether viewers of the presentation are allowed editorial access to it.
   - If not fixed, any accessibility error will prevent the presentation from running.
   - Any accessibility errors that you fix are saved automatically.

3. If you have to compress the media in a presentation, you should always apply the least amount of compression. True or false?

   - True
   - False

4. Which of these statements about sharing presentations is *not* true? Choose the best response.

   - Depending on the cloud provider being used, recipients of a shared presentation might not need to have an account with that provider.
   - Emailing a link is highly preferable over emailing a presentation.
   - Saving to a cloud provider requires subscription to that provider.
   - To share a presentation using a cloud service, the presentation must first be uploaded to it.

Summary: Sharing, collaborating, and security

In this chapter, you learned how to:

- Protect and restrict access to presentations by making them read-only, and by password-protecting them
- Check presentations for compatibility with earlier versions of PowerPoint, and for accessibility by people with disabilities; save presentations to different types of cloud services; and explore different options for sharing them with others

Synthesis: Sharing, collaborating, and security

In this synthesis exercise, you'll ensure the security of a presentation. Then you'll assess its compatibility and accessibility, and make any necessary changes. Finally, you'll share the presentation with others.

1. Open `Synthesis - JT Final Checks.pptx`, and save it as `My Synthesis - JT Final Checks.pptx`.
2. Set the presentation as read-only.
3. Password-protect the presentation.

    Once a presentation is formatted as read-only, sometimes PowerPoint won't allow you to password-protect it. Should this happen, a warning message will display above the presentation. Click **Edit Anyway** and proceed from there.

4. Check the presentation for compatibility, and make any changes you deem necessary to make it more compatible with earlier versions of PowerPoint.
5. Check the presentation's accessibility. Then fix at least five errors.
6. Compress the presentation's media for online use.
7. Save your changes, and preview the slide show.
8. Upload your presentation to OneDrive or to another cloud provider.
9. Email a link to at least two recipients. Confirm their receipt and function of the link.
10. Close the presentation.

Alphabetical Index

Accessibility 352, 354
    Checking 354
Accessibility Checker 352, 354
Animation 230, 232, 243
    Effects 230
    Objects 232
    Shapes 232
    Timing 243
Animation pane 233
Animations 233, 235, 237
    Copying 237
    Customizing 235
    Modifying 233
Animations pane 235
Animations tab 230
Aspect ratio 119
Audio 251, 257
    Audio Tools 257
    Effects 251
    Formats 251
    Formatting 257
    Settings 257
Audio effects 251
    Adding 251
Audio file 251
Audio object 254
    Inserting an 254
Audio Tools 257
    Format tab 257
    Playback tab 257
AutoCorrect options 278
Automatic spell checking 275
Backstage view 18, 179, 296, 344
    Export options 296
    Info pane 18
    Info window 344
    New pane 18
    Printing 179
Bulleted lists 75
    Creating 75
    Options 75
Bullets 75
Changes 289, 290
    Accepting/rejecting 290
    Combining presentations 289
    Comparing presentations 289
    Reviewing 290
Chart data 139
    Editing 139
Chart layout 136
    Changing 136
Chart style 138
    Applying 138
    Changing 138
Chart types 131, 135
    Bar 131
    Changing 135
    Column 131
    Line 131
    Pie 131
Charts 130, 131, 136, 205, 207
    About 130
    Adding 131
    Adding shapes 207
    Elements of 136
    Flow 205
    Genealogy 205
    Inserting 131
    Organization 205
    SmartArt 205
Comments 282, 283, 284
    About 282
    Adding 283
    Deleting 284
    Editing 284
    Managing 284
Compare tool 290
Compatibility 352
    Checking 352
Compatibility Checker 352
Context-sensitive 6
Cropping handles 120
Current slide 6
Curved shapes 100
    Placement and position of curves 100
Curves 96
Custom Shows 335
Custom slide show 335, 337
    Creating a 335
    Presenting 337
    Running 337
Data 148
    Entering 148
Diagrams 188
    SmartArt 188
Document outlines 165
    Importing 165
Emphasis effects 230
Entering data 148
Entrance effects 230
Excel 148
    Enter box 148
Excel chart 138
    Inserting 138
Exit effects 230
File 348
    Properties 348
File tab 18
File types 300, 301
    PDF 301
    XPS 301
Files 296
    Formats 296
    Types 296
Footer 56
    In masters 56

Alphabetical Index

On slides..56
Format Background pane..........................82
Formatting..73, 86
    Gridlines..86
    Text...73
Gettig help...11
    Tell Me box.......................................11
Gridlines...86, 100
    Displaying..86
Groups...6
Guides...100
    Displaying..100
Handout Master view................................304
Handouts..................................59, 303, 304
    Changing the appearance of............304
    Footers..59
    Formatting.......................................304
    Headers..59
    Word...303
Header...56
    In handouts and notes......................56
Headers and footers.................................56
    Date area...56
    Footer area......................................56
    Header area.....................................56
    Number area....................................56
Help..11
    Getting..11
    Tell Me box.......................................11
Hyperlinks..30
    Images..30
    Inserting...30
    Text..30
I-beam..24
Image files..34
    Inserting...34
Images...........................34, 116, 117, 119, 120, 122
    Applying styles................................122
    Background.....................................117
    Bitmap..116
    Cropping...120
    Cropping options............................120
    Inserting..........................34, 116, 117
    Local...116
    Moving..119
    Online..117
    Picture files.......................................34
    Pixels..116
    Sizing..119
    Types..34
    Vector...116
    Vector files.......................................34
    Vector graphics................................34
Importing..165, 167
    Outlines..165
    PDF file...167
    Text..165
    Text documents..............................165
    Word documents............................165

Info..348
    Properties.......................................348
Info window...344
    Security..344
Layout..48, 65, 194
    Changing..194
    Modifying...................................48, 65
    Slide master.....................................48
Layouts..65
    Applying...65
    Gallery..65
    Slide master.....................................65
Line charts...130
    About..130
Lines..96, 98
    Drawing..98
List items..195
    Moving..195
    Promoting/demoting......................195
Lists..191
    Converting to SmartArt..................191
Media...251, 356
    Audio..251
    Compressing..................................356
    Video..251
Motion path..230
New Slide..26, 65
    Layout gallery..................................65
Normal view..7
Notes......................................59, 316, 318, 320, 321
    Adding..316
    Adding a notes page......................321
    Changing the appearance of............318
    Editing..320
    Footers..59
    Formatting..............................318, 320
    Headers..59
Notes Master view...................................318
Notes page...321
    Adding a..321
Notes Page view.......................................317
Notes pages......................................316, 324
    Printing...324
Notes pane...316
Notes view..7
Numbered lists...75
    Creating...75
    Options..75
Numbers..75
Object...167
    Action, assigning an.......................167
Objects...24, 150
    Hyperlinks..24
    Images...24
    Importing.......................................150
    Non-text..24
    Shapes...24
    Text..24
OneDrive...364, 366

Alphabetical Index

Emailing a link to 366
Online images 36, 117
    Inserting 36
Online Pictures 36
Online videos 259
    Downloading 259
    Searching 259
Open shapes 96, 98
    Drawing 98
Organization chart 206
    SmartArt 206
Outline view 7, 320
    Notes, working with 320
Page setup 220
    Changing slide orientation 220
    Changing slide size 220
Password 346
    Protecting a presentation 346
PDF and XPS documents 301
PDF file 167
    Importing 167
Picture files 34
    Bitmap images 34
    Inserting 34
    Pixels 34
Pictures 116, 117
    Online 117
Pie charts 130
    About 130
Placeholders 24
    Graphics 24
    Text 24
PowerPoint options 278
    AutoCorrect 278
Presentation 4, 18, 20, 29, 160, 213, 276, 306, 333, 335, 345, 346, 364, 366
    Blank 18
    Checking spelling 276
    Create 18
    Creating 20
    Custom Shows 335
    Inviting others to share a 366
    Multiple slide masters 213
    Navigating slides 29
    New 18, 20
    Opening 4
    Password protection 346
    Read-only 345
    Rehearsing timing 333
    Saving to OneDrive 366
    Shared location 364
    Sharing 364
    Slide master, adding a 213
    Slide transitions 160
    Templates 18
    Video 306
Presentations 219, 290, 296, 303, 307, 352, 354, 356
    Checking accessibility 354
    Checking compatibility 352

Comparing versions of 290
Compressing media 356
Creating a video 307
Creating Word handouts 303
File formats 296
Recording a video 307
Reviewing changes to 290
Sections, creating 219
Sections, working with 219
Presenter view 330
Print Options 174, 176
    Setting 176
Print Preview 174, 175
Print settings 177
Printing 174, 175, 176, 177, 179, 180, 324
    Backstage view 179
    Notes pages 324
    Previewing 175
    Print Options 176
    Quick Print 179, 180
    Requirements for 174
Printout 175
    Previewing 175
Proofing 277
    Options 277
Proofing Options 277
    Setting 277
Proofing tools 272
    Checking spelling, grammar, and usage 272
Quick Access toolbar 6, 179
    Customizing the 179
Quick Layout 136
Quick Print 179, 180
    Adding to the ribbon 180
Reading view 7
Reviewing content 282
    Comments 282
Reviewing presentations 289
Ribbon 6, 180
    Customizing the 180
Rulers 100
Saving 301
    Export pane 301
    PDF 301
Saving presentations 300
    Export options 300
    Save As 300
Sections 219
    Creating 219
    Working with 219
Shape layers 106
Shape styles 104
    Effects 104
    Fills 104
    Outlines 104
Shapes 32, 96, 98, 100, 103, 106
    Aligning 100, 106
    Creating 96
    Curved 100

Alphabetical Index

- Drawing..96, 98
- Formatting..96
- Grouping...106
- Inserting...32
- Layering..106
- Resizing..103
- Shapes gallery..32
- SharePoint..364
- Slide...57
  - Date..57
  - Footer...57
  - Number...57
- Slide backgrounds...82
  - Applying..82
  - Effects...82
  - Fill..82
  - Formatting...82
  - Pictures...82
- Slide master................48, 50, 65, 73, 213, 214, 216
  - Adding a...213
  - Applying themes...50
  - Applying to slides.......................................216
  - Copying a..214
  - Duplicating a..214
  - Format..48
  - Layout..48
  - Layouts..65
  - Modifying...48
  - More than one..213
  - Tab...48
  - Text formatting..73
  - Text style..73
  - Tools..48
  - Viewing..48
- Slide Master tab...213
  - Edit Master group..213
- Slide Master view...48
  - Layouts..48
- Slide masters...218
  - Restoring placeholders................................218
- Slide notes..317
  - Notes Page view...317
- Slide show.......................................330, 332, 333
  - Keyboard shortcuts.....................................332
  - Mouse shortcuts...332
  - Presenter view...330
  - Rehearsing timing.......................................333
  - Running..330
  - Testing...330
- Slide Sorter view..7
- Slide transitions..160
- Slides..............24, 26, 29, 30, 65, 100, 160, 162, 220, 316
  - Adding...24, 26
  - Adding notes...316
  - Applying layouts..65
  - Changing orientation...................................220
  - Changing size..220
  - Inserting...26
  - Inserting hyperlinks......................................30
  - Moving...24
  - Navigating..29
  - Objects..24
  - Transitions..160, 162
  - Zooming in/out..100
- Slides pane..6
- SmartArt...188, 189, 191, 193, 194, 196, 197, 205, 206, 207
  - About...188
  - Adding shapes...207
  - Charts..205
  - Colors..196
  - Converting lists to......................................191
  - Creating...189
  - Design tab..193
  - Diagrams..188
  - Format tab..193
  - Layout, changing..194
  - Layouts gallery..194
  - Organization chart.....................................206
  - Shape styles...197
  - Shapes...197
  - Styles...196
- SmartArt lists..195
  - Moving items...195
  - Promoting/demoting items..........................195
- SmartArt Tools..193
- Sound effects..253
  - Adding...253
  - Inserting...253
- Spelling..275, 276
  - Checking...275, 276
- Spelling pane..276
- Spelling, grammar, and usage..........................272
  - Checking..272
  - Proofing tools..272
- Starting PowerPoint..4
- Status bar...6
- Styles..122, 148
  - Applying..148
- Table Style Options..150
- Tables...146, 147, 150
  - Cells..146
  - Columns...146
  - Drawing..146
  - Importing..150
  - Inserting..146, 147
  - Rows...146
- Tabs..6
- Templates..20
  - New pane...20
  - Previewing...20
- Text..............................24, 73, 165, 169, 230, 231
  - Animating...231
  - Animation effects.......................................230
  - Appearance..73
  - Creating WordArt.......................................169
  - Entering...24
  - I-beam...24

Importing	165
Inserting	24
Placeholder	24
Sources	165
Style	73
Text box	24
Text formatting	169
WordArt	169
Text styles	74
Formatting	74
Individual slide	74
Themes	50
Applying	50
Timing	243
Animation effects	243
Transition effects	243
Timing Effect Options window	245
Animation types	245
Tooltip	6
Transition	243
Timing	243
Transitions	160, 162, 253
All slides	160
Applying	160, 162
Individual slides	162
Slide	160
Sound effects	253
Undo	100
Vector graphics	34
Inserting	34
Video	251, 258, 259, 261, 306, 307
Adding	251, 258
Creating a	307
Downloading	259
Formats	251
Formatting	261
Inserting	258
Online sources	259
Options	306
Saving a presentation as a	307
Searching	259
Settings	261
Video Tools	261
Video file	251
Video object	258
Inserting a	258
Video tools	261
Format tab	261
Playback tab	261
Views	7
Word handouts	303
Creating	303
WordArt	169
Creating	169
From text	169
Zoom control	6
Zoom slider	100